THROUGH OUR EYES

A Foster Famil Shares Their Secret World

William A. Hunter

Hamilton Books
A member of
The Rowman & Littlefield Publishing Group
Lanham · Boulder · New York · Toronto · Plymouth, UK

Copyright © 2010 by
Hamilton Books
4501 Forbes Boulevard
Suite 200
Lanham, Maryland 20706
Hamilton Books Acquisitions Department (301) 459-3366

Estover Road
Plymouth PL6 7PY
United Kingdom

All rights reserved
Printed in the United States of America
British Library Cataloging in Publication Information Available

Library of Congress Control Number: 2010920173
ISBN: 978-0-7618-5067-0 (paperback : alk. paper)
eISBN: 978-0-7618-5093-9

Cover photo by Michael Jordan of MJProPix.com.

∞™ The paper used in this publication meets the minimum requirements of American National Standard for Information Sciences—Permanence of Paper for Printed Library Materials, ANSI Z39.48-1992

Dedication

For the tens-of-thousands of foster children who struggle to discover the meaning of trust and family;

For my foster children who clung to hope, despite the often painful despair;

For my birth son who surrendered his father to a different path;

For the social workers who dream of a better place for their overwhelming case loads;

To Bob who taught me courage in the face of helplessness;

To Pat who taught me patience in the face of hopelessness;

To Linda who taught me understanding in the face of loss;

To Mike who taught me Faith;

This Work is Dedicated

***

Jason's Journal: My First Foster Child

I strongly believe the past builds us to be the people we are today. Our past gives us choices to change the things that went wrong. I told myself that I would never be like my parents. I would never abuse my children or let anyone I care about get hurt.

A lot of people think that a kid that has been abused will be an abuser. I don't believe that. People I know always want to hear about my past. I endeavor to avoid talking about it because I'm afraid they will label me, see me disabled, or treat me differently. Writing my story and sharing my hurt with you will help me feel more comfortable about it.

This is my story.

***

TABLE OF CONTENTS

Preface: Origin of Foster Care	vii
Introduction: Unconditional Commitment	xi
Final Day	1
Twelve Years Earlier	7
Lined Up for the Slaughter	19
Product of Substance Abuse	25
My Little Knight	37
Honeymoons are Deceiving	49
The Lifeline	57
Desks are for Security	65
Dad is Earned	83
Million Dollar Lawsuit	93
The Birth of an IEP	99
Return to Open Campus	105
Locked Down	113
Sanctuary	127
Coming of Age	133
Tragedy & Victory	139
Life With a Nun	151
Trauma is Forever	159
Leaving the Cocoon	163
Boot Camp	169
First Love	179
It's a Boy	191
You are Loved	201
Final Moments	241
Farewell	245
Closing Thoughts	249
Epilogue	253

Preface:
Origin of Foster Care

To read a book about a foster family requires a clear definition of the expression. The most simplistic description is a traditional birth family that provides temporary care for children brought from outside their home. A more legal term would be that the family has accepted responsibility to provide care, but do not have control or guardianship.

Mankind has wrestled with the care of unwanted and orphaned children from the very beginning. Some societies simply left them homeless to fend for themselves. If they were too young, such as an infant, they would quickly perish. Older children, on the other hand, would learn the rules of the streets to survive, joining a separate social class of riff raff, petty thieves, and gangs. A few fortunate ones came under the control of a caring, parental figure. We find such references in the bible and other historical works regarding the care of orphaned children. The story of Moses is the most famous.

Even in later times when culture flourished, caring for homeless children by an adult outside the immediate family was rare. Most joined the growing ranks of street urchins. As this problem grew, so did methods of control, though most methods were based on economic value such as manual labor. Cultured communities evolved a formal solution such as work houses and church societies. In many cases these children were maintained at the same level as slaves or indentured servants; their childhood lost forever. Some of the religious based institutions provided care and training and were the foundation of the formal orphanage system that developed during the industrial age. A number of these religious based charitable institutions in Europe operated for hundreds of years. I visited one such place in Florence, Italy, the *Spedale degli Innocenti* that opened in 1445, and was reputed to be the first orphanage in Europe.

Foster care in the modern usage, however, did not come about until 1853, when Charles Brace, a minister who directed the New York Children's Aid Society, began the free foster home movement. His idea was simple: to advertise needy children for charitable families to provide shelter. This new concept was driven by the growing number of immigrant children sleeping in the streets. His approach did provide a solution to the immediate social dilemma, but in so doing it created a new problem, protecting children in care. Brace accepted that people were motivated by more than pure charity. Just as with *orphan trains*, when children were sent west to be adopted as work hands; Brace recognized many of these foster homes were using the children as servants. But considering the rampant growth of starvation and disease in large cities like New York, his plan was a bold solution that required little formal government or charitable funding. Brace's imaginative plan to New York's overwhelming crisis is considered to be the beginning of modern day foster care.

Many books and films have focused on the horror suffered by homeless children from this period that continued well into the twentieth century. The aberrant conditions of juvenile facilities, adolescent institutions and many orphanages have been well documented from major litigation cases across the country. Less documented are the more intimate experiences within a private foster home.

Through the twentieth century, foster care has evolved to a formal, government managed business established to protect children. Though historically the focus was for homeless, unwanted or otherwise abandoned children; the system has developed to include all children, with a primary focus on those neglected and abused. Foster care is still dominated by volunteers, but unlike in the past, today's families undergo an intense screening process and specialized education that culminates in legal certification. In addition, foster parents must continue with on-going training each year to be re-certified, while constantly under the watchful scrutiny and management of the welfare system. When children cannot be placed into a foster home due to limited availability of open beds or a child's unmanageable behavior, they are placed in shelters or group homes, and for the severe cases, residential treatment centers.

Sadly, many foster children are never reunited with their families or adopted into new families. Those unfortunate lost souls are abandoned once again at eighteen years old. The industry terms this 'aging out.' A new segment of care has been growing in recent times called transition care, to provide a bridge from this state of limbo to independent living. Transition resources are typically available to youth eighteen to twenty-one. Not unlike foster care, success is highly dependent on the living situation of these older youth. Left in the streets or in shelters, their prospects are very limited, as most still struggle with the ghosts of their past and the fantasy to have a stable home and family. This humanitarian effort is having some positive effect, but the jury is still out on the success rate.

Introduction:
Unconditional Commitment

As people age, they ask the question: Why am I here, which usually leads to the simpler question: What legacy am I leaving behind. This takes about fifty years to construe, so if you are under that age and not pondering that question, don't feel concerned. You have time. If you are over that age and have not thought about this matter, congratulations; you may live longer than the rest of us. My legacy was not planned or well conceived, but fell upon my lap. I had the unique privilege to deeply affect the lives of a few children who floundered in the foster care system.

The U.S. Department of health and Human Services defines foster care as:

> *Twenty-four-hour substitute care for children placed away from their parents or guardians and for whom the State agency has placement and care responsibility. This includes, but is not limited to, family foster homes, foster homes of relatives, group homes, emergency shelters, residential facilities, child care institutions, and pre-adoptive homes regardless of whether the facility is licensed and whether payments are made by the State or local agency for the care of the child, or whether there is Federal matching of any payments made.*[1]

These words evoke few colorful images for the reader. It is typical government bureaucracy that is clinical and dry. The true meaning of this benign definition is reflected in the often tormented lives of these children and their families. This is a memoir of a foster parent supported by a few personal journal entries directly from my children and family friends. This is not a formal dissertation on the social welfare system as defined above. In defense of their sometimes inept decisions, understand the underlying element that defines the foster care business: risk management. To fully accomplish this ideal requires total case control; the methods of which remain cloaked by a veil of secrecy.

To be a foster parent requires nothing short of total and sometimes blind commitment. In many cases, the foster parent must put self-interests aside. They take some classes, get a certificate, and then open their door to the darkest side of humanity. Like most foster parents, I never knew the history or true diagnosis of any child that entered my home. If I was provided such information, I might have slammed the door shut.

Why people engage in this work is no better understood than dissecting the motivation of a soldier who runs into a hail of bullets to carry an injured combatant to safety, even when the prognosis is poor at best. Does this behavior reflect an extreme level of compassion? Or are they blinded by the emotions of the battle with adrenaline pumping so much that they are devoid of concern for their personal safety? Such is the circumstance in foster care for those who open their hearth and heart to a damaged child under the control of government bureaucracy. This is the ultimate example of raising a child by the book, where the key theme for all parties, from social workers to therapists and lawyers, is classical risk management.

Additionally, foster families that open their door to emotionally tormented children will never attain the stability of a traditional family, because none of these children grew up together with the same culture and values. When a foster child enters a home, all the family dynamics are forever changed. Despite this understanding, I dreamt and struggled to attain permanency throughout my years working in this ever changing environment. But I learned over time that such optimism was tenuous at best. We were always a home in flux, everyday walking on eggshells.

My foster children brought more than just an exclusive personality, but a unique behavior pattern developed from their remarkable history, or what the industry terms 'baggage.' They all suffered appalling abuse before the age of speech and reason, and with it post traumatic stress for sure, and for some, serious attachment disorder.

All children directly couple their experiences with self worth. After all, they are the center of the universe. If they experience good and positive things, they are good. If, on the other hand, they experience pain and suffering, they are bad. They accept full responsibility for their experiences. It is how young children learn.

In addition to this negative self value driven home due to constant abuse, my children also struggled with the ever threatening fear of abandonment. Once in the safety of foster care, they interpreted daily events and personal interactions from a haze of disconnected memories. Their over reactive behaviors were hardwired, evolved at the primal level to survive and never to be erased.

These are confused and angry children. For some, the frustration is anchored deep inside, surrounded by an impregnable wall. Others launch out against anyone within reach. In either case, depression, anger and violence are typical outcomes.

In our home, each of us learned and then acknowledged the others' behaviors, and through trial and error, developed skills to co-exist and find our own blissful sanctuary. A colleague once sent me an email with a most appropriate religious quote: "We should see beyond our differences, embrace our similarities, and simply love one another." Foster families must find that path to survive.

To understand the complex world of foster care requires more than a psychological study of abused children, or the professional training of case workers and the political analysis of the bureaucracy that manage their cases. Ultimately, the child's ability to survive their forced captivity within this very controlled environment is dependent on their unique character, the unconditional love of the foster family, and their acceptance by the school and community in which the children live. This managed environment, consisting of the constant interplay between the foster parents, school and community with the massive bureaucracy of state agencies and courts, impacts the child's perception of their world, and in the long-term, their ability to transition from the unique culture of foster care into a more normal social environment of traditional families. Neither child nor foster family can endure this experience without suffering profound emotional change.

Some families will be more traumatized than others depending on the extent of the damage suffered by children placed in their home. The children's trauma evolves as they move from placement-to-placement, forced to adjust and re-adjust to various family values, personalities and regulations. One of my foster sons, who had several different placements in the system, once told me he felt like he had lived completely dissimilar lives. Not one had any connection to the other. The only similar theme was his feeling of helplessness and lack of trust.

Each foster child came to me with the expectation of never leaving. Permanency was the case plan. And despite this promise offered to their starving spirits, they all suffered anxiety of impending loss taught from past experiences that such promises were very superficial. They had heard it before. They remained on constant guard, vigilant of the slightest sign of another move to a new family. This extraordinary sensitivity drove their behavior as much as any trauma suffered in their past.

Studies have reported that a foster child afflicted by loss can suffer post-traumatic stress disorder far worse than soldiers experience from battle. These children are born in the midst of a domestic conflict of which they have little to no understanding. Their perceptions are clouded. At any time their emotions can be under attack in the dark, their minds empty of definition or understanding to past events. Long after the trauma, they are triggered to feel unbearable emotional pain, but rarely comprehend the reason.

Imagine yourself enjoying a moment with your friends when suddenly and without warning you feel your gut wrench. You search your mind for the cause and are left empty. The anguish has no apparent rationale. You feel helpless and confused. Your pain is only elevated by frustration. You feel both anger and unbearable grief. You look for a quiet corner, and cry. Welcome inside the soul of a foster child.

I raised one child through a divorce, which in today's world is more common than not. My separation was mutual, and more important, my wife and I maintained good relations and shared most holidays and vacations together until her unfortunate death from cancer. My approach to fatherhood was not perfect, not nearly so, but I always cared.

The most important lesson I learned with my birth son was to maintain a moral and ethical basis of parenting. One need not refine the Ten Commandments. Keep it simple. Keep it honest. Plainly said, I kept my word, and I owned-up to my mistakes. Both actions were the basis for building trust; the foundation of family security. This philosophy also contributed to maintaining a strong and long-lasting personal relationship with my foster children. The key method to accomplish this goal was direct and honest communications. Children raised without honest dialogue with adults will grow on a foundation of distrust.

In foster parenting trust is paramount to succeed. The challenge to this simple virtue, however, is not so straight forward. Foster parents are not alone. The child is managed by a team with many people involved in the decision process. All the decision makers outside the family unit are paid professionals who go home to their own families without much thought to the long-term impact of their decisions. They are solving daily problems that require instant solutions. They have dozens of case loads that weigh upon their daily work schedule. This can have benefits when dealing with unexpected behavior issues that require support from a professional with firsthand experience, but can be catastrophic when you find yourself trapped between the welfare of the child and the demands of the system. You find yourself driven to protect and comfort by promising that which you cannot control. In many instances, the case workers promise what they know will not be delivered simply to manage the moment. Parents can be caught taking a similar tack out of pity or ignorance. Make no mistake. Within the bureaucracy of foster care, the parent is as helpless as the child.

Introduction

The commitment children require to feel safe is your unconditional love and support. They will coax, manipulate and plead that you never abandon them. Promise as you may with the most sincere intent; you cannot comply. These children are wards of the court, property of the state. You are but the caretaker. Such is the dichotomy of the term foster family. The word family is a pretense, one that older foster children learn all too painfully. It is a dream they will seek to fulfill their entire lives.

This story is my journey through the hidden world of foster parenting. It covers twelve years of service in a murky world seen by few, understood by far fewer. It is a family story; my sons' as much as mine. As such, they have collaborated to openly share their experiences and opinions as they reflect back to their most agonizing memories and tender moments. All names have been changed for confidentiality. We have given an account to the best of our recollection. The children's stories reflect their memories which at times have been clouded. This was very painful for them. Child abuse survivors guard these memories and the emotions they invoke, keeping them tucked deep and walled in. When they allow the hurt to surface, all the suffering and traumas their psyches have worked so hard to suppress will return, and with it the sting.

Oscar Wilde wrote: "Children begin by loving their parents; as they grow older they judge them; sometimes, they forgive them." Foster children do not begin with love, but enter the world with loss and distrust of everyone. Theirs is not love easily given to any caretaker, but earned through a long journey of unconditional acceptance between the foster parent and the child. Some will succeed, while others will suffer through a life of homelessness. Any one outcome is difficult, if not impossible to predict.

Share in our story, feel our throbbing pain and most important, join in our jubilation for we have survived. If you allow yourself to touch their wounds and feel their hurt, you will better appreciate their struggles and understand the true meaning of a foster child's love. It was, and will always remain, the most painful, frustrating and self-empowering experience of my life. One of my foster children wrote me this note during his senior high school year when he took my family name:

First, I wanted to say that I love you, and there is no doubt about that. I just wanted to let you know that you have given me a life that is pretty much a dream come true and I could never ever repay you, Thank You.

You have been the single person I've ever met that has been there from the beginning and that had real love for me through thick and thin. I will always love and cherish our relationship.

Final Day

My last day caring for a foster child began like most weekdays. I was up at 5:30, had a quick shower, and made a single minded dash to the car for my morning ritual, a croissant and coffee. Leaving the house by the back patio, my eyes fell upon a clear glass, Turkish style object that could otherwise be displayed as a piece of glass art. It was a bong in plain site on the patio table. My heart sank and disappointment fumed. I had no need to search out the culprit. It was my foster son, Drake.

At eighteen, Drake was a narrow, solid built kid with olive skin, wavy black hair and brown eyes. He could well have been a model for Greek sculptures of their Olympic heroes, or what the Irish would call: a brawny lad. As a little boy he was cute and adorable. As a teenager he was a fine looking young man with strong handsome features that attracted most girls to his inner circle.

He was very athletic, but shied away from competition. As a high school and U.S. Diver, he struggled with criticism, finding it impossible to separate coaching of his diving form from his personal self-image. Every negative statement cut deep into his flesh. He would rather smack on his back again and again, than endure the displeasure of a coach. The same was true of me, his father. No matter how gentle the criticism, the pain of my disapproval far outweighed the meaning of my words. He never heard the lecture. He was simply too focused on his own hurt and negative self-talk: I am stupid. I failed again. I am bad.

Not being fully experienced in the world of narcotics, I wrapped the bong in a towel with the other paraphernalia on the table, gently laid it on the back seat of my car and drove off to work. I intended to show it to Drake's social worker, Tom, to confirm my suspicion. At my office, my mind wandered as I addressed the morning's email traffic. Learning to manage emotions is a key talent for successful foster parenting. It was a skill I never mastered.

Midmorning I drove off to my foster care agency in Phoenix. Meanwhile, my cell phone was ringing with text messages flowing. Drake was asking if I found something, but did not name it. He was desperately searching the house with a friend. It was Thursday, pool cleaning day. He later told me he speculated that the pool man was the culprit. I disregarded his annoying texts to let him stew. At that moment, I felt no pity.

Tom had been called out of the office. I left the object d'art on his desk and proceeded back to work, anxiously waiting for his call and confirmation of what I suspected. I never did get my croissant and coffee that morning.

I was jerked awake once again to Drake's drug use. I couldn't plead ignorance. This was not the first incident. But after so much exertion to solve this particular issue, I was blindly optimistic he had moved on. His illicit drug use wounded me. However, the need he felt to use weed to cover a deeper pain was far more alarming. What was so hurtful he needed drugs to overcome?

He was pushing me out of his life when he needed a parent most. And yet, his mental state was such that he was oblivious to the consequences of his behavior within our family or society at large. As often as I would lecture him on how his negative behavior impacted the family, he maintained his casual defense that we all had a choice to be affected or not. His voice was deliberate and cold. Walking away and closing off everyone in his life was so easy for him. And to hear anyone complain that his actions caused them hurt was simply not within his grasp to understand. He seemed to lack empathy. Or perhaps he buried it too deep to recover. He would say things like: "Ignore me Bill; it's not your problem. You worry too much," or, "I'll be OK. I'll grow out of it."

I was not so sure he would grow up at all. I loved him and could never understand his thought process. This is the challenge of raising foster children. They are not raised with your beliefs, experiences, or culture as a foundation. But foster families must discover, through trial and error, a method to live together in harmony. And the parents must find opportunities to constantly nudge righteous values in their children's path, hoping they will stop for just a moment to pocket one or two.

While waiting for the call from Drake's social worker I reflected on the recent events of that year. I struggled with three teenage foster boys together under the same roof, a difficult scenario for the strongest family. But in our case we suffered ongoing threats of disruption from forces outside the home, as well as from the boys themselves. Each was battling his own demons that generated fear and insecurity. They were always feeling threatened even when such concerns were speculative. This inner conflict carried by each of the boys resulted in an atmosphere polluted with uncertainty. It seemed that every day someone was reacting to their own triggers or the others' behavior. I could never find a peaceful moment. Each boy was the center of his own storm. When one fell into a lull, another would explode. Someone was brewing day and night.

As a family unit we were paralyzed. Each individual was fighting for survival. The children's' natural reaction was to fight against the slightest hint of loss, each using their unique behavior patterns to outshine the other which evolved from their painful histories. Was I so blind, overwhelmed in a fight I could not win? As I thought about the best approach to give Drake a wakeup call about the consequences of drug abuse, I was not conscious of my own denial as to the relationship of his behavior and the ongoing family conflict. Sometimes parents need a wakeup call more than their children. But at that moment, Drake's drug use consumed me. I was in full reactionary mode.

Drake's case worker was an old hand at dealing with foster children, but by no means an aged man. Lanky in stature, Tom's appearance seemed rushed with unruly dirty blond hair and a fuzzy chin beard. Scooby Doo could have mistaken him for his partner Shaggy. The children jokingly said he resembled Mr. Thomas from the story Narnia. He appeared young, still wrestling at home with a toddler. No matter how desperate the situation, he always carried a caring smile and warm embrace. When I first met Tom, I was unsure of his professional ability due to his very casual appearance. I soon learned to respect his deep commitment to the youth and willingness to struggle with the bureaucracy of the system. He was designed by God for social work both in disposition and patience. And most importantly, he was an eternal optimist; a child of Woodstock.

Later that morning Tom called. We spoke about the pot problem and similar inappropriate activities and poor decisions that were symptomatic of Drake's recent rebellious behavior pattern. I was groping for a permanent solution. How naive of me. Drake's underlying issues were too complex and hardwired. He was eighteen. His psychiatric condition slipped under the wire for years; a misfortune of his passive character. I wanted to contain the problem and get my boy back on track. I was a parent after all, not a clinician.

Tom and I were always talking about his many poor choices that year and how to address his misconduct. We lectured. We warned. We threatened. And we witnessed little concrete change on his part. We invested in a major behavior modification program the prior year and were hopeful he would soon settle back down. However, as he approached eighteen that year, he asserted his adult authority more and more, though sadly, in a very self-defeating way. Drugs, tobacco, traffic tickets, and shop-lifting all pointed in one direction. He was absolutely defiant of authority.

This was not the first time he used weed, but things seemed to be escalating. What upset me most was the blatant display of the drug paraphernalia without consideration of me, or the fact I had another younger foster child, Sam, in the house. I would learn later that my younger boy was well aware of Drake's occasional drug use; a fact that pleased me less. Sam had lost all respect for his older foster brother. Burning inside with disappointment, he felt betrayed.

Drake was my third son; my third experience with the mental and emotional transition of the eighteenth birthday. It doesn't happen on that one day, but builds during the prior year, and then settles during the next. For the youth, however, it represents instantaneous power. How they react most often depends on their place in society at their birthday. Two of my older children had big parties, and likely a few secret ones, but otherwise experienced little change. They were both still high school students. For them, the big milestone was going to college.

My first foster child, named Jason, did have an enchanting experience at Grand Cayman Island soon after turning eighteen. Early one evening he was exploring a small coral reef to test his new scuba flashlight near our hotel. He went to grip a piece of coral to balance himself and grabbed hold of a spotted sting ray. The animal was not receptive to his touch and whipped him good. Off we went in search of the nearest available ice: the bar. Did I mention the drinking age there was eighteen? If not, I likely also didn't disclose information about the two beautiful Australian girls behind the bar. These two gorgeous models played nurse, providing the best sedative a bottle could offer. Those are the kind of memories you laugh about years later.

Drake's test of adulthood was not so amusing. It represented something far more powerful. He was struggling in school, had no plans for college or special skill training, and was generally unhappy with his prospects. He wanted control of his life; a power he had battled to possess for many years. Though he wanted to flaunt it in the face of authority, it overwhelmed and frightened him. It was setting him back.

Aside from the emotional baggage from foster care, he suffered the same issues as many teens today and was unprepared for independent responsibility. As a culture, we treat our adolescents like children and minimize adult accountability. I was no different, most especially raising my children in an affluent community. Drake had chores and eventually got a job to pay for his personal needs. But, like most teenagers, he was protected from the harsh reality of independent living. How frightening it was when he peered into the real world from inside the high wall I built and struggled to maintain. He preferred his world, half in and half out; anything more caused anger, depression, and rebellious behavior. Now at eighteen, Drake launched himself in a dark abyss, anxious for a successful outcome, but truly scared of failure, a fear driven from years of helplessness.

Drake was a product of his past experiences for sure; but more, suffered many of the physical challenges inherited from his parents. His multidimensional diagnosis was masked from professionals his entire time in foster care. In truth, like most foster children, he was years behind in maturity, and had barely begun the process of emotional healing.

If parents have addiction issues, assume the child will too. If the parents are plagued with mental health issues, don't think your good home will be the cure for any inherited genes. Many behaviors are genetic or hardwired by experiences at a very young age. Both elements are the building blocks that establish the foundation for future behaviors. To compound the problem, these children have no understanding of the relationship between their current emotions and the resultant behaviors, and their past traumas. In Drake's case, he was the product of parents who abused narcotics and alcohol, and a father in particular, who never grew up himself and clearly displayed signs of a mental disorder.

Throughout his high school years, Drake was quiet, with a laissez-faire attitude, displaying many of the characteristics of an introvert. Was he his father's son? Is that so difficult to accept just because he was removed from the man's influence at the young age of three? He was also under the care of his grandfather for a number of years. What was his emotional state? Was Drake's father but a mirror of his grandfather? Many destructive behaviors can migrate within a family line for many generations. One of the many objectives of a foster parent is to break the pattern.

Drake maintained a distant physical boundary at all times and showed many of the symptoms of attachment disorder. Because he was always so distant and did not display emotion, it was difficult to fully understand the depth of his personal loss. At times, I feared he was sociopathic. Emotions were locked away in his inner vault; the keys lost years ago. Denial was his common theme. When talking of his past, he would often affirm that the many beatings he suffered under his grandfather were normal to him, so what was the big deal. Can you beat hope from a child? Drake is the proof that it can be done.

His current emotional illness resulted not only from the physical abuse for which he was removed by Child Protective Services (CPS), but years in foster care. The purpose of CPS is noble. The result of a placement, however, can often be cataclysmic. In the end, many simply feed into the criminal system. I worried Drake was on that singular path. Foster care is like warfare, it is a reality of our culture that leaves horrific waste in its wake.

With his misconduct continuing, Tom and I agreed to look at options for Drake to move out of my home where he had lived the last four years. It was time for a wake-up call, or what some would call 'tough love.' A young adult shelter in downtown Phoenix seemed the best option. In such an environment he would face adult reality without the protection of Dad, but still have some oversight and structure. He would need to accept responsibility for the most basic personal chores, and pay the consequences for his poor decisions without me playing savior. However, this action was no different than a decision to place a child into residential treatment or even weekly therapy. The child must be emotionally ready or the results can be shattering.

In addition to his own issues, I was concerned about the impact of his misconduct on Sam. Drake had recently dropped out of his junior year of high school just five weeks short of the term's end, but was not failing. He was smoking cigarettes around the house and hanging out with older youth who were no longer in school. They were not bad kids, but on a different social maturity level than Drake. And worse, though these youth were dealing with adult issues, it was without accepting the full load of adult accountability since they too were still living at home. The attraction to their world was irresistible, and they provided him an escape from the disruptions at our house and a distraction from schoolwork. Unfortunately for him, and for me, their influence was having dire consequences.

Later that afternoon I scheduled a meeting with Drake and Tom at the house to discuss our options. By the time Tom arrived, Drake's anxiety of loss was at an all time high, though our options had petered out. The young adult programs were full with a waiting list, and because he was eighteen and of legal age, we could not force him into a group home or foster shelter, though he didn't know that at the time. He had occasionally used weed, but wasn't a drug addict requiring residential drug rehabilitation. He was sullen and visibly shaken as we discussed the situation and his continued emotional decline. His facial expression was empty, head down, eyes to the floor. He recognized my heartache as I began to cry. How do you express your love, while at the same time, your total disappointment and loss of trust for your son? And after four years, he was my son, even though he still addressed me by my first name, Bill. But when he spoke about me to others, I was dad. A curiosity I did not understand, but stopped distressing over a long time ago.

As the drama played out, Sam's social worker appeared at the door with her supervisor. What was to unfold shook me to the core. Suddenly, the bong crisis was brushed aside and replaced by a far greater calamity. A match lit months before was about to engulf me in a raging forest fire.

Twelve Years Earlier

It's a short flight from Phoenix to Denver. Not much time to consider the day ahead. You lie back, close your eyes, and just relax. My seventeen year old son Nick and I arrived in Denver on a wintery day in 1996 on a journey neither of us could possibly have predicted.

We raced to the car rental bus amongst a hustling crowd, our minds focused on the moment. We hopped in the car and drove off to a little known place between Denver and Boulder near the town of Westminster that the case worker simply referred to as Cleo Wallace. It was boasted as one of the best treatment facilities in the west, thought at the time I thought it was some kind of group home.

I was in my early forties; educated in political science at Rutgers University in New Jersey, and a defense contractor by trade. I was married, divorced, raised a son, and was active in a sleepy little community in Arizona. High adventure sports and long distance running were my true passions. If I wasn't exploring some new rock formation in places like Queen's Creek or Pinnacle Peak, I was running a 10K. I even tried my hand at mountaineering and ice climbing. At six feet tall and a hundred and seventy pounds, people always commented I looked many years junior of my true age. Perhaps they were just being polite or political, but the compliments motivated me to stay in shape.

Chasing after forty to fifty scouts on weekend outings contributed to my physical condition as well. Over the past decade I had served as the local Scoutmaster and was active as an elected member to the governing board of our elementary school district. I was comfortably settled with my life and fortunate to be well connected within our community.

Nick was narrowly built like me, though shorter in stature, a gift from his Dutch mother. He participated in cross country, just like I had done decades earlier in New Jersey. Unlike me, he joined the wrestling team for most of his high school years. Academically he did well, advancing to honors classes by his sophomore year, and registered for college level credit in his senior year. But Nick was not the classic scholastic athletic type. Though built for sports, his character was far more refined. He remained quietly in the background; steadfastly loyal to a small group of friends he had known since fourth grade.

The single aspect that defined his character was being an avid reader. As a teen, Ann Rice and Robert Jordan were his daily companions. In Scouts, while the boys were playing around a campsite during a typical outing, Nick could be found sitting on a log or warming a rock under a tree, book in hand. A stranger might conclude he was a geek. Acquaintances, casual or intimate, knew different. Occasionally his friends would engage him to less serious activity, but no one ridiculed his one true joy.

That cold wintery day Nick and I were on an adventure of a very different sort from our normal exploratory regime; one that did not pit physical strength and endurance against nature. We had shared our lives together more so than most parents. After all, it was just him and me for most of his childhood. A psychologist might conclude we had developed a co-dependency. When he was only seven, we climbed all around Arizona together. When I had my first major rock climbing accident on Camelback Mountain, falling off a lead climb down nearly forty feet to the ground, he was tied to the rock face, observing my every move. Later at the hospital as the physician forced my dislocated shoulder into place, he stood quietly by my side, teeth clinched sharing my pain. On another occasion, while running the Phoenix 10K, I collapsed and was taken to the hospital. As I lay wired to multiple machines, he sat on the bed intently watching my cardiac performance, alerting me of any skipped beats. We were inseparable.

My mind was clouded with the thoughts of our relationship and the impact of a new son in the family as we drove from the airport. I was naively optimistic that Nick would embrace this newcomer with the same enthusiasm that had filled me about being a foster parent.

The weather was gloomy. Spots of frozen snow littered the prairie surrounding the airport. Nick navigated as we headed to Denver, then north toward Boulder. We were still a team. The directions were well laid out and the drive went well. We were even running early for our appointment.

In winter, the area between Denver and Boulder can seem bleak to the uninitiated. Bare trees stand alone in the frozen ground surrounded by tufts of brown grass. The real beauty is hidden beyond the Denver area, west into the Rockies. We both half-jokingly commented about our mutual regret that we were not heading in that direction for a ski weekend, rather than this more serious business. We were anxious. As we turned into the entrance of our destination, our excitement snapped shut, leaving a dull throb. We faced a hospital Emergency Entrance sign, above which read: The Devereux Cleo Wallace Psychiatric Facility for Children.

'What is this place?' I thought. Nick had an expression of confusion and fear. We rolled slowly into the parking area of the visitor's lobby. Nick was reluctant to get out of the car. He preferred the security of the rental vehicle. I was curious but at the same time angry. The social worker had told me he was in residential treatment. I wrongly assumed they meant some kind of group home. In my enthusiasm for getting a new son, I asked few questions, and they offered little information beyond an old school photograph. I never equated the term residential to a facility for psychiatric patients. I would later discover that he had been a patient for nearly a year. The initial social worker who introduced me to the case was leaving the agency and a new social worker had yet to be assigned. His case was on standby since the agency had turned over his maintenance to Cleo Wallace. What sketchy information was provided came through the family developer. They are the agency's front line sales people.

If you are in this business very long, you soon become accustomed to personnel changes and minimal information. I was told by an old social worker once that if the prospective foster parents were ever given the whole truth straight out, most of the children would never get placed. Full disclosure is not a requirement. So prospective parents are spoon fed just enough to get them hooked. Also, as case workers change, key information learned through the relationship with the child can be lost.

Foster children have the unique prospect of experiencing multiple social workers over their time in the system. Many will also endure multiple placements. It all provides them a special skill in flexibility as they learn and re-learn personalities, expectations, and rules. Through these unstable experiences they develop unique behaviors to survive in the system. These behaviors are not conducive to building positive relationships as they mature. They can be left cold and distrusting of people in general and particularly people who represent authority. These are the emotional scars that never fade. I was about to meet one small boy emotionally disfigured with such invisible wounds.

Upon our arrival, we were introduced to a psychiatrist, Dr. U. He was a gentle man with a kind face and welcoming expression filled with optimism. His mellow voice transmitted hope. He spoke of a lonely child who suffered from an extreme case of reactive attachment disorder due to multiple emotional traumas of loss. And at that particular time at Cleo Wallace, he also suffered from serious conduct disorder. Both were significant diagnoses in a young person's life. He was a child without inner hope. The short introduction to his multiple diagnoses meant little to me at the time. I was politely attentive, but my mind was in overdrive trying to imagine this ten year old boy from Phoenix, lost in what appeared to us to be a very cold and repressive facility. I re-engaged with the doctor when he asked, "You ready to meet Jason?"

We waited in a small nondescript room sitting across from an empty chair. Nick had been very quiet, staring down at the ground, his body language declaring his desire to be anywhere but in that room. This was Colorado and the only time prior to that day that we were in this great state was to hit the slopes with skies and poles in hand. Nick had been very supportive of my foster parenting plan. We had talked about it for nearly a year. It seemed as if in a single moment a swift wind ripped the sails from his mast. I too was uncomfortable. Working through a psychiatrist was not my vision for getting a new kid. I was certain no one talked about getting children from hospitals while I was in training. We sat waiting for an eternity of anxious minutes. At that moment, if I had suggested we walk out, Nick would have leaped ahead to hold the door for me.

While we were sinking deeper into disillusionment, a lanky little boy shuffled into the room, head down, with his chin tight to the chest. Doctor U. introduced us. His name was Jason. The doctor gently led him to the empty chair directly across from me. He slouched down. He was lethargic. At first all I could see was his overgrown hair, long dirty blond with no particular pattern as it fell across his face. When he slowly raised his head, I honestly felt a pang of disappointment. His thin, shallow features were overwhelmed by a pair of oversized glasses hung on a rather thin ridge nose. Gazing past me were hazy grey eyes, one seemingly twice as large as the other. His skin seemed almost transparent, his lips parched and pale. I studied his pupils for a few minutes, desperate for a reaction. I always found children's eyes to be a real barometer of their feelings. But that day I saw an empty, hollow being. He was a broken shell, no doubt heavily medicated.

Dr. U. lead the conversation with a discussion about Jason's reaction to a picture album we called *Our Family Book*. We had sent this album of family pictures to Jason weeks ago. It was a great idea presented by our trainer. A picture book that described our family, park-like community, and the many activities we enjoyed. We were outdoor enthusiasts. I had been a Scoutmaster and Nick an Eagle Scout, so we had pictures of our scout adventures. We were very active in rock climbing, backpacking and camping, as well as downhill skiing and whitewater rafting, and so included all those pictures as well. The doctor started with small talk about our interests and how Jason seemed very excited about trying his hand at some of those activities. I was taken aback by the word excited. I found nothing in this little guy that met the most basic meaning of that word: excited. He shook his head on cue with a puppet-like affirmation. The doctor then addressed one of Jason's questions about the book. There were no pictures of mommy. I confirmed his suspicions. This was a point of contention for Jason. He was also concerned about one of the pictures of Nick holding a boogie board on a beach. Nick had a short 'bald' hair cut and looked mean. Nick and I assured Jason, it was only the sun in his eyes, and that Nick was really a nice guy.

It was a short meeting and a good thing too. We were all feeling uncomfortable. Perhaps the doctor picked up on our vibes or didn't want to stress Jason too much on the first meeting. I wasn't sure we exchanged much new information, but we did accomplish one important goal. Jason measured us up. The doctor suggested Nick and I return the next morning and take Jason out for the day. He recommended the *Butterfly Pavilion*, a local visitor attraction. Jason enjoyed a school trip there in the past, so Dr. U. encouraged us to let him be our guide.

We quickly took our leave. Both Nick and I were sharing the same uncertainty about this whole adventure. We exchanged few words driving to the hotel that day. What was there to say? We were filled with misgivings. The place was nothing short of depressive. The winter chill and brown landscape added to the overwhelming sense of melancholy. And worst of all, we learned little about Jason other than he was heavily drugged. I was so green not to even question why that would be so. But I strived to keep a positive attitude, though Nick was already expressing concern that I was in over my head.

In truth, I was completely unprepared. And yet my limited knowledge also provided a complete lack of bias. I met Jason with a clean slate, colored only by my own personal experiences. I had no preconceived thoughts about emotional disabilities or mental illness. I was unrestrained from total idyllic optimism. Years later, this same unbiased optimism would bring me face-to-face with the darkest of all childhood mental illnesses.

I kept repeating in my mind: 'I will love him, care for his every need. I will always be there for him and all will be well'. My attitude with foster children is a model for the adage: ignorance is bliss. We went to bed early that night with guarded anticipation.

***

Jason's Journal (9 Years old)

The day that I left for Cleo Wallace was like any other. It was the weekend. I was at the park with my friend Matt. I spent most of my time at the park or out in the desert to avoid my foster dad Ryan. When I came home for water; something felt different. My caseworker was there. I came in and Ryan, Marge, and my caseworker were all talking in the living room. The moment I came in, there was an awkward silence and then Ryan and Marge got up and left the room. My caseworker sat me down to tell me that I was being taken to a new family. I had two hours to pack. I wasn't so upset about leaving this family. The pain was leaving all my friends and my things. I ran to ask Matt if he would take my three leopard geckos. He was the only one I trusted. I also had to explain what was going on and he was really sad. The family didn't talk to me that day. They seemed happy to see me leave because their family would be perfect once more. My Caseworker helped me pack a few of my clothes and my stuffed bear. We left for the airport.

On the plane, I got really nervous because things seemed odd. My caseworker didn't talk to me throughout the whole plane ride or during the car ride to Cleo Wallace. When we pulled up I was confused because she told me that I was going to be living with a new family. When I asked her she told me that she just said that to get me to come without a fuss. I got mad and jumped out of the car while it was still moving. Once I got out I realized it was too late to run, the gates had already been shut and I was trapped. I tried to run anyway but my caseworker cornered me in front of a building. I started to panic and went into a rage. I wanted to hit my caseworker for lying to me but she stayed out of arms reach. I beat on an outdoor railing. I kicked it until it was completely broken. The staff at the facility saw what was going on, and ran over and tackled me. I started swinging and kicking. It took six grown men to hold me down. I broke two fingers of one of the men at which point they all started beating me with the collapsible batons that the cops carry, until I was unconscious.

I woke up to one of them smacking me in the face. I was covered in blood. They ordered me to take off my clothes or they would do it. They sprayed me down with a high powered hose, and then threw powder all over me. It burned my skin really bad. After that they threw me into this little room about 8x8 feet. It was a lot like a prison cell, but empty with no windows to the outside, no bed, no toilet; just brick walls with a 6 inch window with bars on it on the door for people to look in and see what I was doing. I spent that night beating my fists into the door until they were bloody and I couldn't feel them anymore. I wondered what I had done that was so terrible to deserve this. I finally passed out that night from the pain and exhaustion of beating my fists against the door. I didn't cry that night. I was too mad and confused. I felt like an animal. When anyone came near me I'd get violent. I was a beaten dog, nothing more.

The next morning I was taken to the infirmary. I got really depressed and was too sore to fight anybody. I just shut down and stared out of the window.

Later I was allowed to my room which had bunk beds and two closets, cabinets and a barred window. It wasn't much bigger than the quiet room. No matter how bad it hurt, I couldn't cry.

That night I didn't sleep. One of the staff saw that I was still awake and he told me to go to sleep or he would put me to sleep. I noticed that he had two fingers bandaged up. That was the same guy that tackled me and I broke his fingers. I told him to go fuck himself. I would go to sleep when I was damn well good and ready. He didn't like that answer and came over and hit me over the head with his flashlight.

The following morning I was woken up at 5:00am by getting yanked out of my bed onto the floor. I was told to go take a shower. They handed me a plastic cup of shampoo and then shoved me into the shower with all the others.

Dr. U. spent over two hours trying to talk to me that first day, but I didn't say a word to him. I didn't trust him or anyone that worked there. After lunch he tried again for a long time, and once more I said nothing to him. That night was the same, the staff guy came in and beat me to shut me up and make me go to sleep.

***

The next morning Nick stayed back at the hotel. He said he wanted to sleep in. I knew better. He really wanted to keep his distance from Cleo Wallace. I arrived early and was given directions to a different location on the campus from where we first met Jason. It was a separate building arranged like a hospital ward. The entry was guarded by a security buzzer. A nursing station greeted me upon entry into a large gathering room with lots of chairs and pillows. This room was encircled by the bedrooms with bunk beds in each, a group bathroom and a quiet room. I would later learn that the quiet room was anything but quiet. This was a place Jason spent many hours, and in some cases, days. Clinically speaking, it was an isolation room.

Children were lying around, though not interacting with one another. The smell was sterile, the air thick. Some of the children seemed to be frozen to a single spot on the floor staring into empty space or just rocking on their heels, while others were engrossed in a video game or watching cartoons. Jason was in front of the television. As we walked into the area, he snapped to with a grin that lifted his glasses up his nose. I smiled back. I noticed his eyes were blue, big bright blue. I was immediately reassured. Today would be exciting.

He took my hand and led me to his room. It was medicinal like the rest of the place. A bunk bed stood against one wall opposite two simple desks and dressers. The room was neat and clean, a point he emphasized more than once. On the bed rested a small brown stuffed bear, looking worn and limp. It was no different than millions of others, though it was obviously placed with great care, centered on the bed, head gently resting on a flat pillow. I was formally introduced to his bear named Brownie. The tops of the dressers and desks were bare. Brownie was the only sign that the room was occupied.

I brought a small gift for him, a Pirate Lego set. Lego blocks were big business in our home over the years. It was the only toy that seemed to survive endless wear and tear as the boys grew up. One never throws away Lego blocks. They accumulated in our closet and were always expected at Christmas. He accepted it with a simple 'thanks' and carefully placed it on his dresser. His smile was unwavering and seemed genuine.

I sat on his bed while he grabbed a small gym bag. I suggested he bring a bathing suit to which he gave me a quizzical look; his smile distorted to an awkward grin. I immediately responded to his surprise with the information about the hotel's indoor pool and spa. He reluctantly agreed, regaining his composed smile. Unlike the prior day, he was anxiously tense, constantly fidgeting and talking, jumping from one topic to another, transmitting a stream of random thoughts. When I suggested we leave for the hotel, he grabbed my hand once again and led me to the door. After the signing out formality at the main desk, we were out in the frigid air heading toward the car. He seemed to become more and more animated as we left the grounds, acting the role of a tour guide, pointing out each building on the campus. Little did I realize at the time, but in his mind, I was his ticket out of that prison. Perhaps his first and only hope for freedom from what he perceived to be a much tormented existence.

At the Butterfly Garden we experienced a child poles apart from the one in the institution. He was fully engaged, expressing curiosity and wonder one expects from a boy of ten. He was a most energetic guide, jumping about as fluidly as the insects buzzing around us. For that moment, he was free of the institution and all it represented. He was happy. He was a real boy.

Happy is a simple word used to describe a content child. Most children rarely question it, or go to bed at night anxious for it. For foster children like Jason, it was rare, an occasion to be savored. Residential treatment is a cruel interlude in a child's life. Freely walking out the front door with friends to play becomes a distant memory. Existence is focused on survival and escape, and just every so often, a fantasy of having a family that would never turn you out. Each time Jason was introduced to a new family placement, it soon ended in disruption. Locked away, he became numb, his behavior selfish without the slightest concern for others. During that first visit, perhaps because of his spiritual innocence, he defied his deeply dour condition and allowed himself to be consumed by a tiny flame of hope.

After the tour, we went to the hotel to relax and have dinner before returning Jason to his ward. At first he just wanted to watch television in the room, but agreed to go swimming with Nick after some insistence. As we left the room I noticed he still had his socks on. I picked him up, dropped him on the bed and pulled them off too quickly for him to argue. I was appalled. He pulled back, bringing his knees to his chest, eyes drawn down, face ashen white. His feet were covered with dozens of warts. No toe was untouched. One of his little toes was so engulfed, it appeared deformed. His eyes reflected his shame. His smile was gone. It was a critical moment and I felt his anticipation of my displeasure. The room went tense. I gently took his feet in my hands, while I hardened my stomach to avoid nausea.

"It's no big deal," I told him, "that's an easy fix."

I took his hand and we were off to the pool. During this episode Nick seemed ambivalent. I was so focused on Jason, I was not watching for his otherwise obvious body language. Nick spoke little. He was an introvert, always expressing himself with his actions and facial expressions; that is when his face wasn't hiding in a book.

Once over the horror of his disfigured feet, we all enjoyed the pool; and Jason was animated with all the attention, especially from Nick who tossed him about like a tub toy. But he was very attentive to anyone staring at him. When out of the water, he tended to keep his feet out of sight. I recognized that this superficial physical deformity would be the first of many issues that would need to be addressed. I was not abased by it at all, in fact it gave me something physical on which to focus, a simple engineering problem that I could solve. Dealing with a physical problem was completely within my capability to address. Emotional acting out behavior was not. All I could ever offer was motivation, while obscuring my sense of total helplessness.

Back in the room, we watched some cartoons and he seemed relieved to be dressed and in his socks and shoes. He was still uncertain about me and was clearly seeking reassurance.

"The children make fun of me because of my feet," he said. "They put medicine on them, but it doesn't work. I'm gross."

Jason was not playing for sympathy. This was his true self-perception. Between his oversized glasses, with one lens thicker than the other creating the optical illusion that his right eye was larger than the other, combined with his scrawny appearance and feet overtaken by warts; he had good reason for self-doubt. And his peers, like most children of that age group, used these physical oddities for their own amusement. We learned later that disgruntled, poorly trained or unsympathetic staffers also found enjoyment tormenting him over his awkward appearance.

After dinner we drove back to Cleo Wallace. He was as gloomy as the darkened winter sky. I reassured him we would be back in two weeks. The news didn't appear to cheer him. By the time we returned to his room that evening, he was distant and withdrawn, not so different than our first meeting. We exchanged goodbyes. I never turned back as I left the building and hurried to the car and back to the hotel. I was too afraid to look into his eyes; too weak to see his pained expression.

I felt committed, but not sure to what end. My emotions were more driven from pity than a true sense of connection. He was unlike any child I'd experienced, and after ten years of Scouts, I'd encountered quite a diversity of personalities. His innocence was heartbreaking. His longing for attention and family was all too clear. What was less apparent was his innate ability to manipulate the human spirit. He had established the groundwork of a "honeymoon" relationship. He would capture my heart and soul, strangle my common sense, and leave me stripped of all logic. It was a brilliant survival tactic, though certainly an unconscious act. He baited me to a hook from which I would never break free.

The relationship that was just launched would test my fortitude, which in the end, could only survive, not based on these initial feelings, but a powerful bond built on mutual trust, love, and respect. Those virtues would develop over time in the course of our shared experiences. A foundation of trust was critical to the formation of this relationship. What I could not know was how often and to what extreme levels he would test my commitment, and just how many years it would take to win him over.

During this growth a spiritual bond would evolve in me of an unconditional love, an emotion that burns in your chest and tears your eyes. This is a human bond so strong that you suffer inner pain and joy, no matter the physical distance. For many people, this is the essence of humanity, distinctly separating us from all other creatures. Foster and adoptive parents must take the time and allow the hurt. It is the only true path to permanency. It is not easy. Those people who sustain themselves in the system are battle tested warriors.

That Sunday's return home from Colorado was bitter sweet. This was an emotion that I would often experience during the next twelve years. After months of training and expectations, I was offered my opportunity. Nick was clearly disappointed, having expected an outgoing, energetic, athletic brother ready to hit the basketball courts. Honestly, I can't say I felt much different with one key exception; he had stolen my heart. Whether from pity at first, his weird expression, lack of self-worth or that welcoming grin that spoke so vibrantly, I cannot say. I saw a flicker of hope in his expression. How could I callously extinguish that spark? I was committed to return.

I reported back to the case worker with reserved enthusiasm. They encouraged me to go back in two weeks. I agreed.

This was the beginning of my journey, no, my adventure, experienced by few and yet occurring all around you. I was one of tens of thousands of foster parents. For a dozen years I struggled as the intermediary between the system and the child. To the state I was a caretaker, in fact, an employee paid to provide basic needs. Many of us, as self-destructive as it is, get emotionally involved. You begin to feel the child's trauma and at times feel as vulnerable as they truly are. Over time I would feel like a servant to the system, with no more power and authority in my own home than the State Ward I sheltered.

I cherish the memory of Jason's smile that first day I picked him up from his room at Cleo Wallace and that animated little guide at the butterfly garden. It has and will always bring more inner spiritual happiness than any career accomplishment or material acquisition.

Lined Up for the Slaughter

Over half a million children are hostage to the foster care system due mostly to substance abuse, with nearly 20% in care for more than 3 years. In my state, the number of children in care has risen from six thousand in 2002 to nearly ten thousand today. Depending on the study, as many as 50% of these children have been sexually molested, many while in foster care. There is no national system or code of conduct. It is all regulated by the states with services dependent on available budgets. The law and state policies continue to establish an increasing legal basis for removal of children without any direct correlation to the available budget for their care, especially mental health services. While the government preaches a "better safe than sorry" philosophy, a single mistake can permanently damage a child and their extended families. Any child removed from a parent abusive or not, regardless of the well meaning intent, will suffer emotional trauma. The study titled: *The Impact of Foster Care on Development* from the University of Minnesota, suggests that foster care is actually more damaging to children than abusive homes.[2] Trauma from loss of security while developing into adulthood cannot be overestimated.

Study after study has been completed. Reports have been reviewed, analyzed and published. The statistics are daunting. Large numbers of foster children end up homeless or incarcerated, many before 18 years of age. Over half of all foster children will experience clinical depression because they are so deeply unhappy with their lives, many of whom are filled with unwarranted self guilt.

In addition to the use of physical management, the system depends heavily on the use of psychotropic drugs to keep these children stable. A 2004 study of Texas children with Medicaid coverage found that decisions to give some children three or more psychotropic drugs was largely based on behavioral and emotional symptoms rather than conclusive diagnosis of a specific mental condition. The children are medicated to attain a short term behavioral solution, which poses questions about appropriateness, benefits, and risks to their long-term health: mental or otherwise.

Children suffer trauma from unexpected stressful situations. As a result their sense of security is splintered and they suffer a complete sense of helplessness. It is this vulnerability that shatters their childhood at a time when they need the warmth and love of caring parents. Sadly, foster children fall into the hands of a committee. And though many foster parents try to be the gentle hand to guide, love, and offer security; in the end, the decision makers are at a distance which results in a continued loss of trust as foster children experience one betrayal after another. Is it possible for a case worker, meeting with a child once a month, to have any concept of the child's emotional situation? How many stressed out children would dare speak out to an authority figure so distant in their lives. To a young child, a month equates to a very long time. Many of these children have already suffered other traumas from physical, sexual or verbal abuse, but now must endure perhaps the most threatening of all, emotional loss which is as traumatizing as any life-threatening event that may have happened during their early childhood.

When a foster home opens the door to one of these children to greet them with a broad welcoming smile, what enters the home is a child overwhelmed, frozen and numb. They are disconnected at many levels. They have been cut off, sometimes overnight, from a prior placement or recent family tragedy. They are instantly paralyzed and soon develop many behavior and mental conditions in response to the past and ongoing traumas which cause odd reactions to everyday situations that we all take for granted. At best, they develop neurotic symptoms. For example, many show clear signs of attention deficit and hyperactivity disorder which may be a reactive behavior resulting from severe attachment disorder, rather than the more straightforward learning disability. They are ever alert, surprisingly so. Through a complex arrangement of filters, each evolves to protect their core being. Their interpretation of events is always clouded, forever affecting the way they see the world and interact with family, casual friends or within an intimate relationship.

Many foster children lock themselves away in their rooms and hide in video gaming, leading the foster family to a false sense of security. After all, the child is not raging with anger. Others will turn to drugs for relief or harm themselves.

The system's greatest challenge, however, are those children that lash out against the world with all that anger built up over years of emotional suffering. At some point, many stop caring about themselves and no longer appreciate the needs and concerns of others. Combine this lack of empathy for others with cruel abnormal adult behaviors witnessed or suffered upon them, and these children become most at risk for social trouble and may never safely exercise self-management skills to make healthy decisions for themselves or others in their adult lives. These graduates of foster care are most dangerous to the community at large for deviant behaviors.

Success in fostering a child requires case workers to keep the children managed and the system afloat, while containing costs and risk of litigation down the road. In foster care, risk management has evolved into a fine art, the result of which is not necessarily in the interest of the child, but provides cover for the State and all the agencies with which it contracts.

Arizona spending is one of the lowest per capita on education in the Nation. Foster care suffers from the same dilemma. To compound the problem, Arizona has chosen to contract most case work to private agencies. Each organization operates under an umbrella of their own objectives and budget goals, as well as their own business agendas. And as with all large organizations, they are driven by personalities, people who themselves have a personal history and bias that compels their decisions. These agencies compete with one another for foster parents and case loads. They all want the better, easier cases, attempting to avoid the harsh reality of the badly damaged children with pre-determined poor prognoses. Those are the children condemned to a childhood under the control of CPS, the agency that has been assigned to accept and manage any and all cases to which they are called. Sadly, CPS case-loads are double that of some of the private agencies like the private agency that sponsored me. And these case loads can reflect the worst of our society. Many of these children, who are the most difficult to manage in a family environment spend their childhood in group homes. In these clinical surroundings they learn new and unique survival skills quite different from a normal family upbringing. These learned behaviors that met their needs in an institution, work against the child when they transition to a normal community environment.

Jason spent many nights in such places during his early years. He once told me that people would show up at his group home and just stroll about, talking to children here and there. They were introduced as helpers, visitors and new aides. From the children's perspective, they were foster or adoptive parents on the hunt. This is also the source for new intakes for the many agencies with licensed foster parents, so these same children are interviewed by a multitude of intake personnel. Such activity raises their hopes for a moment in time, just to come crashing down when the social worker or prospective parent does not return. The new children in the system always put on their best manners and quickly learn the value of a strong smile and bright open eyes. But the more seasoned youth who have suffered multiple disappointments tend to accept their fate and keep a distance. Why suffer the indignity of rejection once again. Jason was one of those children, carried by a tide of injustice from birth.

The path to fostering is unique for every foster parent. Most good and decent people have thought about saving a child in desperation. Many of us are filled with great aspirations as teenagers, sometimes too focused on the depravity of society. We naively dream of a better world. In truth, most of us become engulfed by our own needs and keep the darkness at a distance. We feel a pang of guilt during that missionary advertisement showing a starving child in some far off continent, or driving around our own town, passing a family holding that all too frequently seen sign: *Will work for Food*. For most, it is a passing reflection and we continue on with our daily lives. Others will add a little extra in the offering plate next Sunday, or cautiously open the car window to pass out a few dollars.

A few will dive deep into the murky sea of foster care, innocently thinking that a good home with caring parents and love is the simple solution. After all, they parented their own children, suffered the ups and downs, and the children eventually moved out, got jobs and settled down to become contributing members of society. This is the true test of success. How hard can it be?

My involvement began late in life. Nick was a high school junior; and I a successful senior manager with a large defense contractor. We lived an upper middle-class life style, not over indulged, but well provided for, living in an affluent community in Arizona. People become foster parents for a diversity of reasons. There is no right motivation, just a real desire to be a good parent and have the commitment to go the distance. The latter is the most difficult and least understood element of this business by new foster parents in training. I was such a person, filled with excitement and desire to get the training behind me and start a new family.

How novel, I thought, to get a son that is out of diapers, but better, has learned basic athletic and academic skills. The hard work was done and I could enjoy that best part of fatherhood and take pleasure in father and son interaction and activities. What a deal!

My journey started from stories told by co-workers about their adopted children from distant countries like Russia and China. They spoke of hardships, unexpected medical problems, but always with pride and love in their voices. They were pleased with their new children brought from a world of poverty or lost in overcrowded orphanages. I spoke with Nick about us following that path, and soon inquired with licensing agencies.

One day at lunch I was in my office completing many endless forms toward this end when an ancient engineer from years past sat down during a coffee break. He loved to chew the corner of his Styrofoam cup while sipping the warm liquid down. He had heard about my endeavor to adopt a Russian child and asked in his flat sarcastic manner, "Why?" I told him about my political science degree with a minor in Russian studies and how I felt I would better understand a child from that culture. His sarcasm grew.

"You don't understand our culture? You know, American?"

I was caught off guard, but responded something like, "I think that's a lot harder."

I won't continue the dialogue here as his language became irate. His message was clear. Why are you getting a child from Russia when we have so many homeless children in Arizona, and they speak English! He emphasized the English.

I really had no honest answer. The next day, feeling very guilty, I called Catholic Services and asked about adopting a child. They told me about the very long wait, and on and on. I was surprised after getting the lecture about so many homeless children just the day before.

"I didn't know people were adopting so many teenagers," I finally cut in.

Silence was the response. Finally she apologized and advised me to call another agency, a private foundation, from here on called the *Foundation*. She continued on that it was not adoption, but permanent foster care, which she assured me, was just as good. I called, was directed to a family developer (the social worker responsible for recruiting, licensing and training), and the rest is history.

The Foundation had the unique position in Arizona that they case managed their children. In other words, this agency provided the social worker that interacts directly with the youth. Most other agencies provide services, but leave case management to CPS. When I was first licensed, they also were the legal guardians. These children were the elite in the industry. The Foundation, not unlike many large charitable institutions, was established by a corporate giant. He left the greater part of his wealth to the organization and so it is well funded. Resources, financial or clinical, are rarely an issue. They tend to intake children who demonstrate the most excellent character to be successful.

The training was not too hard, but time consuming, requiring a drive to Phoenix one evening a week for a couple of months. A home study was performed by the family developer. For this training, this person came to the house for a more personal interview with Nick and me. Throughout the training the instructors would talk about children with issues, mental health problems, and defiant behavior, but always cushioned by the great experience of helping a needy child. Of course, I minimized the ugly and focused on the positive.

After a few months I was ready for my first charge. It wasn't long before the call came to meet with the family developer to discuss a prospect.

Product of Substance Abuse

Jason's history is not atypical of children in foster care. He lived a pattern of disruption and placement changes, with an occasional shelter thrown in here and there. He never kept relationships much more than a year or so, not in a home or school. He was wound up tight most of his childhood, vigilant of the slightest aggression toward his personal space.

A native of Phoenix, Jason was born and raised in the center of town, not the business area, but a very poor and run-down area north of the city center. He had siblings, though I did not make their acquaintance until months after we first met. He spoke very affectionately of them, especially of his brother Martin. He missed them very much and felt betrayed that he was taken away to Colorado. This was a wound that would never heal throughout his childhood.

The other children had blamed him for the loss of their family. The catastrophe of foster care was placed squarely on his tiny shoulders. In their minds things were fine at home until he was born. And at the time, they all believed his paternity was different than their own. He was not their real brother, but rather the son of mom's boyfriend. Jason's dad was the man who replaced their real dad, the man who brought drugs and abuse into their lives. He carried this shame like a rag doll. This humiliation aroused deep insecurities as he took his siblings' attacks to heart.

The Foundation did an intake on Jason when he was around seven years old, along with his three siblings. At the time he was living with a dedicated CPS foster family that did not want to change agencies, so he was required to change placements. Looking at the memory photo album the family gave to him, I would say this was probably his best and happiest placement. This was the only home where Jason was not restrained with physical force. Temper tantrums were dealt with in a calm, but stern fashion. He was asked to go to his room to let off steam. His punishment was always the same; loss of his mattress for the night. He never really complained sleeping on the floor as long as he was permitted to stay with his brothers.

Temper tantrums and raging were Jason's way of dealing with the pain. Some children focus all their anger inside which results in depression, others like Jason, force it out upon the world. We call that raging. It is a violent, explosive outburst of built-up anger or anxiety. To truly comprehend the experience of a raging child requires first-hand observation. It is difficult to describe in words. Think upon your experience with a toddler's temper tantrum. Imagine a little child jumping up and down, clenching his fists, face glowing red, demanding to have his way. Now change the toddler into a full size child of 60 pounds or more, an independent person now riding his bike and playing basketball with his friends. You have a super charged temper tantrum. The clenching fists can take you down, the body movement can push you over, and the facial expressions and foul language terrorize your soul. That's raging!

This family never provoked his anger. They also provided lots of structure, which was important for all the children, as it instilled a greater sense of security and safety. This loss may very well have been pivotal in the development of serious behavior issues down the road. Certainly, he was too young to understand the politics of losing a home over an agency change or planed transitional placement. He could only blame himself accompanied by all the emotional suffering. Prior to this placement, his life was totally dysfunctional.

Jason suffered a variety of childhood traumas from both his birth family's dysfunctional behavior and living in neighborhoods overtaken by gang violence. He lived in an addiction infested house. How much of his memory is a reflection of the facts and a mixture of visions from media exposure combined with a young impressionable mind is difficult to know. He remembers witnessing neighborhood shootings, and in particular an incident where he was hiding near a gunshot victim. He was street smart and fighting for survival was a lesson he learned early in life.

Jason recalls an incident when his brother Martin was out on the apartment playground. Jason came on the scene to join his brother, only to find that Martin was not playing. He was on the ground getting kicked and beaten up. Jason jumped on the back of one of the attackers but was quickly thrown off. The older kid spun around and slashed the front of Jason's legs. He then turned toward Martin with the knife. Jason grabbed the kid's legs to tackle him to the ground. He was too young and stood no chance, but nonetheless reacted to defend Martin. Jason was stabbed in the lower back. He jerked in a panic, slamming his palm into the attackers face. The attackers ran off leaving Jason bleeding and Martin unconscious on the ground.

For Jason, his memories are very real and his interpretation of people and his environment all stem from these early tribulations. It was during those years that he developed the survival technique of rage and flight. As a young adult he still occasionally has one recurring nightmare where he is attacked. In the dream he kills someone and gets shot three times in the chest. At times he is uncertain of the reality of these dreams and will burst out of bed with a knife in hand.

Jason's birth family was solid, working middle class. Pictures of him as a baby portray a normal home. His older siblings confirm that prior to Jason all was well in their lives. The parents broke up before Jason was born, and the mom immediately brought home a number of suspect boyfriends that she introduced to the children as uncles. So often in foster care boyfriends, people with no prior relationship with the children, cause irrevocable damage to all parties. This was certainly the case for Jason and his siblings. The parents may have been occasional drug users prior to their breakup, but with the entry of these new boyfriends, narcotic use grew, and with it, family disruptions. The mom sold herself and her daughter for drug money. The daughter was being sexually exploited at only twelve to strangers and was offered to the mom's boyfriends for fun. One particular boyfriend was very abusive to the children, but especially to Jason, who was too young to escape. The belt was his weapon of choice against the toddler. The mom was so afraid of him she listed the boyfriend on Jason's birth certificate, a fact that haunted him with terror for many years.

Some days the children were locked out of the house, and other times, held captive while the mom and her boyfriend entertained guests with long drug orgies. One can only surmise what things were done to the children while the parents were in an induced state of ecstasy. How can we imagine how children perceive a world where their caretakers' emotions fluctuate from high and noncaring to irritable, angry, hostile, fatigued, agitated, or depressed? While at other times they may act psychotic (seeing or hearing things that are not real). While the adults woke up from these drug parties with no memory of their strange behaviors, the children suffered nightmares. They were not high during these drug activities. In addition to observing their parents acting strange, the children were exposed to abnormal sexual behaviors and general neglect.

To survive, the children developed a co-dependency with one another. Jason's caretaker was his older sister. She was the only person who provided him affection, though she was just a young girl. His best friend was Martin who was only a year older. The eldest sibling was their protector. While his sister stayed with Jason & Martin, the older brother was scrounging the neighborhood for food or selling cans for money. He was also vulnerable in a gang infested neighborhood where older boys taught their younger siblings the fine art of street fighting using the odd-placed white boy as a regular target. He habitually found himself running from senseless violence, more times than not, finding his face the target of flying fists.

Jason remembers the children sharing a can of corn for dinner, and learned early that the garbage at McDonalds provided the best chance for a meal. It was an older sibling who had since moved out who eventually called CPS. The children were removed, but split apart into different shelters. They were soon taken in by this older sister that made the initial report to CPS, but she was only nineteen and too young to handle so many. Soon after, the boys were fortunate to be placed together in their first foster home where they stayed for a while. They were returned to mom, but she soon fell back to her old tricks on drugs and alcohol. The sister played mom and elder brother was out scrounging again.

Jason described his removal from home this second time occurring while tying his shoes to go play with his brother Martin. Two police officers came to the apartment with a social worker to remove the children. The worker took them together, but dispatched them into different homes. His sister was taken to a girls group home, and then Jason remembers they drove around for a long time. He thought they were lost. Next, the elder brother and Martin were dropped off together. Jason was left alone in the car and dropped off sometime later at another shelter. His only memory of that first night was being forced to strip and stand naked while strangers examined him, noting every bruise, scar, and identifying mark.

A sore point for Jason was that his older brothers were always together, while he was placed alone. Because he was the youngest, he would be placed in a different shelter than the older children. This is very common in foster care. This was as devastating to Jason as his life at home. He would be moved multiple times. He always shared with me that his greatest anger with the system was always being separated from his brothers.

The day Jason was taken by CPS, his world was shattered. During his early childhood in foster care, CPS worked at reunification with his birth mother, and for a short time, he was placed back with her. The reunification plan failed. She was an addict and unable to provide for his care. She was in and out of jail and continued associating with troublesome boyfriends. This was the early history of what was to be my first foster son. This was only the beginning of what I call his primal baggage. This traumatic history at only three, forged a human experience against which he would struggle his entire childhood, and continues to endure. Like is the case for all foster children, these early experiences were just the beginning of a tightly forged pile of behavior drivers that played a significant role in his future conduct.

Jason remembers one of his early placements when he was reunited with his brothers and they all shared a bedroom. It was a large family with other children in the home with them. His fondest memory of this placement was learning to use a bow. The dad was an avid hunter and took the children to northern Arizona on a hunt. Jason shot his first deer during that trip; a prize that provided them all with dinner. This placement was also where a dark secret of his young childhood transpired.

One of the teenage girls at the home would call Jason into her room when she was babysitting the children and his brothers were outside playing. She took him in her closet and in the darkness, fondled him and then performed oral sex. She also forced him to 'pet' her. If he refused or didn't do it right she hit him until he did. His brothers discovered the secret closet at some point, though they teasingly thought the two were just kissing. His brothers would sometimes open the closet to surprise Jason with his 'girlfriend,' which only resulted in Jason getting slapped for the interruption. This sexual routine continued his entire stay with the family. This act sexualized Jason as a young boy; an experience that can have far reaching consequences especially when a boy enters puberty. Jason kept this shame hidden for over a decade. He continued changing placements until he was discovered by the Foundation.

After the Foundation concluded their intake process, the children were placed with their first Foundation family, a newly licensed home. The foster mom was courageous taking four children, especially considering she had a mentally challenged daughter at home. They were her first and last planned placement. At that time, the Foundation was a new agency in Arizona as well, so they had limited experience with intakes and no skilled families in their inventory. To place four children in a new foster home was a high risk, particularly when they all suffered from multiple placement disruptions, not to mention serious abandonment, neglect, and abuse from their birth family and some of the subsequent foster placements.

After about a year, Jason lost his placement with this family. The mom enjoyed Jason, but her husband did not care for him and frequently teased him into a rage. Like so often in the past, his rages would be followed by a trip to the roof. Due to the stress on the family dealing with so many new children, the case worker decided the parents needed to be relieved of the most difficult behavior problem, Jason. This disruption resulted in a split from his sibling group, not just a foster family, and so the trauma was all the worse. Had the case worker really understood Jason's fear relative to placements without his brothers, they might have taken a different tact. The loss of the home was minimal compared to the loss of his brothers. The Foundation would learn years later that it was his sister that should have been removed. She was later molested by the foster dad, who is now serving a long prison sentence. In rare cases, a foster home can be as dangerous as the family who initially caused the child to come under the protection of CPS.

With this disruption, Jason was now dealing with both the loss of the CPS placement, where he was happy with his brothers, and this new Foundation placement where he was also happy with his siblings. He was moved to a new foster home with Ryan and Marge, another family unprepared for a foster child with so much damage, and who would have little control over his primal drive to survive. His move was done with the usual quick and un-ceremonial transition. He was picked up at school by a social worker and taken to the new home.

This family lived in an upper class neighborhood and belonged to a prestigious country club, projecting an air of affluence and strong family values. They regularly attended church dragging Jason behind, forcing him into the car, rarely dressed appropriately.

During bible class one Sunday, the teacher was talking about God and Jason asked why his prayers were never answered. Jason was told he was going to hell, to which he told her to go f... herself because he was living in hell and charged out of the classroom. Jason honeymooned early in the placement, after which time he recognized the true nature of this family and their hidden issues. Marge and Ryan had marital problems and argued regularly. Their two other children were not receptive to their new brother with whom they had to compete for attention. No doubt they were also suffering from the daily disruption of their parent's marital arguments.

On one occasion when Jason raged and slammed the door, Ryan responded by slamming the door himself and screaming at the boy. Ryan then pulled the door off the hinges. Jason tried to grab the door back, but was pushed back. The door provided him sanctuary. He locked it at night to provide a sense of personal security. His only other safe haven was the roof to which he had access from his bedroom window.

During this fight, Ryan became so infuriated he grabbed Jason and threw him across the room into his pet gecko tank, shattering part of it. A glass shard cut into Jason's back. He then grabbed at some of the broken glass and charged toward Ryan, who fled the room. Jason remained in his room, bleeding on the carpet. After that incident, he carved a wooden knife that he kept under his bed. Jason has many scars; most are deep in his soul. But the fading marks on his skin he displays with both shame and honor.

Ryan had anger issues equal to Jason's, which resulted in more traumas for him. Ryan's anger was triggered more regularly as he and Marge's marriage deteriorated. After a while he reacted to minor childish accidents, not just in response to the raging. Jason remembers an incident when he fell over a table, knocking a boom box into the pool. Ryan responded by throwing Jason into a cactus.

During these explosive arguments between Ryan and Jason, Marge would disappear. She was unable to deal with Ryan's anger. Over time, their fights escalated to include the topic of Ryan's physical abuse of Jason. Ryan only became more enraged and took this out on Jason. Whenever he would act out, Ryan grabbed the boy by his neck or hair and dragged him into the car. He would then drive away from the house up an isolated hill nearby and hit Jason and then push his small body down under the front dashboard threatening him to stay down until he stopped ragging. This restraint only escalated Jason more, resulting in many hours of physical conflict. During one such incident, Jason threw a glass bottle at Ryan's face resulting in several stitches to his lip. This incident only escalated the mistreatment of Jason.

His stay with this couple was short lived and the Foundation moved him once again, this time to residential treatment in Colorado with the story he was moving to another family. Jason's story of that very distressing period at Cleo Wallace can only be told by him. In fact, he never fully opened up about much of this part of his life until well into his twenties.

How many times can a child suffer abandonment before they lose hope? This was my first foster child, a young boy swept off to a psychiatric facility far from home; an institution, sadly, that had only recently been under public assault for allegations of abuse in the death of a resident teenager.

Now would be an opportune time to provide some insight into my own history. All of us carry scars that flow and ebb throughout our lives, mostly working quietly in the background of our daily behavior. But every so often, usually during the most troubled episodes, they rise up and stare at his from behind a polished mirror; triggering us to bring closure with the past, through the present.

I was the middle son of three boys, raised in an executive lifestyle in New Jersey. Dad was a finance executive who worked in downtown New York City, and later closer to home in New Jersey. We were not deprived of material luxuries. Some would say we were spoiled in many ways. I remember one home that sat on a wooded acre surrounded by a stone wall. My older brother had a suite on the third floor. My room resembled a library more than a kid's room. Mom had a traditional sitting room in addition to the living and family rooms. Dad boasted an English tavern downstairs with all the trappings. He named it after Mom, *Colette's Tavern*. We skied in Canada and vacationed in Florida every winter to sun on the beach and go fishing. Dad spent nearly every day on a boat, his pole in one hand, a can of beer in the other. I caught my first marlin at 12 years old. To the neighbors, all was perfect.

My father was of Scotch-Irish ancestry. His family emigrated from the Belfast area in the early 1800s to Illinois. Our ancestor, James Hunter was a Master Blacksmith with his own business. His son, James Jr., with a limited education, left the Midwest and married into a wealthy textile family and eventually made his mark on Wall Street, which in those days literally traded in the street. My dad's father was well educated and served on General Pershing's staff in World War I. The climax of his career was serving as president of a national publishing firm.

Every family has a romantic love story in their genealogy and my grandparents held that honor in our family. Grandpa fell in love prior to departing for France during World War I. He married just before shipping out. Grandma joined the Navy Nurse Corps to follow her love to France. The family has many of their love letters. Though he survived the war intact, despite a German machine gun ambush, Grandma did not. She wrote letters home about the horror of seeing young soldiers, no more than teenagers, physically and mentally torn to pieces. It was more than she could bear. She returned a morphine addict, a condition that she and the family suffered until her death. To my father, she passed on her misery, for him to carry to his death many years later. The horror of war does not fade with the death of the witness, but is passed to their descendents after them, and sometimes many generations beyond.

Dad was the youngest of four brothers and a sister. They were all traumatized living with a woman out of control most of her life. Dad would tell stories about coming home from school, finding his mom lying on the sofa completely lost in her own world. Like children today, my dad was drug savvy. Dealing with addiction and alcoholism is not unique to our generation. Addiction has been tearing at the fabric of family life for thousands of years. His father was a tough old soldier and took on the roles of mother and father. My grandfather was likely a child of physical abuse himself, and the children never missed getting hit for the slightest infraction. My dad suffered a broken arm once from such an encounter with his father. When I studied my family genealogy later in life, I discovered an old photograph of my grandfather as a young boy sitting with his parents on a beach. It had the appearance of a happy family moment during a carefree trip. The boy's arm was in a sling. I have always wondered about the cause. Like my dad, did he too get his arm broken from an angry father?

My dad's greatest loss, to which he never recovered, was joining the Army to follow his older brothers in World War II. This decision was against his mother's wish. He was underage. She died while he was serving in the Philippines. This one act of defiance haunted him his whole life.

My mother is French; Parisian born. The daughter of a shipping tycoon, she was raised in great wealth. While a child, Mom told us stories of going to school in a limousine and living in a grand apartment in the center of Paris. But her childhood came to an abrupt end with the invasion of France in May 1944. Her father, an Army Colonel, was a World War I hero and with the invasion of France, he took to the battlefield once again. He left the family behind on a farm in Normandy where he knew they would be safer than at their home in

Paris. He returned a few months later a broken man, though he was awarded the French Legion of Honor for saving his battalion from capture.

My mom was the eldest of six children. To understand my mother, one must have knowledge of European history during those dark times. They lived under German occupation, Gestapo terror, and the American invasion of Normandy. Her father walked her to the beach soon after the invasion. She will never escape those images. The family came to the United States a few years after the war's end.

My parents met at a hospital in Larchmont, New York where my father was recovering from malaria brought about during combat in the Philippines. It was a typical love story of the period. She worked with the nursing staff. The rest can be imagined.

Dad was a young accountant, Mom a dedicated housewife. My older brother was born appropriately one year after their marriage. My mom was French Catholic. Dad was Presbyterian, but Catholicism won the battle in our family. Religion is non-negotiable to the French. My brother and I were two years apart and enjoyed a close relationship, either as best buds or worst enemies. During our younger years it was more the latter. We shared a bedroom until I was about ten years old. Life was good, but strict. Mom wore the pants in the family. Dad brought home the paychecks and handed out physical consequences. We knew we were in trouble when Mom would say, 'Wait 'til your father gets home,' in her broken French accent.

The worse and most embarrassing belting I remember was when my brother and I were fighting over the front seat of the car one Sunday morning. No doubt we had been at this often and Dad had enough of it, or perhaps was just burned out on some other issue. I found my pants pulled off and the belt whipping my bare body to the view of the entire neighborhood. Lots of my friends were out and about, including my girlfriend across the street. Little did Dad know at the time, she already had the distinct honor of examining that little nude package he was beating to a pulp!

I learned many years later that my dad was an alcoholic. I remember the fighting, but I was too young to understand the issues. I only knew Mom and Dad were angry with each other. My most difficult duty as an adult son was to take my dad to the hospital for rehabilitation. Had I not taken that step, I would not have a mother today. She was dedicated to her family and lived with and hid his problem for our sake. Who can ever know what is right. Families do what seems best at the time. My mom was protecting her nest. He died of multiple organ shutdowns at 67. Too much alcohol and tobacco which was all learned as a young soldier, stole his life. To this legacy, my brother and I took the opposite tack. We don't smoke and only drink in moderation.

We attended Catholic school with the Dominican Nuns. One needs an education in Catholic school disciplinary methods of the time to even begin to understand how that went, especially for me, a very hyperactive, mischievous, and angry kid. I was one of the few students at that school who earned a spanking by Sister Superior in front of the fifth grade class. I was in third grade at the time. To this day, I don't know what I did to deserve the tribute. But I did run away frequently. Perhaps that was the cause.

On one occasion I convinced a friend to leave school with me. I didn't want to run away alone that day. He was all excited having never left school before. Like me, he enjoyed the thrill of disobeying the nuns. We took off at lunch, heading through a wooded area near the public high school. While elated during the excitement of the run, we were attacked by a group of older boys. It was to be one of the most dreadful experiences of my youth. I was so scared I wet and soiled myself. The boys threw me against a tree, calling me a smelly pig. They forced my friend to the ground and gang raped him. At that time I had no idea what was really happening. I cried. He screamed, gagging on his own tears. They hurt him and I can never forgive myself for his agony. I saw the blood and remember the confusion of their delighted expressions and his absolute terror. After they took off, he just laid still, moaning. We limped to my house. Mom was out. We cleaned up. We pledged to never tell anyone. We kept our promise. Our friendship ended that day.

No narrative can describe the traumatic emotion of this horror. Such treatment of a child creates the same images as the word holocaust. The expression on my friend's face will forever haunt me. I had a child watching television in my home once who spoke to me about a similar incident he suffered. His name was Michael. A boy character in the movie was raped. It was a minor scene, where the rape was only alluded to, and then the scene jumped to an image of the boy limping away. Michael kept asking, "What happened, what happened?" He knew! Seconds later, he bolted to his bedroom and wrapped a blanket tightly around his shaking body. We both flashed back that evening, a pain few can understand. He could never know just how well I understood his anger and pain that was already branded in my memory. I once tried to describe the absolute indignation of such abuse to that boy's parents, but fell far short.

The foster care system has many of these tormented souls within their grasp. In fact, some statistics estimate that as many as 50% of all foster children are molested, much of which occurs in the system after they are removed from their homes. Many of these children are passed over for adoption due to the stigma attached to this sexual damage. Discrimination is ripe throughout a system that puts risk management above all else. While spending time with this foster child he described many other incidents in his life, the most current involving an older teenage boy that occurred just two months before seeing that movie. I saw him as an easy target, a victim to anyone who wanted him for pleasure. I once told him that if I heard of anyone touching him, I'd kill them. I must have spoken with great fervor, because he turned and gave me a frightened look. He didn't know why, but he felt the sincerity of my threat.

I also had the distinction of being a bed wetter (enuresis) until I was ten or so. I would hide the sheets everywhere around my room. Looking back on it, I wasn't too bright. Spankings do not stop children from wetting the bed at night. I know this from personal experience. Showering does not remove the stench well either. I know that from the same personal experience.

I ended my bed wetting era one summer at camp. I attended that camp each summer, though in those days children went away for two months, not one week. My brother loved camp. For him it was respite from Mom and Dad. I was not so pleased. Beat me, please, but don't send me to camp. I hated camp. The whole episode of the long drive, getting settled in the cabin and the car leaving me behind was dreadful. I would cry for weeks, even after repeating this routine for many years.

Despite the annual threats that I would stay the whole summer, I usually found a way to get home early. Getting really sick and confined to the infirmary was very affective. But it took lots of work. This was a Catholic camp run by the Pallottine Order. Income from the camp supported their cloister. Once after returning to my group after one of those infirm moments I told the counselor my mommy told me I was going home. My older brother was in ear shot and curtly denied my statement. My cheek was abruptly back handed. I remember looking right at my brother, restraining my tears. He looked shocked and hurt. That took the sting out.

A kid leaving early was not conducive to a good balance sheet. I did run away, but the camp was very isolated, so they would always find me. They used a basement under one of the old barracks to serve punishment. No meals were allowed during cellar detention. It was dirty and smelly with no windows other than a flat grill to the outside. Once in a great while a courageous friend would drop a candy bar and a few words of friendly encouragement through that grill. These were the children who had once been imprisoned themselves. They understood. I would just sit on the floor for hours staring up at that grill... waiting. Mice were common at the camp as all the wooden structures were old prewar army buildings. I was never bitten, but heard them rustle. The worst was spending the night in the cellar. The grill was dark and the mice seemed to move about more, or perhaps the quiet of the night just made it seem so.

I will never forget the cellar. When Jason talks about the quiet room my gut wrenches. I've worked hard to put that memory behind me. And like his imprisonment in the quiet room, the cellar did not have a toilet, though the brothers were kind enough to provide a bucket that we kept with us until our sentence was served. I suffered the worst rashes at that camp.

I did have one memorable experience at summer camp; a young camp counselor who cared. He woke me every morning before the first bugle call so I could change my bed and take a shower alone. I admired him for not poking fun at me like so many others had done over the years about my bed wetting. Within two weeks, the bed was dry. It was a simple act of kindness that will forever be remembered. That was my last year in summer camp. I don't know all the details, but I and another kid ran away, and when caught by some counselors, we were beaten up. The other kid had an appendix attack and was rushed to the hospital. I was rushed to the cellar. As I wrote earlier, it was hard work, but I always found a way to get picked up early from camp.

    At times when I think back on it all, I am happy there was no Child Protective Services around my neighborhood where I grew up. I might have been taken away. At times, I showed up at school more bruised than not from the belt. But, I love my family. Like my foster children, I am a product of my past. I fully agree with Jason when he wrote, *"Our past gives us choices to change the things that went wrong."* I accept their faults and would hate the world had they been taken away from me. God has a plan for us all.

My Little Knight

During my second visit with Jason at Cleo Wallace, I decided to share with him our most devoted sport of that time, rock climbing. Our destination that weekend was the Boulder Rock Gym. It was a risk. He didn't seem especially athletic. I'd seen children's spirits as easily broken as their self-confidence enhanced by the challenge of the rock. It all depended on their attitude and personal expectations. Jason wanted to please. He was working the most important sales job of his young life: Himself. What a difficult effort for him to show himself off as the finest son while deep down he questioned his existence and self worth each and every day using negative self talk that was constantly validated by insensitive staff and fellow psychiatric patients.

During this visit we followed the same routine, same hotel. But this time the psychiatrist asked us to keep him overnight. Early Saturday morning we drove to Cleo Wallace to retrieve him. As was the case on my last visit to his building, I found him waiting in front of the television. He was overwhelmed with excitement. We had not told Jason of our plans, but just the thought of getting out for the weekend provided a tremendous motivation to let down his institutional guard. He was more effervescent than before, truly alive and spontaneous. He pulled me to his room and showed me the completed Lego set. His sense of accomplishment glowed in his wide eyes, his expression filled with triumph. I inspected it carefully with pleasure. The Lego was an obvious success. That was a relief since another kit was waiting at the hotel. Once he saw my acknowledgment of his achievement, he grabbed his bag and without a word, headed for the door with Nick and me in close pursuit. The whole room seemed more animated that morning. Some of the children even waved goodbye with the words "good luck." He was on top of the world and from the moment we got into the car until I returned him the following day, he never stopped talking. His medication intake was clearly on the decline.

He talked with barely time for a breath. To the untrained ear, it sounded like babble, sharing disconnected thoughts. He described past placements and people in his life. He used the term 'mom' and 'dad' so many times in so many different contexts that I lost comprehension of just who he was really talking about. But there was one mom he never referred to with that title, his birth mother. He always called her Connie. The idea of a child having so many families was still very alien to us. In his case, he was in at least a dozen placements prior to this current stay in Colorado.

***

Jason's Journal (10 years old)

I went to school at Cleo Wallace and did other activities such as football, swimming, gym, and art. I didn't really like playing football because it just gave the staff the chance to hit us. I didn't really like swimming either, because they would toss us in the deep end in our snow clothes and tell us to swim or drown. I made the mistake of trying to help my roommate Jimmy because he started to drown and no one would help him. I pulled him over to the side, where I was met with a boot to my face. The staff person was very angry because I interrupted their fun. They made me tread water until I got so tired I couldn't move. And if I tried to grab the wall they would step on my fingers or kick me in the face. I got so tired that I came over to the wall and when the guy tried to kick me in the face I grabbed his foot and made him fall back and hit his head. The other staff pulled me out of the water by my hair and hit me with their batons. For my actions, I spent a day and a half in the quiet room. I only got one meal thrown on the floor and had to go to the bathroom in the corner.

Gym and Art were my favorite things to do, well not gym so much because I didn't want to interact with anyone; I just wanted to be by myself. I really liked art and started getting really good at drawing and sculpting. I think I liked art so much because when I'm creating it nothing else matters. I can be in my own world. I had a bunch of pictures and sculptures that I kept in my room. One day we were out playing football and it was supposed to be two-hand touch, but the staff guys always played tackle. I got tired of getting hurt so when I got the ball and the guy came to tackle me I threw an elbow and ended up breaking his nose. When he got up he started punching and kicking me and then when I was on the ground he kept kicking me in the stomach and stomping on my head. I blacked out and woke up in the quiet room all bloody. I only had one meal a day thrown on the floor and I had to use the bathroom in the corner. When I was sent back to my room all my artwork was gone. It was broken, torn up and thrown on the floor.

For a short time I got to hang out with the older children because my older sister was sent to Cleo a little while after me. It only lasted about a month or so because she escaped. She hit the lady in charge of the door locks in the head with a sock filled with batteries. Then she had someone waiting outside for her. Once she was gone I was by myself again. I was angry. She left me. She didn't take me with her. She was always my protector. She was gone for several months. I learned years later that she prostituted herself to survive, just like when we were children back home so many years ago.

***

We had a great experience at the rock gym. Nick had an opportunity to play the role of a big brother, teaching Jason all the basics about balance and how to use his legs to power up. We also enjoyed taking pictures. Jason hammed it up the whole day and was certainly not camera shy. He took to the walls like a spider monkey. He was a natural, maneuvering his small frame easily from hold to hold, talking incessantly the whole time. Driving back to Westminster, I was burned out, but pleased that he was happy. He soon fell asleep, and Nick and I understood the true meaning of *silence is golden.*

After this second trip I decided to write a story for Jason that reflected his struggles at Cleo Wallace and the final goal to come live with us. My plan was to mail him a chapter each week. I developed a story line about a little orphan, living in a fortified city, who had to fight his way through many obstacles to become a squire, and later a knight of the castle. Each character reflected a real person in his life. The Wizard, for example, represented his psychiatrist. A healing maiden was named Lady Cleo. I was the Duke of Hunterston, fighting a war with the Norseman (representing his inner demons of the past) with my fellow knights, one of whom was my son Nick. Of course, his brown bear Brownie played a major role in the epic. The book helped us both cope through a very difficult time. For him, it offered a connection to me when I was not with him and demonstrated my commitment as the story cheered him on. It would provide hope and understanding during some of his more difficult moments after I would leave him to wait for another visit. As for me, writing this short story allowed me to share in his fight, if only in fantasy, and to express my own anxiety about the future. The story represented our journey through darkness and light; always reaching for the hope for final closure of permanency. The story line caught the attention of his psychiatrist who began including it in Jason's therapy work; and so evolved *The Little Knight of Hunterston.*

The path for Jason in the book was clear and direct. He met many challenges along the way, but with each success he matured a little, always moving in a forward motion toward the ultimate prize of family. In reality, it is not so simple. Normally, when children feel safe and secure, the family can move forward toward stability and normal relations both in the home and within the community. This is one of the first of many false assumptions new foster parents grabble. You bring a foster child into your stable family environment, but the very inclusion of that child into your family with all their emotional baggage will test the strength of your family's foundation. What will emerge can be very different than what existed prior to embracing this new child. No family can take a foster child long-term and remain exactly as before. Change is inevitable, and for our family, that change began during the many visits to Cleo Wallace.

Throughout that winter I spent at least two weekends a month with Jason in Colorado. Sometimes Nick would join us, other times not. I think his choice was more dependent on the selected activity than anything else. The biggest trips were skiing. We were dedicated snow worshippers and this was Colorado, one of the world's top skiing regions. Jason would learn to ski.

We took Jason on his first ski trip to a small practice run near Boulder. It was just large enough for Nick and me to warm up and for Jason to take a ski lesson. It had always been my philosophy that my children take their first lesson with a professional instructor. After they learned the basics of how to get off the lift, turn, and stop, I'd take over. It was cowardly of me, I know, but it did work well and they never suffered any major injury on the slopes.

This was the first trip when Jason began to show some sign of being a normal annoying boy with a temper. He was not at all happy being dumped with a group of strangers while Nick and I were off to do some serious skiing. He asked to stay with us pleading with all the promises of obedience of the most faithful student. But I stuck to my plan. It always served me well in the past and I assured him that this trip was no exception. As we waited for the class to start, his complaints increased, but now grew to include whining about cold hands and frozen feet. Finally the ski instructor appeared with an expression of excitement as he called everyone together. I stayed just long enough to see Jason encircled by the group. I quietly disappeared. I felt guilty leaving him like that, but the mountain was calling and Nick was quickly losing patience with all my attention focused on our future family member. Both Jason and I were dropping our polite facade and settling into a normal relationship.

After some brutal first runs and a couple of moguls (bumps purposely sculptured into the ski run), we regrouped for lunch. I was disappointed with Jason's lack of progress. He had been stubborn and had no interest in learning from the instructor. He wanted to be with us and was just as over-sensitive as in the morning, though worked to cloak his anger. After lunch, Nick hit the slopes again, while Jason and I worked together on the beginner or bunny hill. As the afternoon wore on, Jason accomplished all the basics and was now ready for a challenge. This geeky looking kid was quite the athlete!

It was a long day trip, and we returned to our hotel in Westminster late that evening. Like all our prior activities, it ended well with Jason fast asleep in the car. His self-control, however, was beginning to wear thin. He had been working very hard to maintain the façade of a well behaved and mannered boy who followed directions. He was an angel in all ways. He was, in fact, a little too perfect. Cracks began to show during this trip, but at the time, I was still in a dream world myself, and overlooked the obvious symptoms of what would come. In hindsight, having a knowledgeable professional with us, but quietly in the background, would have provided critical information regarding his triggers. That is, specific incidents or actions that caused a radical change in Jason's behavior. We all have triggers. Physical ones are obvious, such as a child ducking when an adult raises their hand, even if it was not done in a threatening manner, a habit developed from years of physical abuse. Jason had a menagerie of abandonment triggers to which he would react.

The turning point in our relationship occurred the following month during a major ski trip to Keystone, deep in the Rocky Mountains. We planned an extended weekend, and I equipped Jason to endure the coldest conditions of the Colorado Rockies. He even wore a fashionable and very colorful jester style ski hat, bells and all. At this point, the little guy was skiing more in control and keeping his bottom well off the snow. He felt more comfortable alone on the smaller slopes, while Nick and I tackled the Black Diamonds. After several runs, Nick would take a break in the lodge and I would check-up on Jason. He enjoyed showing off his quickly acquired skills, while at the same time always playing the ham for my camera. Of all my children, he was the most photogenic.

I was also impressed with his table manners and personal hygiene. After being told in training to expect anything, including biting toe nails or blowing snot out of their noses, I was prepared for the worst. What I had was a military cadet. Throughout the weekend, people commented about my very polite and pleasant little boy.

His joy radiated with his expression, and I no longer saw that queer looking face with the one bulging eye. I saw beyond his physical characteristics and now perceived the real person: His delightful attitude, stubborn attention to perfection, and most important, the way he looked at me. The discomfort of our earlier visits had melted away, replaced by a new powerful bond of hope and commitment. I was content in the knowledge that he trusted me now. I saw this in his every action. In foster care, it takes many years to fully comprehend the true meaning of the word trust. It comes from the very primal element of our being. Some might philosophize that it is developed at birth or never earned at all.

Our return to Cleo Wallace from Keystone was especially painful for us all. It was the longest we had been together as a family. Even Nick appeared grim. This was the first time I saw Jason moody as we returned and cry while I said goodbye. This was but one of many farewells that tested my emotional fortitude. You feel so helpless, as do they. It was around this time that my interest in Jason changed over into a passion. At the same time, staff people at his ward were commenting on how he had transformed in just a few months. They were all cheering for him to get discharged. Or at least I assumed so. Sadly, one staffer was more sadistic than supportive of his little charge. As winter broke, change was in the air.

With each proceeding visit our bond grew. He was always in high spirits upon my arrival with a completed new Lego model in hand; then sad with Sundays and the impending farewell ceremony. I too was heartbroken just seeing his complete change in mood as I would leave him sitting on his bed alone in his room. I remember spending endless hours talking with the family developer and social workers at the agency advocating for him to come home to Arizona.

"Patience Bill, it takes time. It's painful, but it will all work out in the end."

The visits continued regularly, counted by the increasing Lego models now littering his and his roommate's desk and dresser. His room too had transformed from a sterile cell to a living, breathing home filled with memories and hope for the future. He had found his will to survive and to fight another day.

On one of my last visits I arrived especially early. Jason was given permission to guide me around the campus with the last stop at his classroom to meet his fifth grade teacher. This visit would be my introduction to Jason's deeper behavior issues. At the time I was so captivated by his innocent desire to have a family, embraced and secure, that I completely missed the true and far reaching nature and long-term impacts of that behavior.

***

Jason's Journal (10 years old)

My routine consisted of eating, group therapy, arranged activities, meeting with Dr. U., the quiet room (isolation), and random beatings. After months of the staff guy coming in at night and beating me, I got sick of it. So the next time we had art, I stole a clay cutting tool. I waited in my closet cabinet until I heard him coming. Once I was sure he was close enough, I pushed the door open as hard as I could. He fell over and I grabbed his flashlight and started beating him on the head with it. When he was dizzy and close to passing out I grabbed the clay cutting cool and I was just about to stab him in the neck and chest when one of the other staff members threw me into the corner of the cabinets. My head hit the cabinet right next to my left eye. I blacked out.

I came to in the infirmary strapped to a bed. I asked the doctor what had happened, he told me that my roommate almost beat me to death and I was very badly injured. Another of many lies I will never forgive. From that point on I was kept on medications enough to keep me in almost a comatose state, so I wouldn't be violent towards the staff anymore. After a long time that seemed like weeks in the critical care building, I returned back to my building.

I was on so much medication I couldn't fight anymore. I watched and observed the staff rotate. I was going to escape. Every night around 11 pm a train would go by. I couldn't see it but I heard it, and I remembered passing over tracks on the way in. I was just waiting for the right time. It was around that time I met my Dad, Bill Hunter. He took me skiing, rock climbing, and I guided him through the butterfly pavilion. During the final plane ride back to Arizona, I thought back to what happened to me the night I was going to kill that guy. I think that most people would say it was self defense, but I just saw it as murder.

I tried to forget, to pretend that it never happened. I survived.

***

It was a rather warm March day, at least for Colorado. I had flung my jacket over my shoulder as I proceeded down that familiar concrete walkway to his building. As I approached the entry, screams pierced an otherwise serene morning mist. The sound was eerie and unfamiliar; rising and falling from high pitch shrills to a low guttural chock. I was buzzed in and turned toward the television, Jason's usual spot. He was not there. I turned toward the staff desk; my eyes were met with a harsh look of disdain.

"He's in the quiet room," a staffer said with a sharp tone. "He will be in for some time, so you should go to the lobby. We will call you."

I was confused, and honestly irritated. I had just arrived from a long flight and drive from Phoenix. I asked if I could help and the response was a firm negative. Suddenly, I heard a body crash into a metal door near the staff area, and the screams amplified, and I could smell the pungent odor of urine.

I sat over an hour in the main lobby. Now the wind was blown out of my sails, at least for the moment. My mind was scrambled, impulsive thoughts exploding in all directions. What if? What if? My thoughts kept wandering. A gentle hand firmly grasped my shoulder. It was his psychiatrist.

I wear my emotions. I have no poker face. My expression and body language transmit my thoughts to everyone around me. When it comes to emotional response, God gave me a double. Dr. U. sat next to me. It was during this short talk that I was told of the very deep loss that Jason had suffered multiple times in his life. His behavior was his mind's way of keeping the body alive. His entire behavior pattern was about survival.

"He wants to go home with you," he calmly said, "and we have assured him that is the plan. His real struggle is just beginning. He fears your loss. That uncertainty is already tearing him apart."

I was confused. Who was talking about loss? I didn't even get him home yet. I argued and argued that I would never leave him, and pleaded for a resounding affirmation from the doctor. But he just shook his head and told me that Jason may never trust anyone again, least of all himself. He told me that the boy needed to develop belief in his personal worth before he would allow himself to be loved. It seems so obvious to me now in hindsight, but back then all I could picture in my mind was this frail little boy, burning his vocal cords raw and bruising himself, and worse, that smell. What was really happening in that room?

I laid my head back in the chair staring at the hygienic white ceiling. I thought about going back to the hotel, but felt too weak. I'm not sure how much time passed, an hour or two perhaps, when I was startled by Jason running into the lobby, crying out my name with that old enthusiastic popping smile, holding his glasses against his face. He snatched my hand, pulling me up from the chair. We were off to his classroom. He seemed completely transformed from what I imagined was behind that locked door just a few hours earlier. What I had not seen after those many pleasant visits was the uncontrolled anger. His raging was at a primal level. It was this behavior that was one of the key disruption behaviors that landed him in the institution and was far from in control.

I learned years later the trigger that caused Jason to get himself locked up that day. While anxiously waiting for me in his room, a staffer cruelly engaged him. Perhaps the guy was having a bad day, or was burned out on Jason in particular and enjoyed tormenting him in retribution. The staffer told him he would be in Cleo Wallace forever. That no one could love such an ugly kid. My visits were just to mess with his head. Jason attacked him. His meds had been drastically reduced in preparation for his transition, which no doubt made it more difficult for those responsible for his daily care and management. He earned his place back in prison, where he had spent so much time during the past year. How much is reported to the medical staff in these residential treatment facilities about these 'minor' staff infractions and off hand comments targeted at the children? Institutional placements add new trauma. In some cases it cannot be helped as the professionals must weigh the better of two evils. There can be no doubt that as one problem is addressed, another will arise, and in some cases, as a direct result of staff abuse of their power within the walls of such facilities. Most of the children who have suffered similar incidents like Jason, will give a resounding affirmative to that question:

Yes, I was hurt.
Yes, no one believed me.
Yes, I was confused.
Yes, I trusted no one, not even the nice doctor.

In truth, Jason's behavior evolved from past traumas compounded by continuous abuse at multiple levels in foster care. How foster children survive is a credit to our species.

His last visit was in Phoenix. It was late March and the weather was glorious. This was his first trip back to his home state since his incarceration. At that time, I lived in a two bedroom home. It was a great room floor plan with bedroom suites on either side. To accommodate both boys until Nick went to college, I transformed the Master Suite for the children. Though enthusiastic at first about moving into the larger room with the master bathroom, Nick soon learned the annoyance of sharing a room with a younger brother, especially one still in grade school.

During this period in my life, I was at the height of my Scouting career and an active member of the local school board. As such, I had many friends with grade school and high school children. One such acquaintance lived just across the street. They had three boys and the youngest son Junior was Jason's age. I had worked to develop a friendship between the two through letters, pictures, and of course, my story: *The Little Knight of Hunterston*. In the story, Junior was the Duke's squire who befriended Jason. During Jason's first visit to my home, the two became best buds and would be inseparable during the next two years. I believe this friendship was a major contributing factor to Jason's quick acclimation in the community.

This home visit was another very bitter sweet experience. Jason was ecstatic when he arrived. Since we shared so many pictures of the home and neighborhood with him at Cleo Wallace, he felt very comfortable from the start. He spent most of his time just hanging out with Junior. Freedom was his for the first time in nearly a year.

I brought home all his things that the agency stored at their office in downtown Phoenix. A bicycle along with boxes and boxes of toys collected over the years from each of his placements. Unlike many children in the system, he did not move in with a few clothes stuffed in a plastic garbage bag. His bike was rickety, so I had it repaired and ready to go when he arrived.

I didn't really see him much, but I felt his presence everywhere in the house. Perfect order was quickly transforming to chaos. I loved it all. My greatest joy was just seeing him content. Direct participation was not required, just observing his wide smile was satisfaction enough.

Driving back to the airport was brutal... tears, begging, and holding my waist with an iron grip. He was overwhelmed with the fear of more loss and was too immature and untrusting to envision the final goal of permanency, even though it was just two weeks away. I felt his pain, but by this point was secure and confident that the plan was finally closing. He was behaving like a baby wanting to be held, and just put down in the crib. Though I would not understand this extreme primal behavior for years, I would soon be dragged down into its dark depths.

These early months of my first encounter with foster care were not at all what I expected. I had a wealth of experience working with middle and high school age teens, but none of it seemed applicable to deal with his primitive behavior tied to fear of loss. I had no knowledge from which to draw strength during this journey. It was like digging a tunnel without a map or compass, ever hopeful of finding just a sliver of light or a rush of fresh air to lead me out to familiar ground.

I learned years later that the social workers, though much more experienced and armed with reams of historical data, were as lost in this dark realm as me. We were groping our way through an unknown maze that changed direction without warning as Jason's mind developed and regressed in an ever changing wave. His thoughts continued to move in unpredictable directions, but always at the core was fear of loss. We were all trying to see a picture with just a few of the puzzle pieces, and since childhood is so short and fleeting, the picture was in constant motion. From medication to cognitive therapy, it was as much guesswork, followed by trial and error, as true science.

I know it was very difficult for Jason those last few weeks. He suffered extreme anxiety waiting to leave Cleo Wallace and have a home, always hesitant to be too optimistic for fear of the return of that burning and unforgiving pain of loss and betrayal. He built up enormous self control to keep himself together during our transition period, a psychological demand well beyond his capacity. His emotional walls, though thick and hardened over time, were cracking, waiting for the slightest trigger.

His scheduled day to come home permanently was April fools, which only compounded his self-doubt. Nick and I met him at the airport. Back then, prior to 9-11, people were allowed to wait at the gate for arrivals. I was nervous, while Nick calmly sat reading one of his vampire novels. He arrived on schedule. One small package of a boy weighing in at some 60 pounds, dirty blond hair still uncut, sparkling blue eyes, and a backpack with an old, very worn brown teddy bear hanging over the top. This was the end of a long and difficult trial, but just the first step of an even greater journey that would take us both into new and unchartered territory and test the very fabric of our character, passion and commitment. It was to be a true test of the very meaning of unconditional love.

Cleo Wallace was the most frightening experience in Jason's life. No one can know the truth of what behavior management practices were used on the patients or the private behaviors of specific staff members. Karen Bowers wrote in an article for the Denver News before Jason became a patient:

On the afternoon of December 21, Cleo Wallace employees became convinced that the Foundation had lost control. Two staffers grabbed him, intending to escort him to an isolation room. When he began struggling, four other employees joined in. Using a controversial method of restraint that Cleo Wallace staffers refer to as "the Illinois system," six men pressed Casey face down on the floor. One man held his head, another arms, another legs. Three staffers lay across his back, a procedure that, according to the autopsy report, literally prevented the asthmatic Casey from drawing air into his lungs.

When Casey quit struggling, the staff members released him. By then he was dead, face down in a pool of his own vomit. An accident, said Cleo Wallace directors--their staff had used the restraint for years with only minor injuries to staff or patients. An accident, said the Jefferson County Coroner's office.[3]

For sometime afterwards, people marched on Cleo Wallace, carrying signs that read, "People are dying to get out of Cleo Wallace, and "Cleo Wallace, restrain yourself!" This is where my first foster child received his most disturbing education, which was the aftermath of a brutal year with a foster dad, Ryan.

Honeymoons Are Deceiving

That first day home could have easily been written for *Father Knows Best* or *Leave it to Beaver*. He was elated with his room and the idea of sharing with his new big brother. We hung a large rope woven hammock over his bed and filled it with stuffed animals. They were all there from Nick's childhood and what Jason had kept from his own past. Brownie, however, remained tucked in on the bed. In those days Jason was not one to sit around admiring his new digs. Junior was barking at the door and the two were off. Jason was anxious to explore the area and Junior was proud to show off his new prize, a dedicated personal friend.

During those first few weeks we followed standard operating procedure when adding a new member to your household. We discussed everything from bathroom use, bed time, play time, homework schedule, and the most annoying topic: chores. Jason really enjoyed sharing a room. Nick provided for him a sense of security at a time when he had little trust and good reason to be filled with fear. He told me years later:

"My first night with Bill was happier than Cleo Wallace. I had a bed with a bunch of stuffed animals and the room was full of Lego models. I shared the room with Nick (Bill's Son), but it was okay because I liked him and he would put on the *Braveheart* soundtrack so I wouldn't have nightmares."

I had lived a simple, bachelor-style life with Nick. I divorced when he was still a young boy, and we grew to develop an unspoken understanding of what was required to keep the house and yard clean. He was a bright kid, motivated student and hung out with students with similar interests. He was in various high school sports during the school year, as well as boy scouts where he attained the rank of Eagle. What I'm admitting to is that he was an easy son to bring up. He was well behaved, though had a mischievous side like any normal boy. He had his period of suffering the school bully in fourth grade, times of loneliness and feeling isolated from his peers, but in general, he was involved in the community and kept himself occupied in positive activities and relationships. Oh yes, he was a book worm. A fun day out was not to the Mall or baseball game, but to *Barnes and Noble* or *Borders*. Vampires and historical novels were his passion, his true escape.

With Jason in the home I needed to provide more structure. This new child came from a much managed environment and was not ready to just fall off the ship and swim free. I can say this now, but don't be fooled. I had little real understanding of that issue at the time. I was simply following my great training. After all, it was easy to talk, write rules, checkmark chores on the refrigerator, but quite another to enforce it all. This was most difficult for a single parent, especially one blessed with a son who had near total self-management skills from a very early age. He was a latch-key kid from fourth grade, living in a secure, walled community where the greatest threat was from a stray golf ball.

During this period of adjusting to our new 'baby,' I looked for something that he and I could share together and continue developing our relationship. I soon realized I was competing with Junior for his attention, which during the first weeks was just fine with me. Nick seemed content to be an older brother available for guidance and horsing around, more of the latter. He was focused on finishing his last year of school, then moving on to NAU. School, sports and hanging with his friends were his priority. Jason and I were left on our own with Junior never far away. As Nick would remind me for many years, Jason was my idea. For me it was a second chance at fatherhood. He was ten, a perfect age when Dads know everything and are seen as near god-like beings. I couldn't be more pleased.

School was the first real challenge. It is always problematic with foster children because they get moved so often, and rarely settle down to build strong academic skills or long-term relationships with peers. Each move means a new school, new teachers, and new friends which sums up to discomfort, fear of rejection, fear of failure and everywhere reminders of past people and places lost.

With the new placement, we wanted to provide an environment for him to experience success. Jason had been accommodated in an institutional classroom at Cleo Wallace and had suffered academic losses with all his prior raging behaviors. The decision was made to pull him back one year. At first he was not agreeable, but once he learned he would be in the same grade as his new friend Junior, all was well and he clearly appreciated the logic, or at least he gave us the impression he understood and agreed. He also physically fit in well with younger youth due to the nature of his small stature resulting from his failure to thrive at Cleo Wallace.

We were fortunate that the school was very close to the house so he could walk, offering an additional sense of freedom and an opportunity to build self-confidence. He had a lovely young and creative teacher who was willing to go the distance for him. She had patience and a very maternal manner, to which Jason always responded with an exceedingly positive attitude. He always wanted to please people; it was his key driver, which I would learn later, was also a key trigger for anger outbursts otherwise known as rage. His desire to gratify was tied to his drive for perfection, which was tied to his self-image, and on and on to fear of rejection and ultimate loss. His mind had this equation memorized. When he perceived that one element of that equation was in play, he reacted to the anticipated outcome, loss, real or imagined.

After Jason was enrolled in school, I continued a dialogue with his new social worker assigned to the case, about a joint activity to build our relationship. After discussing a number of options, we decided to follow through with the story line from my book and build a tree fort, the private sanctuary of the little street urchin who became a knight. Now you need to use your imagination on this. We live in Arizona, and yes, it is a desert. In fact, I had a large multi-armed Saguaro and Ocotillo in my front yard. I do not recommend using either cactus for a tree house. Our home was designed around a central courtyard, Spanish style. This courtyard area was open to all the rooms in the house. Beyond the finished covered area was a garden shaded by a centrally positioned orange tree and off to the side, an old peach tree. For those of you that live around orange trees, you know they can have very thorny branches and are thick with foliage, and therefore not good for a tree house. This left only one option, the peach tree. At first I was wary, but it turned out brilliantly.

We designed, measured, calculated and made numerous trips to Home Depot to examine and price wood products and steel brackets. After a week, we had a viable plan that included attaching the main frame to the corner of the house with the balance of weight taken by a four-by-four post on the opposite corner. We built the fort around the tree which provided just the right filtered shade during those hot Arizona days. This project was perfect for the purpose. Jason was motivated as he always wanted a tree house. What boy doesn't? His friend Junior was as excited, and some days, even more so than Jason. And I enjoy woodworking and was able to share my knowledge and enthusiasm. All was nirvana at the Hunter residence.

He was doing well in school, and the teacher believed I had made up the story of Cleo Wallace to get sympathy and special treatment in the classroom.

Jason was clearly a well mannered little boy. The neighbors told me much the same story; a perfect gentleman. I bought it bait, line and sinker. After all, that was my little ski buddy from Keystone; the angel who built all his Lego models that were neatly displayed for me on every visit. I was doing well. But, of course, nothing is truly perfect. The household grew a third, and that total growth was one high energy kid who tracked in dirt. And what area of the house he missed, his friends were sure to cover with their own mess. After about three weeks, I decided it was time for a family meeting. Now I am not big on formal family meetings. In the past I just left Nick a note or if a major issue, we would talk over dinner. But I was a foster parent now and felt compelled to follow the training and guidance of the agency. A family meeting sounded reasonable.

So one night after dinner I assembled my little family. Nick was his typical character, half in a book, half listening but not expecting anything important enough to interrupt his reading. Jason was his nervous little self, sitting on the floor eying me up. I opened this first session with my complaint about everyone not pulling together to keep up with the basic chores. Everyone had their list, so let's go over it again. Since Jason was the youngest, I thought I'd start with him. He was unable to sit still anyway.

"OK Jason, let's talk about your job here."

His fidgeting abruptly stopped, his body went rigid, and his face hardened with the color of blood; after which a curdling scream rose from the deepest part of his throat.

EXPLOSION!

I was stunned. I was confused. I was at a loss for words. Immediately I went into consolation mode. "It's OK, Jason." But I couldn't get much out with his screams interrupting my every word. He sprang to his feet; fists clenched, raised in an almost evangelistic fashion. His words were crisp and to the point.

"Why does everyone blame me? Nick's not doing anything. He's always reading. This sucks. I hate you."

'Hate me?' I thought to myself with horror. He put a hard accent on the last word as he sped out of the house into the garage. I quickly followed in pursuit. Mistake!

I had to explain myself. Another mistake! Entering the garage I found him punching and kicking my car. This was a fairly new car, mind you, and I was still at the keeping it waxed every week stage of ownership. I leaped toward him and grabbed his arm while yelling at him not to hit the car. Big Mistake!

Then I stared him down while still holding one of his arms. Bigger Mistake!

Remember the quiet room at Cleo Wallace? I didn't have one of those facilities. In fact, I had no place void of breakables. He pulled away from my grip and ran to the other side of the car. His well tuned survival instincts were now fully engaged. As I continued my dialogue on how he completely misunderstood my intention, he grabbed a piece of lumber and aimlessly swung it about. I chased after him around the car, finally catching up, just a foot or so away, face-to-face. Biggest Mistake!

Those once big round beautiful eyes narrowed to deadly slits and struck fear through my heart. If eyes alone could kill, that would have been my last day on earth.

SLAM!

I got the full blow of his newly acquired weapon across the side of my chest. It did hurt, and not just a little. He dropped the lumber and ran back into the house. To demonstrate that I had not learned any useful lesson yet, I followed him to his room where I was suddenly stopped by a door flying in my face. Normally a closed door remains at rest. Not this one. Jason was testing the wood's elasticity, pounding it again and again with his head, fists and feet. This was my little, adorable son, my Knight in shining armor? Don't be fooled by the slender, underweight, photogenic foster child. Though only 60 pounds at the time, he carried quite a punch. Did I forget to mention he studied karate at some point in his youth and was trained to break boards? No, I probably didn't; and neither did the Foundation.

***

Nick's Journal (17 years old)

My experience with my father's foster care journey has been limited. When I think back on it, I did that on purpose. I was in the house with Dad and Jason for a portion of my junior and senior year in high school. After that I was on the sidelines, a spectator. I was present for the show, but was able to leave and go home afterwards. What influenced me most was Jason's "blow up" as I call it. One day at home, the cause forgotten, I see Jason's face red, upset about something. He is butting his head into the wall... I was stunned.

I walked out of the room, passing Dad without saying one word. I lied down on the couch. My mind was blank. What Jason was doing was not processing. The thudding in our bedroom changed, Jason was now butting his head on the door. All I can think about was "nothing."

I am not a confrontational person by nature. Or an angry person either. My Dad and I had legendary arguments which lasted 5-10 seconds. It was the Scottish in our blood. Afterward, we went and had dinner which was the French in our blood. For myself, I don't stay angry long. People who I don't get along with, I wouldn't socialize with. You could say I am the king of apathy. I don't bring emotion to people I don't care for. They are not worth the effort.

My nature influenced how I dealt with Jason and his "blow ups." I never understood them. Dad gave me explanations, but in my mind it didn't matter. Here was a kid who didn't have control. I reacted the only way I knew how, I ignored it. At the time, it was easy to do. I would leave the house, hang out with friends. How was I to handle some kid head butting walls and doors?

People are interesting, you like hanging out with them. Making friends and having fun. Other times, people are nuts. They do things that cause you to think, "What is going on in their mind?" As we get older, we realize people are who they are. They can't help it. Jason couldn't help what he was doing, but I couldn't help him with it.

I tried to become Jason's big brother. We hung out, the regular things boys do. We fought and made up. But I was at a distance. When it came to Jason's other side, I didn't get involved. The sad thing is I wasn't supportive for Dad during his entire foster care experience. As I said before, I was a spectator for most of it.

After Dad moved to Virginia with Jason, I stayed behind and moved on. Dad had to raise Jason, I was not involved anymore. You can say there was a separation emotionally. Jason was my brother, but I was unprepared for what that meant.

***

I was helpless against the locked door. Oddly, Nick was still in the living room on the sofa. Apparently he hadn't heard anything important yet.

In desperation, I called over to him to help, and I heard a faint reply: "This was your idea, I'm going to Tom's house," as the front door slammed shut.

Tom was Nick's closest friend, a relationship that went back to fourth grade. The friendship was tested that year as Nick spent more and more time with Tom, and even spent a number of nights to avoid watching these raging dramas.

I just sat on the floor, leaning against the door as it and my back received blow after blow. I called to him to stop. I'm sure I was very repetitive as I groped through my mental files for the recipe to fix this problem. I also questioned myself. How did I let something so simple, get so escalated. Then I used basic parenting survival skills 101. I threatened him with punishment if he didn't stop immediately and open the door. Fortunately those doors were solid wood. Had they not been, the door would have opened, but not in the traditional manner, and my other side would have been smashed. Was this his way of showing his desire to stay with me?

I maintained my position against the bedroom door, holding my rib cage, which at this point was really smarting. Time had stopped for me, and impulsive, useless thoughts ricocheted in my head. Moments like that are when you question prior decisions and even your sanity, about spending endless hours in training to share your home with such a kid. Your tranquil life now shattered, you look for sympathy from those around you. There was no one around me.

After half an hour, all went dead quiet. I waited a while longer and then stood up, turned the door knob, and to my surprise, the door swung open. No Jason in sight. A more careful survey revealed a small lump on the bed, and indeed, he was under his blanket with Brownie in hand. The monster had transformed back to that gentle little boy. I sat on the bed and gently brushed his sweaty head. He turned around and embraced me, crying like a baby, coughing out "I'm sorry" over and over again. I melted. I had my little darling back. 'How odd,' I thought. As I left him to sleep, I examined the door on the inside; his head had indeed left its mark, along with his fists and shoes. These physical scars were used by Nick to remind me that this was all my idea.

That was my first of many raging incidents with Jason. Some I observed from beginning to end, a special gift for having been the trigger. Others were well underway before I was on the scene, usually coming from work, to help manage the outcome. In truth, I don't think I ever did contribute to controlling those anger episodes. I merely provided the escape route for him to hide from the world he had just terrified into chaos.

That night was too quiet. No rustle of little feet as Jason would sometimes run from one end of the house to the other after a bath, towel flying above his head like a royal standard, and shouting "look out, I'm come in through Nakee!" No music blasting from the kids' room and no friends congregating in the living room debating anything for arguments sake as teenagers enjoy doing. Nick didn't come home that night and Jason just slept. As for me, I was up most of the night analyzing the day's events, searching for a rational explanation. My mind was racing, but without a set course or fixed goal.

What did happen at Cleo Wallace? Was it really the best in the west? I learned years later that not all youth agreed. It was reported in the *Boulder Weekly* in 2004, that Danielle Jackson, a former teenage resident alleged: "I gained nothing of value from my imprisonment at Cleo Wallace, I did not belong there."

Finally I came to the only rational conclusion. I would call his social worker in the morning. I finally collapsed from exhaustion. I awoke a few hours later to the harsh reality of my alarm... time to go to work.

That same week another major incident occurred that I was not advised of until much later. Nick and Jason enjoyed rough housing almost daily. Nick was a member of the high school wrestling team and always wanted to practice his moves. Jason was the perfect dummy. But Nick always took it further. Once wrestled down, he would hold him and play the 'typewriter' game. Nick would punch the keys on his chest: "dear mommy... bing," *carriage return*, "I love you... bing," *carriage return*. You get the idea. While fighting to get free one morning, Jason squirmed over and Nick moved to smack his butt, a friendly, wrestler's smack. Well, he missed and hit his back. Jason flipped from playful into a deadly fury. He dashed out of the house and took off on his bike. Just four houses down, his handlebar hit a tree, flipping him off the bike and onto the road in front of an oncoming car. Traffic screeched to a halt. The driver jumped out of his car to offer assistance, but Jason threatened him to stay away. He formally introduced himself to the neighborhood. Incredibly neither the bike nor Jason was damaged. He hopped back on his bike and continued raging around town that morning. Nick just assumed he had gone to school, and carried on normally. But he was in no state to confront a classroom, so he tooled about until he tired out, and then went home waiting for school to let out later that afternoon. I never learned about this incident until much later.

The Lifeline

When all seems hopeless, you don't call 911, you call your social worker. Now this is a topic of hot debate among foster parents. Though everyone has a passionate position, it really just depends on your personal experience, intimacy and the dedication of the social worker. I have always been fortunate to have had the very best. Though I am sure they questioned themselves many a time during some of our most difficult moments as they worked hard to maintain an outer expression of calm to broadcast a sense of total situational control. Trust me, it works.

The day after I was smacked with a two-by-four, Jason awoke with a jolt and danced off to school not unlike any other day. Though I was anxious and guarded, he acted oblivious to my constrained behavior. I experienced the first step toward adult trauma. He, on the other hand, was in his element, seemingly carefree and ready to begin a new day, or what I would soon learn, his cycle.

I called the social worker to vent, nothing more. I needed to talk to someone. Contacting friends or family seemed counterproductive. After all, they all told me I was crazy to take Jason in the first place. When we decide to open our home to foster children, we sometimes lose sight of our bigger community. We talk about our dreams, but rarely ask for consent from anyone but our most inner circle, our spouse for certain, other children in the home perhaps. We inform and discuss, but rarely open the forum to debate once we have made up our minds to move forward.

I was a single parent, so spousal agreement was a singular debate. Nick was my only son living at home and was most agreeable as long as it did not commit him. That simply meant he was not taking on any additional responsibility that would defer him from his usual activities and personal goals. That was fair. Though I anticipated he would evolve into the big brother role, as well as be a support "parent" for me. Never assume! My relatives, on the other hand, were most critical of my plans:

Why take on another kid when you are near the end.
One more year and Nick goes to college.
You need to focus on his needs and not get diverted.
The kid came from where?
Are you crazy?

I heard the word crazy a lot back in those days; and at times I indeed questioned my sanity, or at least my ability to make rational decisions. For every argument thrown at me, I had a counter. But in truth, there was nothing rational about taking Jason. He was terribly damaged with a long history of violent behavior and disruptions, though I was not provided the depth of his case file at the time. Trust was no longer within his grasp. He was solely on survival mode, a behavior that evolved from years of abuse and loss. On the outside, he was enchanting with his bright eyes, wide smile and adventurous spirit. Below the surface, however, was a fully grown demon feeding off his inner gut, claws tightly clutched around his heart, denying entry to anyone. He was a self serving creature, a taker for sure. But beyond the demon, locked even deeper inside his spirit was a will to overcome his past, to break free and join the world of normal childhood he so longed to enjoy.

This hunger for a normal life is common among many foster children, especially those with such horrific damage that they are managed most of their young lives, kept a safe distance from ordinary family life and peer play. From psychiatric hospitals and residential treatment facilities, to group homes and therapeutic foster homes, the negative messages are clearly communicated, despite every attempt by social workers to counter the obvious. Even the more standard support services such as Individual Education Plans, group or individual therapy, and that dreaded monthly visit to the psychiatrist for a meds review communicates: I am different, I am wrong. Every unique program instituted to help these children, by their exclusive design, compounds the self destructive messages to the child that they are isolated, that they are different, not just disabled, but unwanted and discarded. Negative self-talk is routine. Even the best raised child can fall into this trap, especially in adolescence. Negative self-talk is silent; permeating their souls and poisoning all your good intentions as it feeds on your every attempt to build up their self-esteem.

This sounds very reasonable when discussed in a rational dissertation. Not so when you are struggling to live a normal life: stable, secure and predictable. Once more, no matter how well you learn their behavior patterns and triggers, they will always surprise you at the most unexpected time. They will defy your reasoning and bring you down into their world sooner than you could ever think possible. Before long, you find yourself in the same denial, the same protective mode, and always on the alert for a strike to your very soul. The longer you embrace these profoundly damaged children, the more an objective voice is necessary to maintain your sanity, keep you and the child on the right path and most important, to protect the flame of hope.

The social worker, sometimes referee, is perhaps the most important person in your life. If you are blessed with an experienced, knowledgeable, and above all, committed professional, your child has a chance and your family will survive to be stronger with a well developed social conscious. Through the foster parent and social worker, these children are forever imprinted with the importance of good parenting, despite the long-term effects from their past of drug addiction, alcoholism and child abuse. An experienced social worker, hardened in the field, is critical to survival in the system for both the child and the parent.

No amount of education can provide this capability for either parent or social worker. It is not unlike war. Watching a movie or documentary on television is no equal to hardened battlefield experience. It is the personal participation that creates the personal traumas from which both learn and grow. If the parent is a raw recruit like I was, then the key is to build confidence, and not get dragged down. Again, this is one of many responsibilities undertaken by our social workers otherwise known as case workers.

During Jason's transition to my home, the Foundation decided on a female social worker for Jason since he was now living with a single male, I guess to provide that maternal touch. Being a single adult household was actually considered a plus for Jason, as he had a history of playing adults against one another which stressed the marital relationships. This young woman was my first working encounter with a social worker. She was young, patient, and interacted well with him. She was Hispanic by heritage, short in stature with a beautiful round face filled with a warm and gentle smile. Her tone was calming. She never raised her voice with anger of any kind.

My emergency meeting at the agency opened with the barefaced fact, the honeymoon was over. But this was the worst it would be. He was just adjusting and releasing his anxiety of the new placement. After nearly a year of intense therapy, expectations were high that this would be his last placement. The major issues which were the cause of so many prior disruptions were behind him. The meeting was a complete success. I was composed and had already put the incident behind me. I left the agency office filled with that good old blind enthusiastic attitude. Little did I realize until years later, that the immediate trauma he was suffering was from the very institution that was sought to cure him: Cleo Wallace.

After that first major raging incident, the case worker set up therapy with a psychologist named Linda. Almost every foster child gets the therapy treatment. It's the cheapest solution for the state, a one hour session each week or so. Most children are very resistant to sharing their problems, even less their feelings, with a stranger. After most sessions Jason was usually angry and non-compliant. He complained about being asked "how do you feel about this or that." He always told me he didn't know, but would say stuff just to get her to stop bugging him. My future foster son, Drake also hated that question and would just shrug his shoulders and look down. Another issue for these children is that therapists and medications remind them that they are not normal, a condition they spend great energy to hide.

Prior to Linda, Jason had participated in other forms of therapy. His most memorable session, which he still complains about to this day, involved anger management. He remembered entering a room filled with anatomically correct dolls which were unforgettable for a little kid. The therapist asked him to release his anger by hitting a 'coach doll,' a large air filled punching doll with an angry face. He pulled back like a major league hitter and slammed it so hard, the head popped off. The therapist responded in a very serious tone, looking him straight in the eyes and said; "you will have to pay for that." Some traumas occur while resolving trauma.

Years later with me, one anger release that Jason enjoyed was a large kick bag I hung from the back porch. It was sturdier than the coach doll. He wore through a number of these sand filled, canvas giants. He also wore his knuckles to bleed during the most rage filled episodes. This was one place where blood stains were always evident. Perhaps for Jason they were like scars, marks of honor.

Honestly, I was never comfortable with the bag approach to anger release. In my mind, it only encouraged a violent form of emotional discharge, rather than developing more socially appropriate methods. This would be a point of dispute between us for many years. Often I would quietly move the bag to the garage, but if enraged, that was the first thing he would look for and when he did not find it hanging on the back porch, it only escalated his rage. But now it was focused on me!

I was with Jason for most of his therapy and psychiatric sessions. He was very insecure and unwilling to participate alone. One concern the clinical supervisor spoke about after meeting Linda was her physical resemblance to his last foster mom, Marge. Since that was a failed placement, she was concerned about how he would interact with the therapist. I'm not sure if that mattered to Jason and he certainly never raised that issue himself.

Jason learned that art was his only true escape. As he matured, we learned he was truly a gifted artist. My most prized Christmas present is a pencil drawing of a lemur family that hangs in my office. Picking up on this interest, Linda had a small marker board for him to use. On each visit he immediately took the board from beside a chair, sat on the floor and drew, rarely looking at the therapist. Sometimes she would just talk to me about how things went the prior week, rather than ask Jason for his thoughts, never forgiving him the question, "how do you feel about that?"

As with many stressful situations, one day during an otherwise normal therapeutic session, he raged. I can't remember all the specific triggers, some were obvious in home. The marker board went flying, his language escalated with voice pounding, and he tore out of the office. By this time I learned not to follow too close but keep him in sight. He spun around the hallways, and then down into the main lobby raging the entire time. Heading toward the main door, he confronted a security officer head on. The officer, ignorant of the situation, stood in his way, but maintained a safe distance, and asked Jason to cool it. Jason slowed his progress, clenched his fists tightly and walked straight past the officer and outside, then continued his raging all around the building. I just walked to the car and waited. This was one of the few times I was actually pleased. Finally, a professional working with us witnessed this explosive behavior. Now I'd get some serious help. The passenger door whipped open and my little bundle of joy plopped down, body rigid and fists still clenched tight. He fell asleep on the way home, his deadly expression transformed to pure angelic calm.

Once home, he sprung awake and dashed to his room.

Thud . . . thud . . . thud. . . .

I carefully opened his door following the blunt sound. On the closet floor, sitting with his legs tightly squeezed against his chest, Jason was rhythmically banging the back of his head against the wall.

Thud . . . thud . . . thud. . . .

As I approached to comfort him, his eyes tuned at me, but I saw no anger, no hate, and no killer instinct. They were hollow. I saw the little boy from Cleo Wallace that first meeting with Dr. U. He stared through me, his head continuing to a beat on the wall. I placed my hand between his head and the wall. He continued without interruption. After a few hits on my hand, he slid over a little and continued on the bare wall. I cried. I didn't know what else to do. I picked him up like a baby and laid him on the bed. I was at a loss for words. He pulled his pillow to his face and continued banging. I left the room.

I was stunned again. After speaking with a friend in the neighborhood who was a medical doctor at the local Air Force Base I learned that institutionalized children may exhibit this head banging behavior due to a lack of stimulation, anger, and a need to provide their own form of rhythmic stimulation to the brain. In Jason's case it may have been a combination of issues that resulted in an internal calming effect. What did I bring into my home, that now I was too far emotionally connected with to walk away?

During the next session, Linda was very vigilant to his reactions and steered clear of the "how do you feel about that?" question. While Jason drew on the marker board as if nothing had transpired just a week ago, Linda confided to me that he was one of the worst hardwire cases she had seen in a long time. Her prognosis was not good; she knew no cognitive therapeutic cure. The best that could be hoped for was that he would develop tools to overcome his violent reactions to his environment. It would take years. That's when you ask yourself, "and so what are we paying you for?"

But I saw something that day after we left her office that she did not witness.

Thud . . . thud . . . thud. . . .

It was weeks before I had the courage to discuss it with his social worker, who seemed to shrug it off as no big deal. To see a ten year old boy in such a helpless, fetal and self-hurtful position strikes terror in your heart, most especially when it is the child you call your son.

I soon learned that cognitive therapy or what some people call, couch therapy, doesn't work well with children. At least it never progressed well with any of mine. Their minds are not developed enough to make the connections. They are still too primal. Jason was with Linda for a few months or so, but things never really improved. We tried others over the years, but for young Jason, giving him a therapist was as helpful as putting a hammer in his hands while raging. He simply was not ready. Some people are not prepared to face their issues until they are well past adulthood.

One mental health expert that did have success over many years with Jason was his psychiatrist, also named Linda. He was her patient before Cleo Wallace and remained so well after he turned eighteen. Like with the therapist Linda, I always sat with him, even as an older teenager. It just seemed to work better for him. The meetings (medication reviews) always started with a conversation between the doctor and me, and then she would turn to Jason for confirmation. Mostly he agreed, a few times he did not. We never argued. He was always polite and seemed interested in the doctor's explanations of how the medicine helped him control his anger. She did not ask that forbidden question: "How do you feel about this or that?"

The medicine that worked best for Jason was Zoloft. If we could get his thinking to engage before his reaction equation engulfed him, he was better able to maintain some control, at least enough not to flip out in public. But like most children, especially when he hit adolescence, Jason fought the meds, believing that meds represented illness, therefore if he didn't take any meds, it was a symbol of his normalcy.

During these first few months, the case worker shared more of his history, though little of his mental health or behavior issues. It was then that I learned he had a father in prison, incarcerated just miles from our home. Jason was terrified of this man, who was his mom's boyfriend. His brothers and sister always blamed Jason for the family break-up and their confinement to foster care. Everything was good at home until Jason was born. In reality, it was not, but this was their perception from early childhood. The older children simply lived in a world of denial. It was easier to blame the little brother, especially since he was such a difficult baby that no doubt raised tensions in the home. Jason remembers one instance when he was having a tantrum in the tub and his older sister, who took most of his care in those early years, held him under the water to shut him up. She nearly drowned him; a memory that haunts them both.

Social workers always try to keep children in contact with their birth family. For most the goal is re-unification. At least that is the initial permanency plan. Visits are arranged, despite the pain they cause for the child. Most foster parents dread these visits because the children come back to them angry and hurt with the resultant behavior issues that the foster parents are left to manage. In Jason's case he was given the choice, but his case worker always raised the issue during every visit. Jason had no interest. His mother was distant. Most visits that were arranged with her children failed, as she would not show up. Her divorced husband left the state never to return.

Jason's father, on the other hand, wanted contact. He sent Jason greeting cards that he drew in prison. Like Jason, he was very artistic. He had an attorney appointed by the court to protect his paternal rights and press for contact. After mounting pressure from the Foundation, Jason agreed to a telephone call. It was arranged at the Foundation Offices in the presence of several staff and me. There is no forgetting Jason's expression when the man's voice came on the speaker phone. It matched the horrific expression of World War II photographs of children behind barb wire. He said little during the conference call, but was clearly shaken from the experience. He pleaded on the way home that afternoon to protect him from his dad. His only memories were being beaten with a bull whip. A sound that was so hardwired in the deepest part of his cerebellum, that they caused serious issues years later when diving in high school.

Though the most frightening memory was when this man would pull his pants down and threaten to cut off his penis while pressing a knife against the skin.

I was not convinced this man was his father. Though I did not have access to the extensive files at the Foundation, he resembled his other brothers too much. They all had very similar features, right down to the pale skin, blond hair and light freckles. I asked the case worker for a DNA test. I had no legal rights, but the agency must have had the same concerns at some point, and since the relationship was so volatile anyway, they agreed a couple of years later. The father agreed as well. The next month the results were in and the findings were as we expected. For the first time in his life Jason was free of a very painful history, and more importantly, felt a closer kinship to his siblings. He was no longer the outcast.

Desks are for Security

Teachers require unique talents well beyond academic knowledge and skill. They confront a diversity of characters with as many different motivations and behaviors. Within the student pool are also emotionally damaged foster children, as well as many who are on the cusp of family crisis and are equally injured. I can never sing their praise enough for their dedication day in and day out. Jason was one of those special cases that required unlimited patience. One fact I learned early was that he had to act out somewhere, either home or in school, both were fair game, but rarely did he have significant issues at both places during the same period.

He loved his teacher. She was young and maternal. She was also inexperienced and completely unprepared for such a damaged child. Though Jason had just transferred from a residential treatment program where he attended classes in the institution, he did not come to this new school equipped with an Individual Education Plan (IEP). This is a key document to provide special services for disabled children. This program was developed and enacted by law to provide educational support for children who are not within the average range, as well as provide federal protection for them to be kept in school. Some children are so disabled that the school will contract outside their districts for services, but most try to keep the student contained for the student's benefit, but also to keep costs to a minimum. In the case of foster children, they are typically categorized as emotionally disabled due to post traumatic stress or one of the symptoms of this disorder such as Attention-Deficit/Hyperactivity Disorder. In Jason's case, his behaviors were far more serious. He was dangerous to himself and others. A behavior pattern I minimized for many years.

This lack of special education support, we would later learn, was one of a number of major mistakes. In hindsight, he should never have been placed in a public school classroom directly from the hospital without a transition classroom first. Fortunately, unlike many of these children, he did not have ADHD, for that she counted her blessings. He was, however, extremely insecure and overly sensitive to criticism. He was hyper-vigilant to anyone who might threaten his security, either physically with me, or emotionally within himself. Both were fragile, so brittle in fact that his confidence could be shattered by the slightest comment. Such was my own experience with his first rage at home. By talking to him first from the start of the family meeting, though my intent was to be courteous to his age and nervousness, his interpretation was that I blamed him, and from that perception came the total threat of loss. He escalated without the slightest sign of trouble. His young teacher was soon to experience similar outbursts in a classroom of thirty other children, all vulnerable to disruption, especially from a classmate who lashed out with such rage to frighten the most hardened soldier.

To compound his raging behavior, Jason went ballistic when touched. He created an imaginary space around his person, and anyone who entered was fair game for a violent reaction. His cognition would close down and he became a deadly animal fighting to the last breath. Touching his shoulder to get his attention in the classroom did not result in the anticipated effect. She understood the power of real rage when he was triggered one day when the class was moving to a different room. As she physically approached him while raging, his desk went flying across the classroom and the contents splattered across the floor. No, he didn't push the desk, he threw it.

Things started out well the first few weeks. As always, Jason honeymooned in the new environment. He put on his best behavior along with his engaging smile and willingness to help in the classroom. His first rage at school was several weeks after the rage at home, but once started, continued throughout the remainder of the year. Though I did not see another major explosion at home for a couple of months, his teacher was suffering through his outrageous behavior weekly. And worse, he did not have an emotional attachment to anyone at the school, so he rarely completed his normal anger-calm/hide-forgiveness cycle I witnessed. At best, he would collapse into the self pity segment, though often he remained highly charged. I also learned from reports of these episodes that Jason had quite an extensive four-letter vocabulary, which I had not yet personally experienced during our several months of Colorado visits or recent transition at home. For me, he was just a little package of cute and cuddly, with eyes that drew you deep into his raw soul.

The first call, like most throughout my many years with Jason, came completely by surprise and always during work. I was fortunate throughout my career in Arizona to live in close proximity to my home, an absolute necessity for successful single parenting.

"He is under the desk and won't come out," a woman opened in a pleading voice.

It took a few questions to establish that this was his teacher at the school talking about Jason. In short time, that would never be necessary again. Whenever the phone rang with a pleading voice, I knew it was Jason in trouble. Calls from the school were a new experience. The worst incident with Nick was his freshman year, when after getting pushed by a bully, he knocked him down. The result was a week suspension that he served with honor. Never an incident did we endure again...until Jason!

I asked the obvious, "Can't you just pull him out?"

"Oh no," came a quick snap, "he screams and kicks like a wild animal. I don't want to hurt him. He's so scared. He is a darling you know."

This was the one and only teacher that described Jason as darling while dealing with a rage. Most found him scary with piercing eyes that could kill. She implored me to come to the school immediately. The nurse was in the classroom by that point and all the other children had been evacuated. They hoped he would tire out, but as the afternoon wore on and school was soon to end they were now desperate for other options. And no, the school didn't have a quiet room.

When I arrived the classroom was bustling. The principal was outside the door with others I did not immediately recognize. They cleared away to allow me entry without introductions. The teacher and nurse were inside. Under a desk, tightly crunched into a near fetal position on the floor was my little bundle of joy, shaking heatedly, with expletives exploding from his lips. I dropped to his level, looking straight into his teary eyes. My last encounter with the dark side of Jason was a complete failure. But this moment seemed very different. I felt him drawn to me, not pushing away. It was magic, and I'm certain the others in the room were convinced I had a gifted touch. He dropped his guard and literally fell into my arms. Like a young child, he laid his head on my shoulder, while his entire body fell limp. Without a single word, I left. I was proud. We were making progress. I placed him ever so carefully into the car, snapped the seat belt in place and drove home. It was less than a mile, but he was already asleep. I carried him to his bed, laid him down with his bear. He gently turned on his side, his knees pulling up to his chest, his expression filled with angelic peace. Oh, was I the fool!

I closed his door and went to the kitchen for a caffeine refreshment to calm my nerves. Some readers may find that one contradictory, but let's continue. As the coffee was brewing,

Thud . . . thud . . . thud. . . .

I was curious since I had just laid him down with such tenderness. I cracked the door. He was in that same tight ball, Brownie in hand, rocking back and forth on his bed, banging the back of his head on the wall. When I set up the room I placed his bed against a corner thinking it would help him feel safe. Little did I know at the time, but I provided him easy access to head banging material without ever leaving his 'nest'. I sat in the kitchen sipping my coffee,

Thud . . . thud . . . thud. . . .

I studied music at the college level and can assure you, the rhythm was perfect. Several times that afternoon I went into his room and gently laid him back down. He would pull his knees tight against his chest with Brownie squeezed inside. His eyes were as empty of expression as the rest of his face. I saw no anger and when he would return my gaze, I felt as though he was looking past me. Each time I left, just a few minutes later,

Thud . . . thud . . . thud. . . .

I drank a number of cups that afternoon as the sun fell below the horizon. Nick came home, but quickly left with backpack in hand. I felt no desire for dinner. A hard rap at the front door snapped me out of a gloomy mood. Opening the door I dropped my head to see little Junior with his standard grin from ear-to-ear. I explained without giving away the true nature of the situation that Jason was in for the night. But before I had the door shut, Jason sped past me out the door. He waived a relaxed goodbye with Junior in tow. His eyes were bright and cheerful, his smile inviting.

We had a number of such incidents that year, though the school staff learned how to deal with him. They found my involvement was not reducing the number of outbursts. And frankly, I was not adjusting well to his head banging and body rocking in the closet or on the bed. They also learned that touching Jason was one sure way to escalate him to super strength. His mere 60 pound frame may never have been imposing, but once injected with the adrenaline of his internal fears, he transformed into a wounded animal. Worse, if he was cornered, he would leap out in a frightening offensive attack.

Most people, both school officials and local police were more than understanding. I am sure my position on the governing school board didn't make anyone more comfortable about this situation. And though the superintendent maintained his calm and humor when we spoke, I felt his frustration. Dealing with the politics of running a school district brought on enough stress without the added strain of the constant behavior challenge of a board member's child, especially a very outspoken member who had strong community support for his election. I was very thankful for his help those years and his ability to maintain a division between school political issues and Jason's problems.

I remember one incident I was called to during those first few months, when he ran off into the school baseball fields with a police officer in hot pursuit. I was expecting a lecture from the officer and perhaps a trip to the local station. Instead, I was greeted with a friendly smile. Jason had given ground by the time I arrived, and the two were just talking, though with a clear distance between them. Jason leaped to the car as he had done so often now, saddled up with his seat belt, head down, and eyes to the floor. These were never good times to talk. Asking what happened or why, was not productive. I tried a few times in the past and it only escalated the situation more, or if he was calm, simply re-engaged him to start all over again. When we got home that day, he simply walked directly to his room.

Thud . . . thud . . . thud. . . .

Perhaps I was over indulging. But I never punished him, not then, or years later. We would talk afterward, though these dialogues were probably doing me greater good than him.

I found two opportunities for any meaningful discussion, the car and the bath tub. While driving, I had his full attention. He had no distractions and no place to go. If he became too tense or I hit a nerve, he would put the radio on. That was my cue that any further dialogue would be wasted. The bath was also a great time to get his total attention. I would sit on the floor while he soaked or played in the suds. I always poured lots of soap into his bath water raising the bubbles over the top. Jason played hard and was usually the stinker by bedtime. Not interested in traditional bathing techniques that involved using such tools as a face cloth or bar of soap; I was dependent on the soaking affect of lots of bubble bath. It usually worked. These approaches for discussion provided relief for us both. I delivered the lecture with a sense of accomplishment. I did my paternal duty. Jason felt relieved the lecture was over with the least pain.

During these talks I usually was calm. After all, the crisis was over. But there were times when I was so burned out. I would lash out in anger, which never resulted in a good outcome for either of us. He would escalate. If in the car, the dash board suffered the brunt of his anger. If in the tub, I was sure to get more of the bath than him. After the blow up he usually went to his room and hid in his closet under a blanket. I would go to my room with a heavy burden of guilt, waiting for thud . . . thud . . . thud. Nick, of course, would escape to his friend Tom.

Hiding under a blanket or in his closet was a last resort for Jason. His first choice for safety was up high. No joke. When he became stressed, his fears spiraled and with it, his complete lack of self control. He was as frightened of himself, as anyone around him. A primal instinct drove him to go high into trees, towers, or the nearest roof, anything that would provide a sanctuary from those pursuing him. Jason once told me a story of how, after running away from home to escape being beaten, he climbed a tall cottonwood tree. The fire department was called, and one of the men was hurt trying to pull him out of the tree. His small stature was unintimidating. Most learned quickly not to be fooled twice. Once escalated to a fury, he was lethal.

Jason did experience success at school that first year, not just behavior outbursts. He maintained good grades and was never in traditional trouble. Don't worry. He made up for it in middle school. One of Jason's triumphs that school year was his Indian dance performance for the end-of-year talent show. Nick learned hoop dancing from a Native American while a Boy Scout. He performed at camp fires and Eagle Scout ceremonies. Jason was impressed with Nick's skill and the many different symbols he created intertwining the hoops while never losing a step to the beat of the drum. Nick was more than pleased to teach Jason and pass on a special gift known by very few people.

Jason was a stubborn perfectionist. Through a number of temper tantrums and flying hoops, however, he learned the basics. It was a unique bonding opportunity for both boys. I made him an authentic breech cloth from woolen material acquired from a local trading post in Phoenix. He practiced often at home, and though apprehensive, especially about wearing a breech cloth that covered little; he performed brilliantly to a very appreciative audience of grade school children. It was a major coup for him and had a positive impact on his self-esteem, not to mention his reputation in the community, which up until then, was not very complimentary.

Another activity that helped build his confidence was rock climbing and backpacking. My first hike with Jason was at a small wilderness area near Strawberry called Fossil Springs. It was the perfect location for a first hike. Less than two hours walk, with the final destination being beautiful warm springs that flowed into a deep creek, shaded by huge cottonwood trees. He was a real trooper, the weight of his pack pulling him quickly down the canyon trail. And though I had brought along a support crew of Nick's friends, all senior Scouts, he was completely self-reliant. The wilderness was his element, his attention drawn to the abundant wildlife at every corner.

We set up camp as I had done with the Boy Scouts for many years, and immediately dashed off for the springs just below our tents. Extending off a wide branch of an old cottonwood tree hung a worn climbing rope that had only one purpose, to swing high up and drop into the creek. The ritual was always the same. The boys would toy with the rope, throw it out and catch it back, and test the water with a gentle touch of a foot to the surface...each one looking at the other to go first. After this opening sacrament, without reservation, someone would just grab the rope and go flying into the water, followed by the whole crew. At first Jason just watched with envy. He wanted to go, but was obviously scared. With a little nudging from Nick and a hoist to catch the rope, he was in the water. That was one of many cheerful weekends with Jason. To the casual observer, he was the happiest little boy on earth! And secretly, I was the proudest Dad with my two sons.

I never saw Jason in any other light than my son. In foster care, that can be a lethal mistake for a parent. Never fall victim to such emotions; they are the property of the state and when problems arise, the agency will be certain you and the child feel the full weight of that fact. I believe this is a key reason why no matter how much you try to reassure these children, they never feel the same security of a normal child. Their fear is well founded from personal experience with the foster care system, and they know better than anyone that their security is tenuous at best. They are helpless within a system even adults cannot always understand. They struggle for control, and struggle to feel some sense of personal power. Unfortunately, the very effort for control can lead to the loss of a placement. Once they believe all is lost they work to sabotage the relationship in order to control the loss, rather than have it forced upon them. How often I heard that lecture from the social workers during the most difficult behavior problems, followed by: 'just hold on' or 'don't give up!'

I also charged out against his wart problem which I promised him during his first time out with us at the hotel in Colorado. And with that, I learned about the State's Comprehensive Medical and Dental Plan (CMDP) that provides care for all these children. I received a list of providers, looking for those in close proximity to our home. Don't believe the list. It is not updated often and many of the physicians opt out due to lower than average reimbursement schedules and lack of timely payment, as well as the vast number of children in the system that can quickly overwhelm their practice. The first time Jason was really down with the flu we entered a medical group office that resembled an emergency room at a large hospital, the floor littered with sick children crawling, running, and crying wall-to-wall. The floor was literally covered by juvenile bodies, shaking, vomiting, and otherwise miserable. The smell was insufferable. After about two hours waiting, I left to take him to my family doctor. I paid the bill without complaint. We waited ten minutes without an advance appointment. He did examine Jason's feet and recommended a specialist. As you probably already concluded, none of the physicians on his list were in the CMDP system.

After some effort, I located a dermatologist and made an appointment. The best I could get was five weeks away. We arrived at a lobby not nearly as crowded as that pediatrician group we first visited for his flu. The wait was tolerable and I didn't feel swarmed by diseased bodies. The doctor took a quick count and began the common treatment, dry ice. With the first dab, Jason launched. I held him while the doctor administered dab after dab, but it was soon evident he was not going to settle down. The doctor called for a nurse to help me keep him still, but she had little success and her presence seemed to escalate him more. Clearly frustrated and unnerved, the doctor raised his voice in a strong commanding manner, telling Jason he was scaring all his patients away; and that he was being over dramatic, it didn't hurt so much, just a sting. Jason wasn't buying any of it. And while holding him down so hard, I felt nothing but pity and fear for him and myself. In the end, the doctor admitted defeat. He recommended over-the-counter medication that was acid based and suggested I make it a daily routine. The first night I applied the stuff, he responded with calm optimism. When I reminded him that this treatment did not work at Cleo Wallace, he argued that it was the fault of the staff. They didn't apply it like I did. I had no confidence this approach would breed success, but I was relieved he was agreeable.

I was overjoyed when school ended, a milestone I celebrated during my tenure in foster care. Summers were always the best of times. School increased the children' stress as they struggled to accomplish work or agonize over what they weren't handing in to the teacher. Most parents would have little pity. But foster children suffer two issues which work against their academic success. First, they are behind their age group in academic learning due to the many placement disruptions and lack of pre-school learning at home, as well as emotional immaturity. Second, their constant emotional issues disrupt their ability to stay focused day-to-day, thereby affecting the on-going learning process. This composite problem results in frustration and lack of self-esteem that feeds on itself year after year with never ending negative self talk: 'I can't do it so why try.' Some will take the tact of: 'I can do it, I just choose not to.' It is the same issue, just another way to protect their self-image, though deep down they know the truth. If you confront them too harshly, be prepared for an emotional explosion.

***

Jason's Journal (11 years old)

Junior and I were best buds. We hung together all the time. I soon met another kid who lived near Junior who was from India named Paul. We were the terror of the neighborhood. After dad and I finished the tree house we all hung out there. One day our neighbor was yelling at us for something, so late that night while we were in our tree house we each took a dump and pissed down their chimney. Another night we all dressed like Ninjas and roamed around town to see how stealthy we were. We went right next to a cop who was out looking for children breaking curfew and we didn't get caught. We also liked to make little forts inside big bushes where we would start fires. Spear fishing in the canals was also a fun past time.

Exploring deserted buildings, or not so deserted, was another favorite past time. A large corner grocery store that went bust was our favorite playground. We got in through a garage door that opened a foot or so, enough for us to slide under. While inside we played in the freezers and the office, and had races with the carts. We had head on collisions with one person in the cart and one pushing. Whoever fell out of the cart first was the loser. We also got up on the roof of a local church. It just looked cool. We were testing out everything in those days. On the roof we discovered an abandoned office in one of the church towers that became one our favorite hangout spots.

One of my friends had an M-1000 firework and we threw it into a canal across from the fire department that was full of trash. We figured if something went wrong they would be right there. In didn't go off right away so I went over to check, and it went off, giving me a mouthful of garbage and canal water.

We lived near the community pool and one night Junior and my friends dared me to jump the wall and skinny dip in the pool, two laps. My friends just stood on the wall and watched. It felt kind of weird because everything is free and flopping around.

Our patio home had a flat roof. We invented a new sport, roof racing, because all the patio homes were together. We would run across all the house roofs from one end to the other. Some people yelled out at us, thinking their homes were caving in.

We dressed up like army guys and went out at night. It was cool because the only thing you needed to look out for was the cops. But other than them, the place was very quiet. When we did see people, we just hid in the shadows. Our town doesn't have lots of street lights. I guess we were a bunch of wild guys always looking for action in our quiet little town. It was sure fun though!

***

The summer started well enough, and though it was in the three digits during the day, the heat always dissipated at night. If you have never lived in the Southwest, you cannot appreciate what "it's a dry heat" really means. Jason and Junior spent endless hours playing in the tree house we had built during his first month at our home. It was 10 x 10 feet, allowing plenty of space for two hammocks with room to spare. Entry was through a trap door in the floor that the children could lock from the inside. A canopy of green leaves from the peach tree provided all the shelter they required. Two windows, also with trap door covers, provided for both privacy and protection from counter attacks while playing war. We even brought in electricity for a fan or any other device they required. This was their haven, day and night. Junior slept at our home more than his that summer. I was delighted to see Jason so happy and content. Life was blooming for him, just as we both dreamed during those many visits at Cleo Wallace. Little did I know at the time, but he was also a neighborhood terror at night, releasing tension from a year of psychiatric imprisonment.

The summer was also a good time to meet the foster mom who cared for his siblings. We hit it off right from the start and supported each other for many years after. I now had the unique advantage of having built in respite (foster care term for official, licensed babysitting) with K, and she the same from me. We developed a great working relationship that was indispensible when the children pushed us beyond our limits. We shared many holidays and birthdays together and did Christmas at both homes which I know all the children really enjoyed. What children don't like two Christmas celebrations?

We returned to Fossil Springs that summer too, but this time with his favorite brother Martin. Jason was anxious to show off his newly acquired backpacking skills, and his physical ability to carry a pack down the entire trail. He wanted to show his older brother that he had value. Was he working to establish a new role? Though they lived apart, their spirits were eternally connected, no matter the living arrangements.

Jason was well prepared, Martin not so much. Jason helped, which only amplified his pride. At camp, he gleefully guided his brother around the area to the best swim and jump sites. He was quick to command the swinging rope that so intimidated him on the last trip. He showed his brother the highest jump along the creek which was a dam down river. Only the bravest, older boys ever took the plunge. The water was very deep, but still it required great confidence to clear the dam and rock foundation below. Neither of the younger boys took the challenge that day, which was fine with me. I was in no position to bring back a damaged foster kid. Jason did, on the other hand, with encouragement from the other children, decide to display himself with a nude dip in the lower pool. Just at that moment the ranger came by on his routine inspection of the trail and surrounding area. The two stared eye-to-eye. The ranger moved on with a half-smile, shaking his head; and Jason retrieved his bathing suit. I should have picked up on a not so subtle indication of Jason's character. He loves the challenge of a good dare!

With Jason settled at home and school out, I also decided to start him in Scouting. I had served as Scoutmaster for our local for many years, and retired when Nick grew out of it just before Jason arrived. Nick was part of an elite group of young boys who earn the rank of Eagle Scout. An accomplishment reserved for only 5% of scouts due to the many years of service, hard work and commitment. Our troop had more than our fair share, likely due to the exclusive neighborhood from where I drew youth and the families' strong beliefs in education, community involvement and church. Jason and Junior were both eager to start. Junior's older brothers were active members as well. Our little town is a real Scouting community.

After I left, the troop was run by a few dads that were committed to keep our vision alive. They were dedicated parents who enjoyed being active with their boys. At the time I rejoined the group which by then was under the leadership of an attorney who grew up in Arizona, a real local who knew everybody and enjoyed people. We worked well together, a relationship that would be of great benefit in the near future with Jason. Another key adult was Kevin, a parent who observed and commanded at a distance. He had a key advantage over all of us. He was a psychiatrist. How many troops can boast a psychiatrist on staff? One might also ask how many troops had a member who spent a year imprisoned in a psychiatric institution. He provided guidance and a sympathetic ear during a few major crises with Jason. I am sure he was thinking something like, 'I go on these scout trips with my son to get away from patients.' All kidding aside, he was supportive, never withholding some very concrete advice. So often these professionals give you long winded diagnosis and theories. Just tell me what to do! Kevin was that kind of person.

We operated a high adventure troop, which simply means that we focused more on challenging outdoor activities than the uniform. We did follow the rules, worked on all merit badges and advancement, but were not as integrated into the greater Scouting community as some would have preferred. I believed that families should have a choice, and those that wanted smartly dressed children had plenty of other troops to join.

We were rebellious and proud of it. This is not to imply we had no discipline or structure. I remember one major regional camporee we did attend where the boys were really getting out of hand. A camporee is an organized scouting event where a large number of troops join together for camping and common activities. During this event in the White Tank Mountains, west of Phoenix, my boys just got a little bored and with it, mischievous. The entire troop decided to moon their arch rival nearby. In retaliation, that troop returned the favor. Only when they did it, I was entertaining some senior officials from the local scout council.

After a quick investigation that evening I ordered the entire troop to pack up. Other troops camping in the area were curious, and I remember a few leaders walking over inquiring what was up. They didn't want to see anyone leave early. I informed them we were not leaving, just taking a temporary respite to improve behavior. We were camped in a valley surrounded by rocky, desert mountains. I marched the boys single file with fully loaded packs to the top of the nearest hill; and there they laid out the minimum equipment and spent the night. I had regained control. When scouts get bored, look out! This is a fact any seasoned forest ranger knows all too well.

Another incident that reflects the character of our troop occurred at another camporee. To understand this situation you need to know about an old Scout custom. During the evening's big campfire, any gear that was found out in the field during that day was returned to the owner, but only if he was prepared to do the 'chicken dance' in front of all assembled. Few scouts were left with anything but a very disheartening experience. I knew of many young boys who would rather lose their favorite new knife, than bear that humiliation. The leaders believed it built character. For some boys it may have, but not all.

During one such activity my Senior Patrol Leader told me he had enough and asked if the troop could skip the campfire that night. I refused and told him to find another way to demonstrate their discontent. That night when the chicken dance began and the first article displayed, followed by a shaky little hand declaring ownership, my SPL ordered an about face. The troop turned away, heads bowed to the ground in silence. I was taken aback. I was swollen with pride, even though every adult present had their eyes squarely upon my person. 'I was cooked,' I said to myself, while secretly smiling with delight. The activity ended immediately and I received a call at work the following week from our local Council office in Phoenix. It was an apology and statement of respect for the boys. Whatever they all truly felt, the practice ended in our area because some gutsy boys stood up to adults over an issue they believed was wrong. I tell you these stories to provide you an understanding of the type of youth group that Jason joined back in the summer of 1996.

His involvement was thorough, never missing an event. You would expect nothing less when Dad was one of the leaders. But he really looked forward to going along with his best bud Junior. Whether team building, rope courses, or learning first aid and fireman body drags, he was excited to participate with the other children. I must emphasize here that the activity needed to be physical in nature. Sitting on a bench in the Scout Lodge learning about citizenship was not his cup of tea.

I so often wished his teachers from school could see him in Scouts. He was in his natural element and thrived. We did have an occasional problem, but we typically camped in places where trees were abundant and close at hand. When trees were in short supply, a sheer rock cliff would substitute fine.

***

Kevin's Journal from Scouts

The first time I met Jason, he was up a tree at the Scout Lodge in our town. Some of the boys were encouraging him to come down so we could begin the scout meeting. In the next few years, I got to know Jason through scouting. He was very quiet during the Scout Meetings, either saying nothing or messing around with his friends. He was not very interested in having significant leadership positions and he really found most of the merit badges to be boring. He did much better if we were doing something physical such as a pre-meeting game. As an adult, he was very difficult to get to know. He did not seem to have much interest in the adult leaders. Fortunately, Bill Hunter had filled me in on some of Jason's background and I could offer support when needed. I tried not to spend time analyzing Jason's behaviors, as I was not his Doctor. All the leaders tried to normalize the teenage male behaviors and set limits as appropriate.

When the scouts would go to camp or on an overnight camp out, Jason would be in his element. He had tremendous athletic ability in climbing and endurance in hiking. His temperament would be on: friendly and outgoing or off: withdrawn and sullen. Jason's behavior was difficult to predict day by day and even hour by hour. If he was on, he would be out of his tent, with the other scouts. He would be climbing something. He tended to pick on the younger ones, but more taunting, teasing and horseplay and seldom physical. He scared me from the standpoint of safety. He would wander into the woods, never get lost, but lose track of time. His climbing rocks and trees were often leaning toward dangerous conditions by my perspective. As a parent, I was leaning toward safety first. If he was off, he would be found in his tent, curled up in a ball in his sleeping bag, usually upside down as if to disappear. You knew when he was upset because he avoided everyone. He wanted to avoid drawing too much attention from the adults, possibly for fear of discipline.

An interesting exception to this was when he performed a Hoop Dance at the Eagle ceremonies. I saw him perform this ceremony four or five times. He would transform himself from a young adult to an Eagle and soar. For this, he received much positive attention and rightfully so. The last time I saw Jason perform this was at his own Eagle ceremony. Jason Hunter had become an Eagle!! That was a huge accomplishment.

***

In short time everyone became accustomed to Jason up a tree, whether just playing around or cooling off. Occasionally, a new dad would join us on a trip and quickly get anxious as Jason headed up, up and up to the top. I would always tell them to relax. After all, he couldn't go any higher than the top, so we were good. They would usually respond with a quizzical look of doubt. But Jason would train the most doubting Tom. In all my years with that boy he never fell out of a tree. That record was almost broken in later years when he was sliding down a tropical tree from very high up observing Howler Monkeys in Costa Rica for a most intimate interaction. He found that the high humidity of a tropical jungle resulted in thick, slimy moss growth, making it difficult to get a foothold. If you are into climbing, you know that the greatest danger is not climbing up, but rather, coming down. He did slide more than climb down. At the bottom, my then twenty year old son, covered in muck, looked like my little Jason from years ago in scouts. These are sacred moments for a dad, the kind you take to the grave.

Foster care does not come with many fringe benefits, but one you do get is summer programs and camp. We chose a number of activities for Jason that summer to keep him occupied during the day. Because I was a single parent, he was required to be supervised by an adult. He attended a local tennis program and actually did quite well for such a small guy. He was very responsible and walked over to the courts on his own, never missing a class.

Jason also enjoyed playing basketball with Nick, so I registered him at the Westphal Basketball camp for a week-long away summer experience. This was a time when specialty camps were booming business. Paul Westphal was the coach for the Phoenix Suns, and some of the NBA players would visit the camp, adding to its allure for the children. We have a treasured photo of Jason with Charles Barkley.

Jason appeared excited about going to camp. We had spent the week packing to be sure he had every comfort conceivable, and of course, Brownie. The drive up to Prescott was rather quiet, not typical of the motor mouth kid. Registration upon arrival went well, though he was hyper vigilant. Mrs. Westphal was among the many staff people welcoming the children. When I asked a counselor to speak with one of the head honchos, she turned and introduced herself. She was a very pleasant woman whose maternal personality shone bright. I was confident that would be our saving grace should problems arise after I left. I helped him take his gear to the assigned cabin, and left him in the good hands of Mrs. Westphal. I departed Prescott that day liberated and full of confidence. We were both in need of a break.

I need to confess my greatest weakness: loss. I have never understood the reason or past childhood trauma that drives my total emotional collapse when I lose someone. The loss need not result from bereavement, though I suffered the death of two boy scouts during my tenure as Scoutmaster. One was killed by a drunk driver near Luke Air Force Base, and the other suffered autoerotic death (strangulation by cutting air to the brain while masturbating to increase the erotic effect). The latter was the most overwhelming because the mother called me before the police. When I came on the scene, my young twelve year old scout was hanging limp, an overturned chair to the side. At the time I had no knowledge of this condition and we all assumed he had committed suicide. The coroner determined otherwise. The mother started a crusade, and soon after moved to Texas. She could not let go and grieve in the place where all her memories were revived daily. We all learned later that the scout's younger brother was drafted to manage the chair and put it back under the boy's feet after ejaculation. He was only ten, maybe younger. He panicked, ran away, then hid under his bed until morning. The family never really recovered from this tragedy and most hurtful was that the school learned the following week that the kid was dared during P.E. class. I was asked to do the eulogy at the funeral. For me, death is easier than a living loss. I guess it's because death is permanent and you have nothing to hold on to, nothing to keep the flame of hope alive.

To cope with my heartache when my children are gone for camp, or in the case of my foster children, residential treatment facilities, I gravitate toward physical activities and writing. When the children see me busy cleaning the same part of the house several times in the same week, or pulling every tiny weed in the garden, they know something is seriously wrong with Dad. They know I am suffering extreme anxiety. One of their greatest fears going to camp was that I would remodel their rooms, especially when they were teens and privacy was a key concern. Several years later after returning from a summer trip, Jason found his room freshly painted each wall a slightly different shade of pastel yellow. I was cheering myself up. He was not appreciative of the dizzying effect, but was politely thankful.

When I returned home that day after leaving Jason at the Westphal camp, I found myself alone. It was a terrifying feeling, empty and lost. I should have been exhilarated considering all the stress that we suffered since Jason moved in. I preferred all the anxiety of dealing with Jason's many problems to an empty home. That Monday passed well enough, but by Tuesday the phone rang at work. It was Mrs. Westphal. Jason was not getting along well with other campers in his cabin, nor was he participating in activities. He seemed completely disinterested in basketball and preferred to hang around her Dalmatian.

She was just giving me an update, "not to worry I have handled much worse cases," she counseled. "He's just a little homesick."

Later that day I received another call, more frantic than the first. "He wants to go home, and now." She said. I felt her irritation over the phone. It was all too apparent. It was too late to drive up, but the next morning I took that day off work and drove back north. The scene as I arrived late that morning was uneventful. The place seemed well structured, with a few children walking about, but with an obvious purpose in their step. The majority of youth were on the courts with the counselor/coaches. I caught a glimpse of a large dog off to the side of one of the courts, and with it, crouching down and close, was my bundle of anxiety. In all honesty, mine as much as his. As I approached he jumped up to greet me. I was gifted with an incredibly strong and enduring hug with the words:

"Are you taking me home now?"

I spoke to Mrs. Westphal briefly trying to work a plan for him to stay. Perhaps he just needed reassurance that I was not abandoning him. I hung around the camp most of that day to provide that assurance to him, but distanced myself, observing his every move from afar. No doubt, he was keeping me well in eyesight. That afternoon he engaged with his cabin on the court and received fair praise for his success. But whenever he was off the court, he was glued to Mrs. Westphal and her Dalmatian. One counselor jokingly referred to him as her new pet. As the day came to a close and the children were preparing for dinner and just hanging around, I headed to the car. It seemed the right time to disappear. All was well.

Before I reached the car door, Jason was sprinting in my direction with his arms flailing everywhere, his voice screeching with a panicked tone, and Mrs Westphal trailing not far behind. The scene had not yet played out. I was retreating off stage too early. I turned as he jumped into my arms, holding tightly enough that I could not mistake the message 'You're not leaving without me.' If you understand the characters in this book, you already know the end of this story. I left Prescott that evening with one extra passenger.

A few weeks later we took our annual summer vacation to Catalina Island. If you have never been to this little paradise twenty miles off the coast of Los Angeles, you have missed a special American sanctuary. The island has quite a history involving Hollywood movie stars and the Chicago Cubs of yesteryear, but for us it represents the very highest standards for a family destination. It is safe with the sidewalk rolling up at ten, and it maintains that traditional, not overly commercial, atmosphere. Activities are all family oriented for both children and parents. It is a place where family bonds are strengthened and memories are made.

Jason was besieged with delight. We had included many pictures in our family book from Catalina. He was so animated that week, his eyes as wide as his smile. Jason and Nick tried their hand at parasailing and Nick had his first scuba experience off Casino Point. Our favorite spot was Shark's Cove, where with luck the surf provides the best boogie boarding and body surfing on the island.

We suffered only one incident that week. It occurred while we played miniature golf. If you are in the therapy business, then you already surmised the issue: competition. When pitting each family member against one another, the one with the weakest self-esteem will explode with fear of failure and rejection. Of course, I should have avoided this activity, but it was part of our annual routine that Nick and I so enjoyed. We never worried about the scores in the end. After all, who really keeps those score cards? Somewhere in the middle of the course, a golf club took flight accompanied by a short tirade. We all remained firmly planted, our eyes shifting about for any evidence of a shocked audience. This is a family place. Fortunately, while in his cycle, he noticed some cats nearby and took solitude with their company. Animals always had a calming effect on Jason, which I learned to leverage.

Jason's favorite destination was a zoo. Wherever we traveled, anywhere in the world, count on him to look up the local zoo or animal sanctuary. I thoroughly enjoyed taking him to the Phoenix Zoo several times that summer. He was still the little boy wanting to sit up on my shoulders. Though this was not common for a boy his age, he was still suffering from so many losses and issues from the past that I think he just wanted to be babied. I was more than pleased to oblige. Anyway, he was still small and underweight for his age.

What I most enjoyed was watching him interact with the animals. He spoke to them with such a soothing voice that his innocent intent was plainly transmitted. One of my favorite pictures to this day is from one such visit that summer with him proudly holding a turtle, that brilliant smile expressing his absolute happiness.

During that first summer I also decided to end the skin problem on his feet once and for all. This was one battle I was not going to lose! I had followed the directions religiously using wart remover. I should have purchased pharmaceutical stock for how many bottles I used per week. I was barely able to keep his problem in check. They spread profusely. I went pleading to my personal physician who advised me to take him to a surgeon. He recommended a few, and to my amazement, one accepted CMDP. After an initial evaluation, he was scheduled for outpatient surgery in early August. Finally, I had a victory in sight, as small as it was compared to his mental health issues.

The surgery went like clockwork. His case worker met us at the hospital to sign all the papers as his legal guardian. And with Brownie held tight in his arms, he was sedated. I don't like hospitals; most of us have good reason. They rarely invoke good memories. But Jason was unexpectedly calm. Perhaps the thought of having normal feet surpassed the fear. He was a real champ. He and Brownie recovered quickly and were discharged before evening. Of course, as any parent would predict, the next morning was not so tranquil. With the narcotics out of his system, the pain took hold. Changing his bandages that next day took a strong stomach. His feet were covered in open sores, and the one toe that was so overtaken with warts, was trimmed to the bone. Would it grow back? Parents are given a gift to handle the most grotesque situations with their children and keep their stomach fluids, at least while nursing them. I was thankful he was so young and healed rapidly. After the first few days, he was already hopping around the house with Junior in pursuit.

It was also during this time that I brought him to an eye doctor to get a second opinion about the glasses. What was the diagnosis that required the strange lens? He left the vision center without those glasses, and never required prescription lenses again. It was a major step toward his physical transformation from a toad into a prince.

Dad is Earned

Fifth grade started well enough. Learning from the harrowing experience of Jason's outbursts of the prior year, the school administration arranged for a 'shadow' for that year. Shadows are adults hired to stay with the student throughout the school day, responsible for managing the child's behavior so the teacher does not need to interrupt the class. If nothing else, it provided constant supervision and immediate intervention when necessary. The person who won that special prize was Mike Bolus. He was a young, energetic man who was working toward a teaching degree. He also came with a built in motivational driver for Jason. He was an assistant coach for a local high school football team, and any week Jason behaved, he dunned an oversize football jersey and got to hang with the big guys on the side-line. He was the ball boy.

I never understood his responsibilities in this role, but he seemed to really enjoy the camaraderie of these teenagers who quickly adopted him as their little mascot. The novelty was a great success during the first few months. Though Jason still had his issues requiring time out multiple times a week, Mike was the catalyst to calm his nerves and maintain peace on the campus. Everyone was still resistant to an IEP at the time so not to label him. This shadow was provided without the support of the school's special services.

That fall life was calm at both school and home. This was unusual in Jason's long history in foster care, and certainly my experience. Halloween was always a fun activity for Jason, more so than any of my other children. That year some of his friends engineered a brilliant plan with multiple costumes. They went to the same houses numerous times in different attire, thereby cutting down on the travel distance and time to collect candy, unethical: yes, ingenious: yes.

Meanwhile, things continued going well with the shadow at school and I attended a number of those football games that season, enjoying the action on the sidelines more than the game itself. His smile and bright eyes evident as members of the team smothered him with attention. Mike's support ended with the football season and my serenity was soon shattered with a call from our local minister. As always, I was at work.

He was a man of few words, "Bill, you need to come to the school right now. The police are here."

I arrived at an emergency scene worthy of a television police drama. People gawking and gossiping from the sidelines, emergency vehicles, a ladder truck from the fire department, and of course, the men in blue. All attention was directed to the top of the school bell tower. It was an older school, which was originally built as the local town high school many years ago. The tower was no longer in use. 'How did he climb up in there?' I thought aloud, my eyes surveying the roof and ledges of the school buildings and tower.

"Nothing surprises me anymore about that boy of yours Bill." A deep voice rang from behind. It was our minister.

Why would our minister be at the school? Well, the church is a few hundred yards away. Most things in our town are just a few hundred yards apart. My community is a small sleepy rural community built around a prestigious golf resort. For Arizona, it is very lush with multiple community parks, and giant palms lining the main avenues. The residents, of course, are very traditional giving more to the Republican Party than any other. It is also a town in which everyone knows everyone's business, but at the same time you always have someone for support in an emergency. Church is the center of the universe for most of us. It is also gossip central, where we all catch up on the latest news or occasional scandal, as well as on our moral obligations. Jason was fast becoming the topic of local conversation. He was gifted in that way.

I stayed across the street unsure of what role to play. I was as much in shock as awe. Could things get worse? I let the drama play out, still too new to be much help amongst so many support services. He evaded them all and eventually escaped the school ground and went home. The next time we talked about that event was in 2008. Some events are best laid to rest, or buried more like it. If you drive by that tower today you will notice that the openings are completely covered by metal grills. Little did the school authorities know at the time, but

Jason and Junior had discovered a way into the tower playing after school the prior year. One of many local buildings this little gang explored in lieu of open undeveloped land that was fast becoming a scarce commodity for children's free play.

Curious how it all ended? Jason was able to slide between the floor of the bell tower and an old abandoned office beneath. That's where he hid when the police authorities arrived. From that location, he was able to view the scene below through a vent. Once the authorities moved on to another part of the school in search of the little rascal, he was able to gain access to the locker rooms. From there he left the school through the front door of the gym and joined the crowd of kids watching the spectacle.

During another similar incident, I arrived on the scene with a police car, lights gleaming, door open, and an officer standing firm with his arms resting on his utility belt and side arm. Just before I arrived he had threatened Jason to come down or he would come up and push him off. I stopped the car short and jumped out toward the officer. Turning my head in the direction he was staring, I saw Jason crouched on top of a ten foot tennis court wall. The principal, as always, stood quietly in the background conversing with another administrator. Jason was raving mad, randomly throwing out one expletive after another. I called up to him to come down. I received the same polite treatment as the officer who stood his ground, but at a very safe distance. By this time, the local police were well versed in the crazy kid from the fifth grade. I gradually closed the gap between Jason and me, keeping my eyes fixed to his. I consistently encouraged him to come down. And he equally consistently defied my request. His body was rigid, his fists clenched, and his eyes intent and cold as a rabid dog. I continued a dialogue presenting a calm and caring dad which was a cover for a terrified and anxious foster parent completely uncertain of how this scene would play out. I had but one singular focus; to get Jason into my car without intervention from the police who were still quietly standing by. Finally the officer yelled out to Jason that if he got down on his own, he could go home with me . . . a peace offering. How novel. The words seemed to have caught him off guard as he stopped mouthing off and was clearly deep in thought, struggling, no doubt, with his options under a veil of distrust. At least he was thinking. That was a good start.

In time, he did drop down off the wall without the slightest scratch. The officer kept his word, even after Jason picked up a stick and threw it in the officer's direction. The man was stoic, not that he had anything to fear from this small eleven year old. But he did maintain his calm under such blatant misconduct. Perhaps he too was a dad, or at least experienced enough to realize tangling with a juvenile mental case was not worth the effort as long as he posed no threat to himself or the community. Jason dropped in the front seat, slamming his feet against the dash, again and again. The rage was not over, not by a long shot. I had just moved the action from public view. Arriving home, he tore off to his bedroom, kicking the wall and door. When all was quiet sometime later, he was in the closet under a blanket.

Thud . . . thud . . . thud. . . .

I learned later that this rage began at the school with the principal. Jason was outside on timeout to cool down. The principal approached him and started a lecture which only escalated him more. Lectures do not deescalate raging children. Jason started with the vile language followed by a stone which hit home on the administrator's chest. He then took off for the city recreation center and the safety of the high tennis walls.

With all this family drama unfolding weekly, my company offered me a unique opportunity with a promotion to move to Reston, Virginia. It was one of those critical mid-career moves which couldn't have come at a worse time. Jason was still adjusting to life outside the mental prison and Nick was in his senior year of high school. Despite the disruptions at home, both boys were very happy and content, I was more than comfortable with my present situation. But then that's always when company's smack you with a challenge. Never get too comfortable.

I deliberated over the decision for several weeks. That's a lie. I stressed over it. I wanted to take the job. But wasn't sure how to approach the Foundation. I was still a relatively new foster parent with a limited relationship with the agency and no understanding of the complexity of moving a foster child, still in care, to another state. I was soon to learn how we are not the *United States of Foster Care*.

My initial discussion with the Foundation went poorly. They called a staffing. This was the first time I experienced this intimidating group. A staffing was introduced as a team meeting in which I was an equal member. CPS calls these meetings Child and Family Team (CFT). This is an irony in words; neither the child nor the families are partners on this team. All power rests with the agency. Of course there are management huddles prior to the staffing behind closed doors. This agency operated no different than any major company in that respect. They had their agenda, decided on a course of action, understood the position of the foster parent to better determine their approach, and then had a meeting to work the parent to partner with them to accomplish the mission. This is a very successful model, unless the foster parent is hard headed and noncooperative. At times, I fit that model, and years later it would undo me.

During this, my first staffing, the supervisor was not supportive of the idea of moving Jason. I was reminded of the obligation I took when accepting this child. I guess I missed the class about never accepting company transfers. This was probably when the Foundation first experienced my stubborn willpower. I am a natural fighter and immediately respond to a challenge with sword in hand ready to battle to the death. I must admit that in my passion to win the fight, to defend my foxhole, I sometimes lose touch with the cause. I remember contacting the case worker a few days after the staffing. She was shell shocked with the announcement I had accepted the job in Virginia. I was moving within two months at the most. Another staffing was held immediately and they returned the shock. Suddenly, everyone was sympathetic and ready to take on the challenge. The Supervisor said she was concerned about breaking the powerful bond that had formed with Jason, but firmly warned me, it would not be an easy transition. No doubt, behind closed doors, they were assessing who in their right mind would ever take that raging kid!

The Foundation followed through like champs. An Inter-State Agreement was drawn up, court approvals signed and the local Virginia CPS office notified. It was late fall when we arrived to a very cold and dreary Washington suburb for a house hunting adventure. We met with a realtor and we were off. The first request from Jason was to get a snack at a Circle K. If you are from Arizona you recognize the name as a common corner convenience store. After a short and confusing dialogue with the realtor, she stopped off at a similar place for the children. Jason was devastated to learn that Reston had no Circle K. I dismissed his concern, and we went house hunting.

I was born and raised in New Jersey, so the countryside of Virginia was comforting to me, not so to the children. The traditional colonial homes brought back powerful memories of my childhood, not so to the children. As we moved from house to house, Jason's disposition altered from his initial excitement visiting a new place to mournful. That afternoon we came upon the perfect colonial home. It was twice the size of our Arizona home surrounded by an acre of natural wonder and enough trees to build a fortress. I was in full sell mode to the children. Nick was sold before he left Arizona, as his mind was focused on attending college in the DC area; plus we had already decided he was not moving immediately. Tom's family had kindly agreed to let Nick stay with them until graduation so not to interrupt his senior year.

While on the second floor, I asked Jason which of the bedrooms he preferred. He ran out of the house to the end of the driveway, plopped down and stared away from the house. I was taken off guard. The realtor, an experienced sales person and a mom, offered to intervene. I was open to any support in those days, especially from maternal personalities to which he gravitated. She came back a while later and explained to me that he couldn't breathe and felt sick. After talking together afterwards, she suggested we look at homes that were more similar to southwestern architecture with high ceilings and open layouts. I really liked that house. Had I been like my own father, I would have told the kid to deal with it. But I wasn't my father. She was very reassuring.

The next couple of days were spent enjoying our nation's capitol city, while the realtor searched for an entirely different type of home. Both boys enjoyed all the sights and it provided a respite from our real purpose. The next house hunting day went better. We looked at large townhomes. They were all new, boasting very high ceilings, and open floor plans. One in particular caught our eye. It was a corner unit backed to a large lake, lined with giant oaks. The house was empty and the owner agreeable to a short-term rental agreement while I closed on my property in Arizona. A deal was consummated. Meanwhile, the case worker was closing on all the last minute details for such things as medical care and case worker support services.

During the Christmas break we took a ski vacation to Wolf Creek in Colorado. I wanted as much family time as possible before leaving. Since our first ski trip with Jason, I found this activity to provide such physical demands combined with his natural enjoyment for athletic challenge, we rarely had any emotional outbreaks. In fact, he thrived during family focused activities as long as we didn't play golf. We put all thoughts of the impending move out of our minds. The only incident that trip occurred when we drove home. Coming down the mountain I hit black ice and made the tactical error of changing gears, which on a strip of ice can be fatal. To the right was a cliff, to the left a solid rock face. The children' angels were working overtime and the car stopped just short of death. That was one of those frightening experiences one never forgets, but not nearly as traumatizing as Jason's rages.

Immediately after the holidays, we moved. As planned, Nick stayed behind. I was fortunate to have a good friend, Michael, who was transferring from California at the same time I was leaving for Reston. He chose to lease my house for the mortgage amount and accepted all responsibility for care of the property. He was a most unusual renter in that he regularly raised the rent himself. We left before the movers picked up the furniture, and therefore I was not aware of the extent of wall damage. Michael called me a few days later to let me know that Jason had landed his foot through the plasterboard far more often than I knew. And, as I did know well, never hit a stud. Damn!

Another victim of Jason's rages was our giant saguaro cactus in the front yard. After any serious outburst in the house, Jason would take off for the roof or down the street. Once I was comfortable he was safe and just calming himself, I would wait inside for his return. Unbeknown to me, on many occasions he returned, but not inside. Rather, he was outside attacking our cactus with a steel rod. In this case a kick bag would have been cheaper. The numerous stabbing wounds resulted in a fatal systemic infection. Within the first year, our hundred year old cactus met its end.

Over time, Michael played a crucial role in our family and was soon adopted as an 'uncle' by all my children. While I was in Washington, he kept close tabs on Nick, who continued entertaining his friends at the house as if he never moved. Michael was very accommodating, and being a professional bachelor, enjoyed the company of these alien creatures called teenagers. I remember many calls with questions about behavior concerns and how to best support Nick. He was a novice, but highly intelligent, rational and acutely aware of Nick's emotional needs, though he would never admit to that.

The furniture arrived on schedule and we moved directly into our new Reston home. The day was busy directing the movers and unpacking the critical stuff, as I was going to work the next day. Jason chose his bedroom and kept to himself setting it up. He had a great view of the lake and seemed content. That first evening, exhausted, we collapsed amongst a forest of boxes and disorganized furniture. Nothing really fit well. My furniture, which included a full grand piano, was large and bulky, purchased for a large great room, Arizona style. I was frustrated that evening and over tired. I have no memory of seeing Jason about; though I'm sure I tucked him in that night.

I always tucked him in back then. It was a significant ritual for us both, an opportunity to hold each other in peaceful harmony. I never wanted him to go to sleep angry or anxious about how I felt about him. It was a very simple rite: kiss his right foot, gently put it under the covers, then the left, a firm tuck up both sides all the way up to his neck, followed by a great hug and kisses goodnight. I don't remember how it came to be; perhaps that's how my mother tucked me in as a little child. Bedtime for Jason was a fragile moment. It was when he was the most emotionally vulnerable, at times acting many years his junior. His eyes begged for comfort and security. No matter how badly the day may have been, no matter what my anger or frustration, that moment was always calming, almost spiritual in nature. As with all children, this ceremony quietly disappeared as he matured.

We spent the first week getting settled in the house and exploring the area. Reston Town Center was our favorite hang-out that winter. It boasted an ice rink where Jason learned to ice skate with a desire to play hockey. He bore the very cold weather well, especially considering he was born and raised in Arizona. Ice skating at the Town Center soon became a ritual. I would help him bundle-up and tighten his skate laces then he'd be off with the class. While he was sliding about, I'd enjoy a latte, after which I'd bring him a hot chocolate for his break. I so enjoyed watching him, from his first lesson skating around holding a big plastic bucket for balance, to his more secure racing the circuit.

One night, coming over to the ice with his traditional hot chocolate, he was nowhere on the ice. Heading for the skate barn I found him in a corner holding an ice pack over his face. He had landed on his mouth and chipped a front tooth during hockey practice. He was hurt, though his pride more than his face, but otherwise fine. He was back on the ice in ten minutes. I drank the chocolate.

He also enjoyed the lake area by the house with all the trees. This was a fresh experience for Jason having been born and raised in the Arizona desert.

Sledding was another new skill and he enjoyed going down the hill by our house. On one of his first runs he made the mistaken assumption that the brush along the shoreline would stop the sled. It did not and he found himself out on the ice as he pulled himself back to shore, he fell in. I was not home at the time. Jason still had his guardian angel and survived the ordeal, though freezing cold. That was the first use of the gas fireplace in the new house.

The next Monday I registered him at the local grammar school. Concerned about his history and all the outbursts at his prior school, I asked to meet with the principal. As I described some of the incidents, she picked up the phone and called in another administrator. After a curt introduction I was asked for his IEP. He didn't have one. I was met with two blank expressions. They looked at his school records and the person who had just arrived left the office, only to return just minutes later confirming my report. Jason did not have an IEP. With all the effort from the Foundation, did we forget something important? The principal was cautiously sympathetic. We met his fifth grade teacher and I was off to work, naively optimistic, mind focused on my new job responsibilities.

Jason made a quick friend next door, an Arab boy, who had a gentle disposition. They took the school bus together and seemed to enjoy each other. Jason was adjusting well, though he complained about missing Junior and Nick. I must admit, I too was feeling homesick and lonely. I left a small community where I was very active and fortunate to have many friends and acquaintances. The children would always laugh when people would greet me by name, and I would walk away confused as to their identity, thinking hard on where or how they knew me. Here I was alone. My only company was a few people I knew at work, and Jason. Through Jason's friend, I was able to find friendship with his parents as well. Having children is an open door to new acquaintances in the neighborhood. Children can be more outgoing than their parents that way.

The phone rang one day while I was conversing with an Air Force Colonel on a new project. I must have gone white, because he jumped up to my aid. I introduced him to a colleague and was off to the school. I was escorted to the Principal's office, where sitting in a chair, head down and shaking, sat Jason, surrounded by several police officers. I was stunned and afraid. The principal, seeing my degrading state, led me to a chair and brought me a cup of coffee. She calmly described the morning's events. Jason got into an argument over a pencil sharpener. She wasn't quite sure of the details, but he raged in the classroom, then took off outside. Once cornered against a door, he grabbed a large stick and flung it around at anyone who approached. When not swinging the stick, he kicked and pounded the door. The police were called to control the situation. To do so, they were forced to take him down, and then forcibly carry him to where he sat, still shaking. The principal was very concerned about the younger students in the school, referring to a number of children who were frightened to see police man-handling a little kid. They were too young to understand the circumstances and felt threatened. Jason was suspended, and since he had no IEP, could not return.

He spent most of the day in his room sleeping off the trauma, and no doubt, was physically drained from the incident. I sat in the kitchen sipping coffee, calling the district office for advice. I took vacation time that week, keeping Jason very close at hand, while working out a plan. I was told about the IEP policy and the maximum time the school had to do an evaluation and close on a plan. The administration was very clear that his case would require the maximum amount of time. He would be out of school for months. To make matters worse, the district did not recognize me as Jason's legal guardian, but the State of Arizona. And the State of Arizona was not a resident of that school district. I was now caught in the middle of a political nightmare. During the next few weeks I enjoyed Jason's company in my small office in Reston. He would just sit in a corner and build Lego sets or draw. He was content, and gave little indication of boredom. After a while, several of my customers looked forward to seeing him, commenting that he was the company's new mascot. My boss was not so pleased.

That winter in Reston was dreary in more respects than just the weather. The new house had lost its luster, Jason was out of school, and the job was going nowhere while my personal stress continued to rise. A glimmer of hope came one morning with a call from the district office offering Jason an opportunity to participate in a unique program for emotionally disturbed children. This district was so wealthy they had a special campus the size of a traditional elementary school just for children like Jason. I was delighted. When we arrived, Jason was not. As we entered the building he pulled back. I heard children screaming from behind doors...quiet rooms. We were met by the school's director who gave us the grand tour, while at the same time measuring Jason up, watching his every reaction. I was sold. Jason wanted out. At home that evening, he was despondent, while I was celebrating, talking it up with our neighbors at how this school was our salvation. I called the case worker to share my enthusiasm. She was pleased we solved the problem. Jason refused to be tucked in that night, or for several nights later. I was anxiously awaiting word on his first day of school. The next week the call came. A kindly voice informed me that there was a mistake. The school had a waiting list and could only accept students whose parents lived within the district boundaries and had an IEP. I was devastated. Jason was delighted. He asked me to tuck him in that night. The little bugger!

That night he called me Daddy. For parents this is a memorable event for the moment. Ask any parent years later if they remember the first time their kid used that word. For foster parents this is a milestone event that you never forget. Some children actually start right off on that foot. Perhaps they believe that using parental titles provides greater security. Jason did not. He addressed me as Bill from the very first meeting at Cleo Wallace. But that night, it all changed. I will never know why, and he may not remember, but I will never forget. I adopted him in my heart that night. I re-committed to never let go. It was a pledge that was challenged for many years, by his behavior, the welfare system and my lack of trust in it all. It remained an inner conflict that never really disappeared and one that can only be defended through total passion. This obligation was the foundation of my greatest trauma. One that would haunt me again years later when I made a similar promise: "I will never abandon you!"

That week I called my Vice-President in Phoenix requesting my old job back. He was very hesitant, but understood my predicament. He asked me to hold on while he worked it out with the division president. I returned home the next month just before the harsh heat of the Arizona summer. My home was occupied by my good friend from work, so we purchased a new home nearby and close to my work. Jason was coldly welcomed back to his old school. Nick was glad to be back with the family. The company was more than understanding, though they did require me, as per my contract, to repay the moving expenses of about fifteen thousand dollars. It hurt, but a small price to pay to be home with familiar surroundings and the support of all my friends. If I remember, the Foundation donated a thousand to help out. It was the price of sanity. Key lesson: don't leave home without an IEP.

Million Dollar Lawsuit

We quickly settled into our new home in April. It was not as luxurious as the property in Reston. It did not sit on a hill overlooking a beautiful lake surrounded by tall, lush trees. But it was our place. Home is not just where you hang your hat; it is where you are an integrated member of the community. Nick was preparing for graduation and Jason was rebuilding old relationships, more easily gaining new friends. Our Reston experience, though short-lived, had brought all of us ever closer together, and I think in many ways, provided me the opportunity to gain both boys' trust. Regrettably, as Jason's bond with me grew ever stronger, so too did his anxiety over loss...he cared. At the time we moved back to Arizona, he was with me one year.

Jason survived the last two months of fifth grade. Perhaps the great Reston Rage wore him down or he was just feeling good about himself with the move back to familiar turf. What I did not know was how he was interacting in the new neighborhood. Eileen was one of the first neighborhood kids that Jason met and would become his closest friend during our first year in the new house. Eileen and Jason developed a very special friendship and as the summer wore on I was convinced they were romantically involved at some immature level, at least puppy love. She seemed very affectionate in a sisterly way and provided Jason an opportunity to openly share his daily frustrations, which provided emotional support during many personal crises throughout those early years we lived in that neighborhood.

Junior was back in his life, but not as cozy as when we lived just across the street. I think it hurt him more than Jason who was quickly adapting with new friends and exploring the vast open area around the development which included the Agua Fria River basin. This was a large dry canal used for water management during the monsoon season. In short, flood control with signs that read, "Do Not Enter." To an adventurous boy it just as well could have read, "Please Enter & Have Fun." The area around the canal was open desert with large cottonwood trees scattered about. It was a wilderness area the neighborhood children could not resist.

Nick maintained his community ties, and with May came High School graduation which was a great success. Nick was proud of his accomplishments and ready to start college at NAU. He was determined to be a teacher and follow in the path of many of those dedicated people he so admired at his high school. I wasn't so pleased, knowing the lack of monetary gain for such a career. We talked about it often, but he was steadfast.

That summer was more lazy than usual and would be the last with Nick as a kid. Since Jason still could not be left unattended we hired a full time caregiver. With his raging still very active and negative issues with camp environments, we were reluctant to use a day camp program. Our new hire was a young guy who enjoyed renaissance re-enactment. That's right, those people who dress up and play kings, queens, knights, squires and all that stuff. One of the activities that Jason enjoyed was accompanying him to fairs and shows to see all the armor and weapons, not to mention the actual combat activities. This had an enduring influence on him and for many years later, Jason enjoyed making replicas of swords. I was most impressed with his gladius sword copied from the movie *Gladiator,* starring Russell Crowe. This was also the summer Jason had his head shaved. It was the one and only time he was ever the bald son. Hair or not, he was always adorable. Nick got a summer internship at Lockheed Martin employed in the Information Systems department developing web pages. We didn't travel much, spending our free time landscaping the new house. Both boys helped dig, though Nick, the bigger more powerful late teen, turned ditch digging into a fine art. Jason spent most days with his friends at the nearby Agua Fri riverbed. Though I didn't have a tree house at the new place, the boys worked on their own project in the giant cottonwoods over by the canal.

Jason appeared to make friends easily. Often, when bored, he would set up his hockey net in the street and shoot goals. This activity obtained the intended result of bringing friends to him. Two children in particular nearly brought us to calamity. They lived down the road where he spent many sleepovers. One was his age, the other a young teenager. It was a second marriage for both parents; the father retired military, the mom a dedicated housewife. Jason was never one to advertise his foster care situation. From the very beginning, he used my surname in class, though his official records required the use of his birth name.

After a short while of the children playing together, the parents stopped over to introduce themselves. We started a cordial relationship and I spent a number of evenings at their place. Inevitably, Jason's history would be the topic of conversation. And as usual, with his stories came the expression of utter shock and pity. The younger boy soon became his best friend, along with the Eileen. These were some of the neighborhood children that would accompany Jason back to the canal to horse around. He once told me about a homeless man who lived nearby their private kingdom which worried me, and I advised them to stay clear. There was never a problem.

By midsummer, I again received that ever fearful call at work. Jason was raging at the neighbor's house. I couldn't leave work immediately so I called Nick to get him. Nick arrived to an abusive scene. The mom and children had surrounded Jason in a corner of the garage. They weren't about to let him go. The mom was ranting mad, most of what she said to Nick he couldn't understand. He ordered Jason into the car. At first she argued, but Nick was firm and they backed off and let Jason go. I came home to the police at the house questioning my son. He was visibly shaken; his back was bruised, but physically appeared alright. Without being advised of any rights, or in the presence of an attorney, the police grilled him to which he was more than happy to respond.

"She's a bitch; she wouldn't let me go home," he repeated again and again with fury in his eyes. Here we go again!

The previous day, Jason was invited to their house for a birthday party. It was a sleep over in a home where Jason was comfortable and the parents understood his background well. I never had a second thought about his safety, or anyone else for that matter. Apparently, the party went on much later into the night than the mom expected and she soon lost her patience. Eventually, she did get them all settled down, but in the morning took out her vengeance, demanding they clean her house. The children all started picking things up, some certainly working more than others. Jason melted quietly into the background. She confronted him, while in an angry state, and he took off. He ran to the garage to get his bike with the mom on his heels, both cussing at the other which only escalated the conflict. As Jason pulled up his bike, she grabbed him so hard it bruised his arm, and pulled the bike away from him, ordering him back into the house. He screamed in terror and kicked her. If his rage was nearly as wild as she described to me later, she received a violent blow. She let loose of the bike and he tried once again to escape. While opening the garage door, her eldest son slammed his back to the door, creasing the metal. He broke free from his grip and tried again to get away. The mom, supported by all the children from the party cornered him. At that point she called me and the police. Each time he tried to leave her house, they all pushed him back against the closed door.

As the story unfolded, I was appalled. This is when I learned that, at least early in a police investigation, the one who calls the police first is innocent, especially if an adult is complaining about a youth. This was the first time the police were called out to our home in this town, so I knew the police had no prejudice from prior behavior issues with Jason. After lots of note taking, the police departed; leaving me alone with a hurt and defensive child. I made the mistake of continuing the interrogation to get more detail on what was happening at the party. I felt I knew these people, and never expected such an outcome. Of course, I didn't live with them, so could not have possibly known their true motives. Just as children display their best manners at the neighbor's house, so we adults tend to do the same. We all keep our less agreeable behavior behind locked doors. In response to my questioning, he immediately confronted me with:

"You don't believe me. No one believes me!" He threw me into a guilt trip.

This was the moment I should have drawn from my experience from the third week in April 1996 when the honeymoon ended over a discussion about chores. I must have buried that memory deep. He stamped to his room, slammed the door, and began stress testing the walls. Now Jason had a unique gift. Whenever and wherever he chose to kick a wall, he never, at any time, hit a stud. This was confirmed by my friend Michael who spent many hours repairing holes in my home he was renting. For years, I continued to be amazed at this astonishing feat, which went against all my hopes. I had a firm belief that if he had hit a stud just once and broke a few toes, that behavior would quickly end. The door was shaking off the hinges and the plasterboard was no match for his powerful thrusts. I tried to reason with him which usually failed but provided me a sense of control. I surrendered to the kitchen and soon the house went quiet. When I returned to his bedroom, the door was open and Jason was gone. I ran outside calling for him, and then walked around the neighborhood in search with no better luck. As I was heading for the car I caught site of his shirt under an overhang between an upper and lower roof of the house. I called up to him without success, but at least I now felt secure he was safe. I went in the house and waited. Later that night he was in his room tucked quietly in his bed with Brownie.

For nearly two years our families were at odds. They filed a million dollar lawsuit against the State of Arizona, the Foundation and me. Later the husband filed a consortium claim that his sex life was affected by Jason. Meanwhile, the children were at odds in the neighborhood. During one altercation, Jason and a friend ran into these boys by the canal, each loaded with stones. Jason was ready with a sling shot. No one will ever know what happened for certain, but the police stopped over to file charges against Jason for assault. The boys apparently accused him of attacking them with his slingshot without provocation.

He denied this profusely and I remember when the juvenile attorney met with Jason weeks later in a conference room to confront him, he broke down and admitted he did shoot the first stone, but that they had weapons too. In the eyes of the law, it didn't matter and all agreed Jason should plead guilty. With everything still in flux over the lawsuit, this behavior with the woman's children only strengthened her case that Jason was dangerous. For that particular misdemeanor, he was given community service which he dutifully completed early.

We also were forced into the game of warrants for being too close to each other. She accused Jason of riding his bike in front of her house, and I accused her of driving slowly in front of our home when Jason was playing outside to stare him down in hopes of escalating his behavior in public. That action failed thanks to his improved self-control and in some cases, the presence of his friends. Jason's attorney also counter-sued for illegal restraint and abuse.

The most painful assault for me was her report to CPS that I was neglecting Jason. She asserted that he was left alone all summer without supervision. Within weeks an investigator came to the house with Bret, our social worker. I was interviewed, Bret showed receipts for the caregiver, and Jason too was taken alone for questioning. It was frivolous, but nonetheless hurtful. This would be the first of two investigations into my integrity as a foster parent that I was forced to endure.

In the end the attorneys settled as the legal costs continued to mount to more than the real value of the claim that could only be based on her chiropractor expenses. Jason was awarded ten thousand dollars and the neighbor awarded fifteen thousand. The person who suffered the most financial loss was her attorney who trusted her to pay her claims against the settlement. She took off with the money. I suffered the greatest emotional stress worrying over the possibility of losing my child and my home. You get frightened when the insurance company sends you that letter stating the amount of the suit exceeds the value of your insurance policy for which they are not responsible. Key lesson: foster parents are liable for the behavior of foster children in their custody.

**

Jason's Journal (12 years old)

Mischief didn't stop when I moved to the new house after Reston, Virginia. When we first moved I still hung out with my old neighborhood friends. If I couldn't get a ride, I just took my bike or roller blades. We were starting to settle down in town. I figured we pushed our luck far enough. The only real trouble we got into there was rollerblading across the school cross guard areas when the ladies were holding up their stop signs.

Back in my new neighborhood, however, we were just warming up. When we first moved in most of the area was still undeveloped. We always kept a tractor key with us. One time we started one up and knocked over a portable potty. We also did a science experiment with one of those portables. We were flicking matches at each other and one missed and fell inside the unit. They light up!

When the new school was just completed being readied for the first day, we checked out the roof and turned off all the A/C units. School didn't start on time that year. At night we would dare each other to go streaking around the block. I remember one time we were in the garage getting ready for a run and I was dared to moon the next car passing. I got out to the end of the driveway and pulled them down. It was a cop car. My luck, I guess. We also liked daring each other to skinny dip in other people's pools. Once we were really lucky and found a group of girls doing the same thing. We just watched over the wall that night.

We really enjoyed playing army soldier in the river bottom. We built some forts on the other side inside huge cottonwood trees. I took my dad's rock climbing gear so we could get high in the trees. It was our cool fortress.

Nearby was a diary farm where we went cow tipping, but they were all awake, including a bull I didn't see until it was almost too late. We gave up on the cows, and my friend dared me to smack the bull on the ass. I was hesitant, but it was a dare! The farmer came out and shot a round in the air. We returned another night with a paintball gun, and I'll leave it at that.

We also practiced shooting flaming arrows like in Braveheart. I took a dish rag soaked in rubbing alcohol. It worked. It stayed lit, but when it hit the ground, the rag split apart and lit the grass on fire. It was dad's house so we were OK. I also did a science test on heating a CO_2 cartridge with a blow torch. I used protective goggles and gloves. The cartridge blew up along with the tip of my blow torch.

On the school bus we were rarely on our best behavior. We sat in back so the camera wouldn't see us. My friend and I always had our roller blades on the bus. A few times we put them on coming home. As the bus came to a stop; we would launch ourselves off our seats down the aisle, and then jump over the steps and out the door. The driver would curse at us as we were going away. She reminded me of the bus driver in South Park. We got in trouble the next morning, but it didn't matter. I had a permanent desk at in-school suspension.

***

The Birth of an IEP

The Individual Education Program (IEP) is one of the most valuable tools in the foster parent arsenal. Never leave home without it. After Jason finished fifth grade, the school took on the task of building an IEP package for the next school year. Unlike Reston that promised nothing could happen in less than 90 days, his school had it done in less than a month and arrangements were closed on Jason attending a special classroom for emotionally disabled children at a off campus school. Located about twenty minutes away; it was far from his old campus. This school developed a special education classroom program for their emotionally disordered children which a number of local school districts used, for a price of course. Our school district exported Jason to this program for the year. Problem solved.

I was more than pleased with this tactic. No more calls to the office. We met his teacher who was an expert in the field with unlimited patience and a personality that exploded with maternal love. During our first meeting I took great pains to explain Jason's behavior, while he worked his charming personality. She had seen it all. She was not concerned.

Jason's behavior during that school year was not unlike prior years. However, he now had that all-powerful IEP. But more importantly, he was in a classroom with a professional who knew how to manage him with structure, consistency, educational support and lots of TLC.

The only major issue that required my attention occurred early in the school year. The staff used physical restraint to manage raging. Jason was fully accustomed to this from Cleo Wallace. The approach used, however, was different in that they would get behind the child, bring him down in a sitting position and then tightly hold their arms across their chest. Jason had a pigeon chest and this type of hold restricted his breathing. After a few such incidents, the teacher called me to the school to confirm his physical handicap. She agreed to let Jason sit on the swing set to cool off. It worked well until this happened once when a large group of eighth graders were in the area and teased him. He ran away.

This was one of the very few times I received an emergency call from the teacher that year. Taking off from school property when in a tirade was standard practice for Jason. But in this case, being so far from home, he had not attempted an escape for a long time. When I arrived, I came upon what was now a common sight, the sheriff waiting by the classroom. They had an APB out and just finished a complete sweep of the campus and surrounding farm areas. He was gone. His teacher was visibly anxious for his well being. You either hated him or loved him. She was captured by the latter emotion. I was too. I walked around the campus in a daze, trying to imagine him walking or hitchhiking back to town some twenty miles away. Heading toward the main road that bordered the school, I noticed a very large clump of cottonwood trees, likely over a hundred years old. It looked very inviting while I stood in the hot sun. I walked into the brush and inside was a cleared circle of dirt, perfect for a Sunday picnic. Looking up with hopes of seeing my little boy, I felt the serenity of the scene, leaves lightly rustling from a gentle breeze, and birds chirping as they hopped among the branches. No sign of Jason. I stayed to enjoy the cool shade of these giant desert monsters. A small familiar voice, not much louder than a whisper spoke out, "Are the cops gone?"

"No," I honestly replied, now scanning the high tree branches with great care. I saw nothing, not the slightest sign of him.

"I'm not coming down, not ever. I hate this school. Cops suck."

"Jason, where are you?" I called out, keeping one eye up searching for Jason, and the other to the side to see if the sheriff had followed me. All looked clear. "If the police go away, will you come down?"

"Maybe," He replied softly.

I left the small clearing for the school campus. When I arrived the sheriff had left and his teacher was still in a panic, near tears. I explained that I had found Jason, but was very scared he might get hurt being so high in those old trees. If she was in agreement, I would bring my car over to the main road, park by the trees and take him home. I was certain he would come down once he saw my car within easy reach. After all, it provided his rescue from school crises many times in the past. All worked according to plan, though he came into the car quite the dirty little "Huck Finn." Something too was different, he broke down crying. He had no anger, no clenched fists and was not kicking the dashboard. He just cried. He was feeling remorse, not for the incident, but about his teacher's reaction. Fear of rejection and loss of her was unbearable to him. He was slowly transforming. He cared.

That year we decided to visit Nick at NAU for the Halloween weekend. Jason was all excited to spend the night with his big brother at a college dorm. I was looking forward to a weekend respite and hoped the two would bond more. After quick introductions to his roommate and friends on the floor, I left. Jason was climbing about his brother's loft bed oblivious to my departure. I must warn the weak at heart not to read much further unless you still remember your college days. Though I expected Nick to treat his brother as a child, not a fellow student; I had forgotten to emphasize that point. Upon my return Sunday morning Jason was complaining about some bruises, a bent nose and a severe headache, but otherwise carried an awkward grin with a rather blushed expression.

Driving home he couldn't stop talking about his fun time with big brother Nick and all his college friends. The conversation started about boxing matches in the hallway. Now imagine a lanky sixth grader up against two hundred pound college guys. It was not much of a fair fight, but Jason didn't seem to care. He was proud to have held his own, despite getting knocked down, thrown around into a few walls and generally abused. I was impressed with his stamina. So far things sounded good.

Then he started describing girls' breasts. He had my full attention. I asked just how that came to be. He was fuzzy on the details, which narrowed my focus to his every word. Nick and his friends attended a few parties that night, little brother in tow. His brother kindly allowed Jason to have a drink or so. Prior to going back to the campus they all went off to a haunted house. Jason having just come from the temperate desert of Phoenix was unprepared for the frigid air. He was walking a little tipsy, wrapped tightly in a sweatshirt with his hands over his ears and head down. As the group walked down the main road, Jason bounced backward off a clear wall of a bus stop, stepped to the side and continued walking like nothing had happened, The college kids were much amused and at that point the group recognized it was time to return to the dorm, where they tucked him in under the loft bed and forgot about him, or pretended to do so.

These college students engaged in behavior not appropriate around an underage person. In fact, at least according to Jason, a couple of the girls thought he was really cute and gave him a few kisses. They probably found him amusing under the influence. Further details were difficult to retrieve that day, either because he wasn't talking or more likely, he had fallen asleep as Nick planned.

This was Jason's introduction to life and he spoke to his friends at school of nothing else for months. My little boy was growing up or at least quickly losing his innocence.

This was also the year he received his last stuffed animal. Jason loved these little critters, but he was growing up now and more interested in the living variety. But his inner child was still vibrant when we passed a huge floppy ear dog at F.A.O. Schwartz one day at the Scottsdale Mall. It was very expensive, well outside my ability for a single gift. His eyes were brightly lit, but he was also a realist and not one to beg. His Lockheed Martin guardian angel was looking out for him; because that was the year I earned a rather unexpected bonus. The dog was discovered under the tree Christmas morning to an amazed Jason. At five feet long it was not hard to find amongst the normal size presents in which it was burrowed. He was twelve going on six that morning. However, the dog soon gained the unique place in his room as comfortable cushion for watching television. But I know he always felt the love it represented. He also received a model rocket kit, which opened a new window of learning opportunities. My frightened boy was now maturing into a real teenager. I don't believe I ever let go of my little Jason with his easy-going sense of humor, purity of heart, and that great big imagination when every new discovery was a source of wonder.

After the holidays, it was back to school and stress. We spent many weekends building and shooting rockets that year, and advanced quickly to those giant vehicles that can only be launched in designated areas approved by the FAA. He introduced his friends to the hobby, occasionally shooting some of the smaller rockets at our local park. 1999 started off well and the teacher seemed to have him well in hand. He graduated from her program ready to go back to the main campus for seventh grade.

The summer followed the fun routine of all our previous annual breaks. No school equated to no stress. We were blessed with Alison that summer. This was a young girl, just turned eighteen, who participated in my high adventure troop. When Nick and his friends aged out of traditional scouting at fourteen, I started an Explorer Post. The boys insisted it be co-ed. I was hesitant, but agreed. This was one of those satisfying decisions. The girls brought a new culture to the group, a sense of balance that we all enjoyed. Alison was a natural, maternal being. Even Jason melted before her endless giving heart. They enjoyed countless hours together, most often around our community lake, Jason's old stomping grounds. Alison developed a very special relationship and soon saw the same wonderful human being I came to love.

Jason also began to develop a new that metal working passion that so intrigued him the prior summer, making swords and armor. He was at an age where playing with these weapons was as much fun as making them. He didn't have a furnace and anvil, but he soon learned to find substitute tools to acquire the right look of professional weapons. The lack of a blow torch was good for all of us.

But even with a blow torch and huge metal mallet, Jason was a formidable threat to our serenity when fully engaged in his work. Soon thud . . . thud . . . thud gave way to bing . . . bing . . . bing. He had found a new release, an interest that continues to this day.

***

Alison's Journal: Summer Vacation

I have nothing but fond memories of my summers with Jason. He was always great when he was in my care. Bill had given me some background information and advice on how to minimize the likelihood of an outburst, but in three months, I only witnessed one minor incident. Stories of Jason's altercations circulated around town, but they sounded so unlike the Jason I knew, I hardly believed them to be true. I don't doubt that there were afternoons I was unaware that Jason was out causing mischief with friends, but I don't feel for a second that he was deceiving me. I was just blessed to spend time with Jason in his home, where outside forces didn't trigger his fight or flight instincts. I saw his sweet, true self.

Some mornings, Jason would still be sleeping when I arrived and I'd relish the opportunity to crash on the couch. I was always awakened by one of Jason's signature sneak attacks. As we both eased into the day, he patiently tried to teach me to play the videogame Golden Eye and we both marveled that over the course of the summer I never improved. I continued to run into as many walls as the first day he placed a controller in my hands. Of course, Jason showed no mercy and my rapid death in every game was the source of great amusement.

***

Catalina travel was routine, but we chose the July 4th holiday that year to watch the fireworks over the bay. We brought, Jason's brother that year as well. He participated in a number of activities with us while Jason was young. Jason remained active in the troop, following in Nick's footsteps as the troop hoop dancer for all major ceremonies.

This was also when we decided to provide solid evidence to Jason he was a member of our family, a Hunter. I could not adopt Jason. His mother still maintained parental rights though she could never have custody. The Foundation recommended not taking the matter to court, as this action would only cause trauma, and there was no guarantee he would win a severance. A name change was much easier. July 10, 1998 we all met at the agency office in Phoenix for a grand ceremony. Though Jason never appeared in court, we did have a formal party that included what could only be described as a little Knighthood affair. To the bagpipes playing *Sons of Scotland*, I presented a special Scottish knife, flag and a framed certificate that read:

DECREE OF THE CLAN HUNTER

In the year 1116 AD, King David of Scotland appointed his comrade in arms, William, Chief Hunter in Scotland, and gave him the royal forests in Ayrshire. Upon this land in Northern Scotland – Hunter Clan was born. An ancient yew tree grows in the walled garden at Hunterston Castle. The tree is over 600 years old, and early hunters made longbows from its wood. This tree is a symbol of our strength and longevity, it guards our spirits, and now, it shall guard yours.

Mindful of your courage, honor, and loyalty to the Hunter family, and recognizing within you a spark shared by the clan, I, William A. Hunter, confer upon you our greatest pride: The surname of Hunter; the motto Cursam Perficio; the crest badge of the hound sejant proper, gorged with a crown; and the tartan Hunter.

I hereby declare on the 10th day of July 1998 that you are granted the name

Jason William Hunter I

Bear this name with pride, allowing it to remind you and others of your continued commitment to the highest ideals and virtues which this family has vowed to uphold. Let the motto and crest, remind you of the Hunter honor and your obligation to protect, cherish, and love your family. I grant this honor to you and to your descendents in heredity custody.

Return to Open Campus

Attending an open campus at the middle school was a major step for Jason. After a year in a confined classroom, he was looking forward to less rigid structure and an opportunity for socialization with his peers. This was also the year a new social worker, Bret, was assigned to the case. He was very experienced and soon loved Jason as much as me. Over time we would joke that Jason was raised by two dads, Bill and Bret.

This social worker had the most powerful influence in Jason's life. He understood the core issue, though recognized early not much could be done until he was ready. Little did either of us realize just how long that would take. Bret was medium height with a very calm expression. He displayed unlimited patience with both of us, but when pushed, he had a temper. Jason would experience this on several occasions, as Bret was the only person who had the guts to get right in his face, daring Jason to take a shot at him. But, Jason never did, though I feared the worst at those times. On one specific occasion, Bret came to the rescue after a major rage. When he arrived, Jason was on the roof. As Bret was reassuring me all would be well, Jason came down and gave his car a good kick. Bret was not impressed!

With his standard calm demeanor, Bret made a strong remark at Jason to stay away from his car to which Jason stared back ready to kick it again. Bret and Jason stared each other down and neither would back off. I drew back into the kitchen. Bret returned to the house and Jason took off. I was concerned, but not Bret. He looked at me with a comforting smile telling me Jason would not go far, in fact, close enough to keep the house in sight. As we looked down the road from the living room window, a small figure kept popping around a parked vehicle perhaps ten houses away. Bret soon left and Jason returned to the roof. Before returning to his room, I would be embraced with heavy tears and unlimited love. The cycle was over.

From Jason's perspective it was pure hate or love. Bret was either his hero, or he wanted him dead. Bret was the only person during those early years that had the courage to have a get-in-your face confrontation with Jason and not give way. This relationship continued for over a decade. Years later, after he and Jason discussed an issue over the phone I got a text from Bret that read: 'he hung up on me yesterday...he has come a long way though, he didn't threaten to kill me.' Jason told me that when Bret stood up to the beast within him, he knew for certain his social worker would never abandon him.

Unlike previous years, seventh grade did not start peaceful. Typically he would get the teachers to fall in love with his delightful personality, but that year he was tuned for rebellion. He started the year with his old behavior pattern of rage and flight to solve his internal conflicts. When people faced him down or worse grabbed him, he would launch out aggressively. Though everyone understood, knowledgeable of his horrific past, his constant misconduct simply wore everyone down to the core. I even provided a training class with help from the family developer that year on dealing with foster children in general, using Jason's behavior as a case in point.

Jason was on full alert for any attacks to what little self-esteem he could muster. And worse, his delinquency just set him up for one assault after another. He even had the nerve to light a firecracker at the bus stop the first day of school. As a result of his weekly behavior issues, he spent most of his seventh grade year at in-school suspension (ISS) or was sent home for one to two weeks depending on the severity of the incident.

He earned one of those "go home tickets" when an eighth grader grabbed Jason from behind and put him into a chock hold. Jason twisted his scrawny body around, kicked the back of the attacker's knees and planted the kid's face into the sidewalk. That earned him two weeks suspension. That can happen even when you defend yourself if the other kid comes out looking the worse. Another time a kid threw a punch at him which he caught in mid-flight, then proceeded to pummel the kid. Yes, that was another two weeks out of school.

I was not helpful during this period either. The more people attacked him, the greater my protection. This personal compulsion to protect, along with fear of loss, surfaced as my greatest demon throughout by foster parenting career. However, this fear was also the foundation of my never ending passion to win the battle for his stability. I had no solution, and could only be hopeful that Jason would change with maturity. Cognitive therapy had failed. The Foundation even tried *Eye Movement Desensitization and Reprocessing* (EMDR) therapy once. Bret was getting desperate and was convinced over the years of failed general therapy that Jason was too hard wired. He was filled with primal traumas that needed cleansing.

Eye Movement Desensitization and Reprocessing (EMDR) is an information processing psychotherapy used to resolve disorders stemming from distressing life experiences. The therapist uses a structured approach to address past, present, and future elements of the patient's disturbing memories. It has been found to be very effective in the treatment of post-traumatic stress disorder similar to that suffered by foster children.

Jason and I met the EMDR therapist at the Foundation office one sunny day. Everyone was optimistic about this new procedure that could finally help bring closure to Jason's struggles with abandonment and loss that continued to be the key trigger to his outbursts. Leaving Jason in good hand after being sold on this method, I relaxed in the Lobby with a calm sense of security. No sooner had I laid my head back and closed my eyes, when suddenly I witnessed the quiet professional office atmosphere shatter.

I was later told that the therapist had asked Jason to find a safe place in his mind, then she led him to what we all called "the dark farm," those memories that he had buried very deep for years. He launched. She told us later, that in her entire career, she had never experienced someone flip so swiftly. She was taken completely off guard, as well as the staff. By the time I realized what was happening, the supervisor was on the phone to the police reporting a run-away, while everyone was scoping the trees behind the office. Jason had established several hiding places around the building. Most were high up. However, that day I learned of a new one. On either side of the main entrance drive were brick light boxes. I never quite figured the mathematics of how he jammed his body into the limited volume, but he worked it.

I can't take credit for discovering this spot. I was calling out walking around the front of the building when I heard his tiny voice. I really was confused for a while, repeating as I continued as to ask him where he was. I never would have believed he was able to squirm through the small access door, let alone fit inside this confined space.

EMDR is a multi-phase therapy and it is clear to me now that the therapist missed the critical first and second phase. No one really assessed Jason's readiness for EMDR and developed a treatment plan unique to his needs. The therapist should have worked with Jason to identify some specific issues to process, as well as assess that Jason had adequate methods of handling emotional distress and good coping skills, and most important, that he was in a relatively stable state. Jason . . . stable?

Too bad the therapist didn't come home with us that evening; they may have had better luck with Jason in his closet rhythmically banging his head.

We didn't talk much that day, but this experience only furthered his complete distrust of therapy. Expressing his feelings launched him, drawing pictures got him in trouble with the police, and EMDR turned him inside out.

His anger outbursts continued to escalate and raised fears at the school. Jason spent many days confined to in-school suspension. He was in that room so often that he had his own designated desk. He likely set the school record for the most in-school suspensions. Remember the firecrackers the first day of school? Yes, he was put in ISS, the first and only kid in that class so early in the school year. The next day he and a friend started a fire in a storm drain under the road waiting for the bus. That earned him out of school suspension.

One major incident that brought me to the school involved him mouthing off to the bus driver. Apparently, some of the children were overly rambunctious and kept running or rollerblading up and down the bus aisle. When told to sit down, they used abusive language. I was shocked in my usual protective mode. The superintendent assured me it was all on tape. Bret and I asked to see the tape to determine what was triggering my demon son. We returned to the school the next day to an apologetic principal. The tape had been erased. I spoke to some of the other children on the bus (I was the scoutmaster so had unusual powers in the community). The truth was the bus driver had a far worse vocabulary than the children. This did not excuse Jason's behavior; but it did explain why the tape was so quickly erased.

On another occasion during in-school suspension he was using scissors to cut paper for a project. The assistant principal walked into the room and made a negative comment to him. His mannerism in the way he held the scissors combined with some choice words and his highly developed evil eye, not to mention his ability to throw the scissors into the wall like a ninja star, resulted in out of school suspension. The teacher complained to the principal that she believed her life was threatened.

These incidents were becoming more frequent, with little hope for change. And he was still running away. Whenever he was losing control, feeling thoroughly threatened to the core, he would flee. Left to his own, he simply walked home. But if interrupted in this flight, he would be very oppositional.

I was happy to see seventh grade end. It was perhaps one of the most stressful school terms I endured, likely because he was now maturing into a teenager with no more self-control than he displayed during that first rage at ten years old. We were blessed with Alison again that summer.

Eighth grade was a landmark year. Early in the semester he ran. The incident was initiated in the assistant principal's office. That was one administrator who was at her wit's end with him.

She attacked him with "You're just a stupid little kid. You're side of the story doesn't matter here."

That was a trigger! A chair took flight across the office into the wall. I personally saw the hole in the wall. Jason was very gifted at this type of wall renovation. He then responded with "Fuck this, I'm going home!" And not so lightly, walked out of the school toward home.

The principal had enough of sending school staff after him. She called the police, but never bothered explaining that he was emotionally disabled, or the fact that he could not manage being touched when in flight mode. The police located him walking home and stopped their vehicle to address him. Jason ignored them and kept walking. The officer then approached him from behind and grabbed his arm, to which Jason abruptly responded swinging his arm out of the officer's grip. The officer threatened to pepper spray him at which point Jason immediately dropped to the ground, assuming if he just sat still he would be safe. The police discussed the legal issue of his behavior and offered to take him back to campus. He bluntly refused, keeping himself firmly planted to the ground. He was immediately taken down and cuffed. While in the back seat of the Officer's car, he continued raging, smashing his feet against the windows to break them out. They stopped the car, pulled him out and proceeded to completely restrain him in plastic ties. He returned the favor with spitting and usage of the foulest language.

I was called away from work and told my son was at the local jail. No other information was shared with me. I arrived to a busy lobby, people hustling around, some visibly shaken. At the window I asked for Jason and was immediately brought back to meet with the arresting police officer. A real gentleman, though plainly upset. I explained Jason's condition to which he responded with empathy. He brought me to the cell, and on the floor was a meek and terrified little boy. As he stood by my side as submissive as a beaten dog, I implored the police not to press charges. The police agreed that it was inappropriate of the school administrator not to have warned them, but the sergeant was absolute. The felony charges would hold: resisting arrest. Let the judge deal with it.

This was another episode that took years out of my life from sleepless nights of untold anxiety. This was a felony crime. What could be worse? I spent so much energy to keep him out of the grips of the juvenile criminal system. I felt completely dejected, filled with self guilt, and as usual, anger at the school for not protecting him. I learned later, they were burned out shielding him and felt it was high time he paid the legal consequences of his own violent behavior. That was one principal who was done with him. She wanted him out, and this approach was a quick solution to removing a student with an IEP for an emotional disorder.

I truly feared the outcome, constantly calling Bret for reassurance to which I received his honest appraisal of the situation. I was bluntly told Jason could receive a juvenile sentence. I was emotionally devastated. Knowing his issues and past experience at Cleo Wallace, I was certain such an experience would result in more untold damage. I was fearful of even taking him back in my home after suffering a juvenile incarceration.

The only hope for him was the unique policy of the foster care system in Arizona. The foster care case judge (the children were all wards of the court) was also responsible for hearing any criminal cases against their ward. In this way, a more reasonable head would carry the day. At least his presiding judge understood Jason's history and treatment plan, providing her a more complete understanding to offer a sentence that would not undo all the good efforts of the past.

The court date was set and the drive that day was filled with utter fear for us both. Few words were exchanged. When we arrived, the place was crowded. The routine always the same, sit and wait. His lawyer appeared and reviewed the situation with Jason, and for the first time, advised him that he should prepare himself for the possibility of a prison term. Meaning he may not come home with me that day. The lawyer wanted him mentally prepared to be taken in handcuffs from the courtroom. Depression hit hard. His facial expression was blank, his eyes empty. I sat with Bret who tried to reassure me. But I could feel his own fear for Jason. Did he have the strength to survive juvenile incarceration? Would he come out far more damaged, his prognosis for recovery reduced? As these thoughts whirled through my mind, the call came.

We sat like frightened mice cornered for a feast. Jason sat by his lawyer, head down and shaking. I was with Bret. The court opened up with the normal fanfare. Then the charges were read and the prosecutor charged like the light brigade. He was a young aggressive attorney who was tasked with making an example of the monster who dared attack the police. He pressed for incarceration. Jason's fears were overtaking his common sense, his body went rigid, his emotional response on a tight trigger. Jason's lawyer then spoke. Jason pleaded guilty and the lawyer continued with an explanation of the circumstances of the situation, asking for leniency, presenting a psychological history of loss and abuse, certainly prepared by Bret. The message to the court was clear: a juvenile sentence would only result in greater damage. The judge then addressed Jason about his behavior.

He immediately went on the defense, raising his fists, his voice, and his language to which the judge abruptly stopped the hearing. She slammed her mallet hard pointed straight at him and ordered him to get hold of himself. His mouth stopped, but his body language remained threatening. She told him to leave the courtroom immediately and called a recess. We all left quickly to sit outside. He sat alone. The lawyer asked Bret what next. I kept my own distance. Bret calmed him down and the lawyer confronted him with the facts.

He said firmly, "You are lucky you were not arrested right there in the courtroom. I've seen it done. I'm sorry Jason, but it is now very likely you will be taken in custody when we re-enter the courtroom."

He cried, holding his head firmly with his hands. He always realized too late the self damage caused by his poor judgment. I know he was as much afraid of his own outbursts and raging as anyone else, which resulted in even more self-condemnation.

After ten minutes or so, we were called back into the courtroom. As we entered we all immediately saw a sheriff sitting against the wall, handcuffs clearly visible on his side. Jason was terrified. The judge entered, seemingly calm and opened the hearing again with a direct question to Jason: "Are you in control now?" To which he stood up, tears still streaming from his face and apologized, not only to the judge, but to those of us with him. It was heart wrenching to me. He was clearly not playing for sympathy. His words were earnest. I had seen this cycle play out for years and it still tore my heart out. I wanted to hold him close, but this was not the time or place. More importantly, he needed to stand on his own two feet, to face the music alone. And he did it with honor. Despite the negative circumstances, my young Boy Scout displayed the characteristics of an Eagle Scout: Courage, Honor and Loyalty. I felt great pride, though still filled with the fear of losing him.

The judge asked a few questions and then asked once again for the prosecutor's position for an appropriate sentence, followed by a few words from his defense lawyer. The judge took another recess, but this time asked us all to stay in the court room. My eyes rarely left the sheriff sitting calmly in the corner. She returned quickly and gave her verdict. Jason was convicted of a felony, however, she ordered him to do a large amount of community service to be completed by a fixed date. If he complied and did not set foot in her courtroom again during that period, she would reduce the conviction to a misdemeanor. My heart began to settle back to a healthy rhythm. We were directed to another part of the court, where Jason was introduced to a probation officer and then taken back where he was fingerprinted; a standard practice when convicted of a felony. The drive home was as quiet as the one to court earlier that day. I was exhausted and remember just dropping on my bed and crying myself to sleep.

Locked Down

Our school district continued to grow and costs for sending special education children to other districts escalated. They developed their own program in a remote location from the main campus behind the school bus barn. The program was under the direct leadership of a good friend and Jason supporter, Mr. Dean, a school psychologist who worked his case at the elementary school. Jason had developed a trusting relationship with this man over the years. The facility was very mediocre, a single mobile structure surrounded by a high fence and bordered on one side by the bus repair and storage facility and the rest by a desert preserve. He had nowhere to run. The place was quite a difference from the prestigious A+ Middle School campus. Jason was transferred to this restricted campus for eighth grade due to the incident with the police and his ongoing behavior outbursts. He was also growing into a strong teenager which only enhanced the fear people felt when he raged. In fact, he was not even welcome at ISS anymore.

Once again, our hopes were elevated. Here he would be safe from police involvement in his behavior issues and in the hands of experts. I was looking forward to another year like the one with the teacher at the last special education classroom in sixth grade.

From Jason's perspective, the move was catastrophic. Like all teens his age, he was developing social skills and enjoyed school as much for the peer interaction as academics. Confinement in restricted school campuses slow or stop general social development and in some cases, sexual development as well. An additional hardship for the student and family is the lack of peer interaction allowed and that which occurs is with children with serious conduct disorders. It is always a difficult decision for school administrators to use this restricted campus approach to solve immediate behavior problems. Some children, once moved into a restricted setting, tend to continue a downward spiral; or once returned to an open campus, struggle to adjust and be accepted by their peers. Often these children suffer an additional indignation in the communities, where many families curb their children from associating with them because they do not participate at the mainstream campus.

Jason had been moved around every year, each change due to behavior issues within the academic community. These moves only reduced his self-image which increased his fear of rejection. The moves and large portion of school time spent on behavior modification and not academic work led to his general lack of success, contributing to his increasing behavior problems in the classroom. Let's face it, any kid who is academically overwhelmed will shut down, get bored and lean toward misbehavior for attention.

Our hopes were soon dashed. On the new campus Jason acted out often, far more than in the past. Some of the problems were simply a result of a new school team developing a program in a very difficult environment. The teachers were all developing their structure and curriculums. Some of his behavior problems resulted from his anger about the placement and the influence of the negative peer activity on the campus of which he was a member. In fact, this new facility had a psychiatric hospital. Due to Jason's extreme fear from his past confinement at that facility, the director of the school agreed to let Jason go outside for 10 minutes to calm down. His favorite safe spot was a small pond off to the side of the property.

There was, however, good news for me. I had very few calls to the office, and most were simply to advise me of incidents and consequences so that I would be prepared if he came home whining or still carrying guilt or anger. Considering the limited IEP expectations, the first semester was a success. He may have raged around the classroom or outside within the confines of the facility, but he never ran away or brought the attention of law enforcement. School crisis solved.

Christmas break that year brought the Millennium celebration. I spent endless hours planning an incredible itinerary to Europe. I had plenty of time on my hands now that Jason was under control at his new school. It was the first time Jason and Nick ever traveled abroad other than Mexico. My good friend Michael and I took them for a three week trip to London, Paris and Rome. London was damp and cold, chilling us to the bone. But the children were stoic and so excited about visiting British historical sites, that they soon overcame the damp, chilly weather. My fondest memory with Jason was attending the *Lion King* musical. It was a very special time for the two of us. We enjoyed Christmas Eve at the Victoria and Albert Theatre with the orchestra dressed in 18th century dress and Father Christmas in the lobby. They were less impressed with Shakespeare's Globe Theatre than a dungeon wax museum on a side street. But that's all the fun of traveling with your children.

New Years Eve in Paris was unforgettable. We watched the fireworks around the Eiffel Tower with thousands from around the world. The kids' favorite meal spot was a small crêpe stand just down the block from our hotel. The crêpes were especially delightful to Jason, who bought one almost every time we passed by. I was concerned about the amount of cognac used, but it didn't seem to bother him or Nick.

This was also where Jason lost his cool for the first time on our trip. The trigger was hidden from our notice, but not the action. He took off. I waited and waited for several hours into the evening. I was in a panic. This was before cell phones were a common appendage of American youth. I went to the front desk for help. They first asked his age. To which I responded a mere fourteen years old. They laughed and assured me he would be back with a grin on his face. I was not amused and certainly not reassured. But I was stuck. What could I do other than wait? It was major anxiety time. Nick was on his bed with a book in hand and the television blasting. He was remote and undisturbed. Late into the night, Jason finally showed up at my hotel room with his hand out for money. I immediately went into lecture mode while he was talking so fast I couldn't understand his problem. Or perhaps I wasn't listening. He waived me to follow him back down to the lobby, and waiting outside was an irate cab driver with the meter still running. In broken English he explained he had picked Jason up at Notre Dame Cathedral. That was nowhere near our hotel which was located near the Paris Opera House. I paid the taxi and went to bed. I was too relieved to stay angry. But there is a lesson for anyone going to Paris. Do not walk aimlessly without a map. You will get lost. Better yet, if angry, find another avenue to release the emotion other than walking about town.

From Paris, we rode the train to Rome. This was our last week and the children were tiring. We did see Pope John Paul II, though Jason once again found a way to confront law enforcement, only this time, the Swiss Guard. After we were seated, he had to make a bathroom run and got lost outside the security area. As the time for His Holiness to appear arrived, the crowd's enthusiasm grew more charged. Large groups raised banners and flags shouting slogans of love. Jason's seat was empty. My anxiety grew with the audiences' excitement. As the Pope approached his throne, Jason plowed through the tight seating area, to jump into his chair. He was clearly frustrated, whining about how he was forced to evade the Swiss Guards who didn't speak English. I guess all those ninja nights with Junior paid off.

The excitement faded quickly after the first few churches and saintly remains. They perked up again at the Coliseum, but found the Forum a bore. I guess it just required too much imagination to assemble the ruins into a meaningful site for my non archeological boys. Of course, they found McDonalds, so that cured their diet complaints. But after so long away from home and friends, they were burning out. It was in Rome that Jason's mischievous spirit broke loose and he and Nick started getting on each other's nerves, not to mention mine.

We left Rome earlier than planned and returned home tired, but satisfied. Perhaps we tried to do too much, but I know the boys appreciated the opportunity and to this day they have very fond memories of many of the sights, and most important, the cherished time we spent together.

Jason returned to school and Nick to college. It took little time for Jason to get back into his typical anti-classroom behavior pattern. At that point I found the whole matter of school behavior to be caustic and was now emotionally distancing myself. It was my last survival option. How they managed Jason was completely outside my control. Truly, I have found it an issue with all my foster children. How can I be responsible for what happens in the classroom where the children spend the vast majority of their time. Sometimes parents and teachers alike, lose sight of the fact that our children spend more hours in the hands of the school staff than with their parents. Most teachers have little to know understanding or training on the unique world of foster care within which their students struggle to survive. This lack of hands-on knowledge makes it difficult for them to feel empathy while these children act out in the classroom, and worse, have few tools to deal with the behavior issues that regularly disrupt the other students.

Like clockwork, after a few weeks of peace, I was called to his school. When I arrived on the scene Jason was sitting against a tire of the sheriff's car, bleeding and bruised. I walked directly over to him, but was intercepted by the officer. Apparently, Jason had attacked one of the teachers, who then contacted the police. The teacher, as it turned out, was an untrained aid that was left in charge when Mr. Dean attended a meeting off campus.

This was the closest I'd come to assuming my son was lost. After years of violent raging and disruptions, I was burned out... at the edge of losing my sanity. I was honestly questioning my commitment, continuing to lean on Bret for support and almost daily coaching. Any parent who has had the misfortune to see their child in handcuffs knows the total sense of helplessness, fear, and disappointment. Your anger at the child is intertwined with your own feelings of guilt. I loved him, but his continuing violent outbursts against all authority figures were elevating to a criminal intensity. He was dangerous to himself and others. Even at this escalated level my gut reaction was to embrace and shelter. Such an over protective attitude was not the solution for his long-term mental health. High School was just around the corner. I was emotionally fatigued with no sense of direction.

He raged in the classroom that day, nothing unusual. But without a professional available to deescalate him, the situation was soon out of hand. Jason walked off outside as agreed with the school director to calm himself. The aid was in close pursuit. As he approached the pond, the aid grabbed Jason's arm to get control of him. My boy instantly reacted and shoved it off. The aid tried again and Jason took a swing at him with the intent to force the man to back off. At this point the aid's anger also escalated and he grabbed Jason hard to which Jason responded with a punch to his jaw. The aid then hit Jason in the chest and spun him around, holding both his arms across his chest. Jason cried out that he could not breath, to which the aid responded that if he could cry out he could breathe just fine. Jason then grabbed one of the aid's fingers and bent it hard. The aid responded with a swift kick against Jason's legs and took him down to the ground, still holding his arms across his chest. Jason tried to scratch the aid, who responded with head butts, knocking Jason's head against some large stones that lined the gravel path where they were wrestling. After a short time, the aid had Jason under control well enough to release him. About that time the Director returned to the campus. Jason was calmed and returned to the classroom. Soon after, the police arrived and I was called.

Though the aid acted improperly, especially in light of his responsibility in a special education facility, Jason was the focus of attention. Each time an incident involving an adult hurting him occurred, he felt he was always the fall guy. This compounded his mistrust in social rules and in particular, the police. The sheriff released Jason to my custody. Later that day, we were called by the sheriff's office to bring Jason over to answer a few more questions. Bret and I spent quite a bit of time building Jason's confidence and assuring him everything would be alright. We drove to the sheriff's office all together and arrived early. The officer was not at the station so we hung around outside. As he arrived, we saw one of Jason's classmates in handcuffs. The Sheriff came over to us, shook my hand and that of the case worker. As Jason put out his hand to do the same, the officer responded with: "I don't shake the hand of the people I am arresting," then cuffed his wrist. We were all stunned. Jason was bewildered. After the initial shock, I was anxious that Jason would rage with the officers and all would be lost. When I asked why he was arrested, they wouldn't tell me. I called my attorney who came to the station within the hour.

I ran back to the house to get his medication, Zoloft, and begged the officers to let me give it to him. They finally agreed and I was escorted to a small room where he was cuffed to a table, his head down napping. By late afternoon he was finally released.

We learned later that the investigation centered around drawings that Jason and others had done of the school on fire. This was during the period after the Columbine High School killings, when many law enforcement agencies were hypersensitive to students who demonstrated any threat to a school. I was surprised with the sheriff's attitude to arrest elementary school age children who were diagnosed with emotional disorders and enrolled in a special education campus. Furthermore, the drawings of interest that day were from a book Jason was instructed to keep by therapeutic staff to release some of his anger in a constructive way. The fight with the teacher apparently faded away. After this very stressful experience, I never allowed therapy art in my home again. I was proud of Jason that day for not raging when he was cuffed in such a manipulative manner. This was yet another negative experience for Jason where society demonstrated the use of unethical behavior where the end justified the means. A standard practice used by many authority figures with youth.

After the incident at school with the violent outburst with the aid, and the allegations over his artwork, he spiraled down to serious depression. Bret and I knew we had to take action as his raging was not subsiding with maturity as we had hoped, and worse, he was increasingly getting into legal problems that would likely result in juvenile detention. We all agreed that should Jason be removed from my home in detention, the trauma would far outweigh any advantages from imprisonment consequences for anti-social behavior. I kept him home the rest of the week. During that time the Foundation was looking for a residential treatment center. I was very insecure about losing him, and no doubt he was feeling the same insecurities. Jason was very quiet that week and seemed despondent and distant. Bret believed it was an action that was necessary. The concern for him was finding the right time when Jason was mature enough to have a positive, rather than negative response to residential treatment. He was suffering the anxiety of being taken back to Cleo Wallace from the first moment he arrived years ago. The action had to play out, but this time to build trust.

Bret came to the house later that week, advising us that a bed was available at the local Psychiatric Hospital for an evaluation. I asked to be the one to take him. Bret left. Jason and I were alone at the house feeling helpless. Later that evening I took him over to Eileen's house to cry. Many of his friends came over to say goodbye and join in the cry. I departed the scene for my own secluded emotional outlet. At that moment, he had no confidence he would ever see his friends again. His past was the only experience from which he could draw any expectations.

Bret agreed to let me take Jason alone and he met us the next day at the hospital intake area. I remember they first took his blood pressure and temperature and the nurse offered to do the same for me thinking it would help calm him. My blood pressure was 200/120. She advised me to see a doctor immediately. The evening went better than I expected with pitiful crying, but no raging. He was angry realizing it was a hospital like Cleo Wallace. 'Damn they lied to me again,' he thought. Jason was held at the hospital for two weeks, waiting for a bed to open at *The New Foundation (TNF)*, a residential treatment center in Scottsdale. At the hospital he was treated like a medical patient, including regular vital checks during the day and night. During one night visit from the nurse to draw blood, he grabbed the needle, fearful of being abused.

***

Jason's Journal (13 years old)

Because of trouble at school and with the sheriff, I had a feeling I was in a lot of trouble. Bret and Dad sat down with me in the house to go over my options. They told me that I was probably going to juvenile, but if I showed the judge that I was trying to change and work on my anger, that she would go easy on me. Bret told me that I was going to The New Foundation. He said that it was like a group home for children my age. They gave me a few days to say goodbye to my friends and explain what was going on.

Dad drove me alone, I don't remember seeing Bret. We pulled up to a hospital and my stomach ached and my heart sank. I thought that it was like déjà vu, Cleo Wallace again. I was getting really nervous and started to get mad, but I promised dad that I would never rage again. So I clenched my teeth and held my anger.

At the hospital, Bret and dad met with the doctor while I waited in the hall. I heard them talking about me. I thought about running away, but I couldn't do that to dad.

We checked in at the nurse's station. One of the first things I noticed was they had a quiet room. My face got pale and I felt a little sick. I thought I would kill the person that tried to put me in there. The nurses took my blood pressure and kept asking me about how often I use the bathroom. I thought they were weird. They searched my stuff and took my art supplies. I was only allowed to take my clothes to my room.

I was really confused and again I thought about Cleo Wallace. While unpacking, Dad told me I would be there for two weeks. I got upset and a little mad because Bret told me it would be a few days for an evaluation. I thought that they were lying to me again like at Cleo Wallace; and they just told me a story to get me to come without a fight. I looked up to dad and saw it in his face that he didn't want to leave me or for me to have to be there.

After I put my stuff away with Brownie on my hospital bed, I went back to the front to say goodbye to dad. I didn't want him go. He had to leave. I watched through the hospital glass door as he walked away. Would I see him again? I kept thinking to myself that I had to be strong for dad. I was in a fog after he left me, scared, just curled in my bed.

That night I woke up to the nurses coming at me with a needle. I grabbed it from her hand and stabbed her with it. I wasn't mad or upset. The nurse startled me awake and I just saw something sharp. The guards came in to throw me in the quiet room, but I yelled wait and explained that I was sorry. I did it as a reflex, not out of anger.

I told them that I am not afraid of needles and that if they needed me to do something or needed something from me to wake me up and let me know. So they then took my blood and let me go back to sleep.

The next morning they woke us up to get our weight and blood pressure and temperature. After we got showered and dressed we ate breakfast. I was still upset about being there and I didn't eat with the others. I sat alone at a table by the window and watched the ducks in the pond. For the next two weeks it was pretty much the same thing; get up, check vitals, breakfast, go to group, free time, lunch, group, free time, dinner, free time or movie and sleep. During free time the staff took us out to do activities like basketball, tag football and Frisbee.

Dad was able to visit me and we played pool in the game room, or just hung out outside. He came every day, and sometimes was part of group. We talked about TNF as the next step. I didn't want to go, but knew I had no choice. Having dad there every day made a big difference. It helped me stay calm.

Banner Hospital was a lot better than Cleo Wallace and I never felt like a prisoner. I still had lots of freedom to do what I wanted and the staff was nice. During the two weeks I was at Banner I never went to the quiet room.

There is not much to say about TNF. I was most upset when they told me I couldn't see my dad for awhile. That hurt! But I was prepared during my stay at Banner and knew it was coming. They treated me fair and with respect. I felt safe enough to joke at times.

One rule was that when girls walked by, we all had to keep our eyes on the ground. Later that night, I asked the counselor if I had to follow that rule if I were gay. In fact, I should be able to sleep with the girls. It seemed like a good idea at the time. Like Banner, TNF was better than Cleo Wallace.

***

Visiting hours were also similar to a hospital, so I spent most every afternoon with him. The hospital also operated group meetings with the parents and children each week. At one such meeting we heard from one kid not much younger than Jason, about twelve. He shared his story about how he took a knife in the kitchen, and in front of his mother, cut his throat. Jason and I were pressed close to one another on a small sofa. We had the same reaction; things weren't all that bad at home.

As difficult as this episode was, the worst came when he transferred to TNF. Again, I drove him alone and Bret met us later in the day for the intake. Before giving him up again, we had a leisurely break at the skate park in Scottsdale to help calm him and give us an opportunity for personal time together. On the way over, Jason told me he needed new roller blade wheels, so we stopped at a shop. At the park he tested them out, got over confident, and tried a new 360 degree jump trick which resulted in a tragic crash. His face hit the corner of a ramp and he crumbled to the cement.

Jason arrived at TNF with a severe cut over a black eye. The intake was more intense than at Banner. We had a team meeting to discuss his behavior problems and he was told the rules while sitting quietly with an ice pack on his face. He quickly spiraled down, feeling sad and scared as we discussed his new world. He was particularly upset about the visitation policy. He had to earn visits and they would be rationed.

His duffle bag was inspected and most of his stuff sent back with me. He was taken in a back room where they were starting to do a strip and cavity search. I was handed an approval paper that I refused to sign. I told them he was not there for narcotics and had nothing on his person. I was terrified for him. He didn't need any more embarrassment and personal torment at that moment. The staff person agreed.

Time came for us to leave and we walked outside together. In front of the main building Jason grabbed hold of me tighter than ever before. He cried with mortal pain for me not to leave him and his body shook uncontrollably. We were both helpless. As he was escorted back into the building, I broke down. I lost total emotional control. Perhaps it was from the years of suffering this behavior and the fear that one day I would lose him. At that moment, I had no trust he would return. He felt much of the same fear.

As we were told at the intake, he was not permitted visits while settling in. I was the carrot. The program was designed around a slow reunification. During that first month we were not permitted to communicate, causing me as much trauma as Jason was suffering inside the facility. It was during this period that I suffered my greatest emotional struggle with loss. I never thought about my behaviors in the past when the children were in camp. For me, it was just normal paternal longing. This time it was very different. I was completely overwhelmed with grief.

The Foundation psychiatrist met with me that first week and concluded I was overreacting, and that I must have suffered major loss as a child. If I did, I have no memory of it. All I knew during those weeks is that I felt my soul wrenched from my body. Nick was kind enough to come down from college to provide support at a critical crisis in my life. I wanted my son home, but I was acutely aware of his need for this radical residential treatment.

Jason formed a positive relationship with Steve, his therapist, which was a first. They were both artists, which became the basis of their growing bond. Steve did not sit with a clip board asking Jason how he felt. He just did art with him during their talks. He was also one of the few people who earned Jason's trust. The time period given to Jason for his stay at TNF was followed to the day. This was critical for Jason to walk away from that institution without anger and resentment like Cleo Wallace three years earlier.

Since I was restricted on visits, I sent cards and parcels which were permitted. Each week my family or I sent something to him. Michael, who once rented my house, sent Superman themed gifts. With the first gift he attached a letter that listed all Jason's strengths and at the end noted all the characteristics that define a super-man. Michael had a special thoughtfulness for providing deep meaning in all his gifts to my children. I sent wooden dinosaur models to keep him occupied as well as some DVDs that all the boys in his cottage could enjoy. My uncle Jack, an avid supporter for Jason since he came to live with us, sent the largest model he could buy. All these parcels needed to be picked up at the post office and the staff was complaining. His roommate also protested about the growing volume of stuff which cluttered their room. Though I never intended to pressure the place to let him out to regain floor space, it provided me some amusement during a period of melancholy.

Though TNF was tough, the staff at this residential facility was not cruel like Cleo Wallace. He was also more mature and able to understand the direct relationship between his violent outbreaks and the interment. He was also motivated to cooperate with staff to gain his home back. He cared. He felt loved, understanding the emotional depth of its meaning. He had trust in his parent...me. He may have been afraid, but he was able to embrace that fear with reason from his recent experiences with me. It was a small facility with well trained staff. No one could harm the children, physically or otherwise, without being observed by other staff. When I had time alone visiting, his biggest complaint was repetitive chores and having to look down at this feet when passing girls. I was much relieved. I must confess, I did nonchalantly check his back and never saw signs of abuse.

At first, he earned a few phone calls, and then I was allowed a visit for only one hour in a small room. Later, I was able to take him to a local park for a picnic. I spent great effort to prepare the perfect BBQ experience in this park setting. After picking up Jason at the Lobby, we walked down to the park area just behind the facility and settled on a table under a large shade tree. Before preparing to cook the hamburgers we threw a Frisbee nearby. A teenager passed by our table and nabbed my small BBQ out of the bag and ran off on his skateboard. Jason and I ran in hot pursuit. Jason passed me by and closed in. The guy dropped the BBQ and disappeared. Not how I planned the afternoon, but it did provide a distraction from TNF and Jason felt triumphant having saved lunch.

At the end of the treatment he was permitted a weekend visit home before he was discharged. We filled the SUV with wooden dinosaur models. He was also very proud of his Superman ring which he never took off. It represented his victory over the past traumas. His counselor, Steve, can count Jason as one of his success stories. Jason came back to me physically and mentally superior from that gloomy day of his intake. Not only he was in better control of his anger, his mischievous nature had quieted. He was a young man filled with optimism for the future. Bravo to this institution.

Jason did not return to public school that year. We chose to have him finish the school year at the TNF day program. It was a long commute to and from Scottsdale each day, but well worth. This decision provided safety for everyone. Jason was in a structured environment, where he understood the rules and they were managed with consistency. And for the first time in a year, the family enjoyed peace. This approach also provided his therapist an opportunity to check on his progress after leaving residential treatment to help Jason implement the coping skills he learned. The tragic fear of separation that we both dreaded since Cleo Wallace had played out and we survived. Our relationship was stronger, with an improved ability for honest communication that was not filtered by insecurities and fear. Our relationship would blossom.

With TNF behind us, we enjoyed our traditional Catalina Island trip with renewed faith and trust. Jason was on his best behavior with a new perspective on his anger issues and I was in need of a mental escape, having just suffered the sting of extreme loss. I was an attentive and loving father. The feeling of regaining a lost child is one of relief and exhilaration. You may threaten every form of cruel punishment during desperate moments with your children, but when they fall into your arms after an unintended separation, you melt away and feel nothing but love and forgiveness. Ask any parent just united with a runaway.

Eighth grade concluded without incident and we both earned that summer's excursion to Catalina Island. Instead of just playing on the beach that summer, we earned our scuba certification. Working together to learn this new adult sport established the foundation for a new level of personal growth for Jason who was entering his teen years. And further, in the world of scuba, being young and strong, he was no longer the dependent child, but an equal.

It was a crash course with a former Navy Seal. He had an awesome personality that Jason took to immediately. Though my mediocre student was intimidated by the mathematics, this guy helped him through it with ease. I also saw a new side of Jason on this trip. I was not concerned with the classroom work, it was the diving itself. I was no spring chick. He was there for me, as vigilant as the instructor. For a work trip involving six hours of class per day, it was still very pleasant. At the end of the week we were diving off the boat and even took a night dive before returning to Arizona. I had my son back, and he was truly incredible. For many years thereafter, whenever we dove together he had my back and I never questioned his skill. I had unyielding faith and trust in him. TNF was pivotal. It was the right decision at the right time. Both elements were critical and most difficult to get right. Bret hit it perfect.

Though Jason lost some time with Scouts during the whole TNF affair, he quickly regained momentum after Catalina. He was a Life Scout ready for Eagle. Due to his very active status in the troop during the previous few years, he had over-achieved merit badge requirements. All that was needed now was the all daunting Eagle Scout Project. These projects are glorified community service efforts that the boys are required to plan, schedule and coordinate on their own. These efforts involve many hours and the inclusion of large numbers of other people. By their very nature, they are the single largest growth experience in scouting. Jason chose to improve several parks in our town which involved playground renovation, painting and general clean-up. He pulled it off like clockwork, with dad providing that daily push. He submitted his final report and completed his last Boy Scout advancement board of review later that year.

One thing our Troop celebrated with splendor and ceremony was The Eagle Court of Honor. The ceremony began with a short trumpet call and dimmed lights. We opened with the whole troop walking down the main aisle with lit candles to the music: *Fanfare to the Common Man*; followed by the leaders' quick walk to Handel's: *Awake the Trumpets*. A bugle Call to Colors was a troop standard. Speeches always followed, but the real entertainment was the traditional hoop dance. Jason did this himself, and so needed to do some quick costume changing. I was deeply moved when my two sons Nick and Jason received this prestigious award. The occasion always brought me to tears. But in Jason's case, this was more than a scouting milestone. We survived!

With Cleo Wallace and The New Foundation behind us, this ceremony was a symbol of closure for both of us from the past behavior traumas that terrorized so many people in his life, and an opening for a better and enriched future. As he walked down the aisle of our church that evening to the *Prince of Denmark March,* young scouts saluting him on either side, I saw a caring and understanding teenager. He was both emotionally and physically transformed. This was the climax I portrayed in the fairy tale story I wrote for him so many years earlier at Cleo Wallace. The Knighting ceremony of the Little Knight of Hunterston:

After the long processional through town, Jason finally arrived at the Castle's Great Hall. It was decorated with gold, ivory, jewels and fine wood. The trumpets sounded the final call, and he knelt before William of Hunterston. Tears filled his eyes. His chest burned with pride and joy. It was hard work, and now his day had arrived. All Jason's dreams had been fulfilled. But he also knew that his Knighthood was not an end. But rather, it was a beginning of new adventures and challenges.

I pinned the Eagle badge on his chest, surrounded by all our friends and family who supported us through scouting and most especially during some of our most difficult challenges over the past years. This was a child raised by a community at so many levels. I knew he would never be normal or average in any way. That was impossible. My optimism ended a long time ago. No, what happened was miraculous, he grew to become so much more. My love and respect for him cultivated through his high school years. His fear of rejection and loss, and the resultant raging would continue into adulthood. But like Nick before him, Jason was a mighty warrior. Even while writing this, I cannot help but cry.

Sanctuary

After so much turmoil in his elementary school years, high school was a true respite. While most youth were moving into their rebellious teen years; Jason was quieting down. He was burned out on anger and defiant behavior. He was ready to make peace with the world. He was also at an age and size that teachers stopped touching him, which had been a key trigger in past years.

One key element to getting him on the right path in high school was convincing him to join the swim team. I had known many children during my scouting years that swam for the school, and without exception, they were all good kids. Not saying that none of them had mischievous personalities mind you. I also discovered their average GPA was higher than most sport teams. The other advantage of swimming is all the youth cooperate together, freshman through seniors, beginners through varsity. Jason wanted to join freshman football, but I insisted. It was a great opportunity to integrate quickly, meet new friends and have a focus right from the start. It worked, with one minor issue.

Jason was bored swimming laps. After the first week or so he noticed a small group of girls hanging out around the diving boards. It looked easy enough and he always wanted to do gymnastics when he was a little boy. The scenery around the boards was exciting as well. He spoke with the coach and the rest is history. He made varsity his freshman year and continued to qualify for the State Championship every season. This experience exposed a natural strength that resulted in peer recognition and respect. He brought in points at every meet. He had great team spirit. He was noticed around the school with a welcoming attitude. For the first time in his life, at fifteen, he discovered his own sense of worth rather than a puppet manipulated and controlled to meet predetermined behavior.

After the first season, Jason joined a U.S. Diving team that met at Arizona State University. The team was coached by Mark, a 1988 Olympian. This was a serious team that worked the children hard and followed a pre-planned curriculum. Mark was a tough coach. This was not just a hobby for him, but a passion. He also coached the ASU collegiate team. Jason and Mark didn't always get along well. Mark was no child psychologist and expected unquestioned obedience to his demands. His athletes were required to have total trust, and why shouldn't they? He proved his worth as an Olympic athlete and college coach. But Jason's foster care history taught him not to trust anyone, especially authority figures. He needed time to build that trust and lots of coaxing. Though he established a solid exterior, his emotions were still fragile to the bone and he was still searching to justify his core beliefs and fears. People, who want to control me, will hurt me.

It was an incredible opportunity for a young new diver, but a difficult commitment for me. The facility was forty minutes away and to arrive on time, we were forced to fight evening commuter traffic in Phoenix. Jason needed to get his license and drive as early as feasible. We birthed a plan and sold it to the Foundation. He got a job at our local McDonalds to earn money to purchase a motorcycle. This was to become another good decision from which he learned self-sufficiency and built self-esteem. With the job came the trust to get the motorcycle. Our friend Michael participated in a motorcycle safety class with Jason and helped him choose his first bike, a GS500 Suzuki.

Though the job didn't last all that long, it was his first entry into the work force to learn responsibility. Soon after, he got certified to be a lifeguard and so began his long career poolside. Jason believes one reason he enjoyed this work was all his childhood training sitting up trees and on roofs watching people pass by. Lifeguarding and Diving were his true loves during his early high school years. Both provided personal satisfaction and accomplishment, though I could see the cracks in his façade. The hurt little boy was very much active deep in his mind.

After his first US Dive season with Mark, he changed teams to work with a most beloved coach Barb, a 1976 Olympian. She was one of those saintly people who coached for the pure joy of it. She loved the opportunity to coach great talent, but was just has happy showing the smallest child the very basics and cheering them with delight when they accomplished the simplest feat. Barb was maternal, so a perfect match for Jason. She was patient to the end with him. She could coax the most frightened child off a three meter board, then sympathize with their tears or dance to their delight. Words that best describe her personality poolside include animated, excited, energized, and at times totally outrageous. When a diver made the effort on a new dive, she was doing a jig poolside. The parents enjoyed her style as well. She provided real entertainment. She was also most humble, and was one of the few adults outside our home who demonstrated honest respect for Jason as an athletic peer and certainly not treating him as a mentally damaged foster child. She is a true Olympian in all respects, and her divers loved her for it. She impacted more young lives than she could possibly know. Jason is on the top of that very long list.

Through Barb he had the unique opportunity to host 2000 Olympic Gold Medalist Laura Wilkinson to lunch as part of a motivational visit with the local U.S. Divers. Jason asked her how she overcame her fear. How did she first climb up the ten meter platform and overcome the staggering height? Her response was astonishing from one who had recently brought home the gold.

"I never lost my fear. It's always there," Laura told him.

She then illustrated how she focuses on the dive, and that if she is off the platform for even a week, she needs to rebuild her confidence. That was not the magic secret he expected. Laura had that same joyful smile and humble character as Barb. They were both symbols of what great athletes should represent for youth.

Jason had been groping for years in search for the answer to explain his own fears. He had yet to understand that the mental block was deep in his own psyche, unrelated to diving. As the earth orbits the sun, so Jason's issues orbit his horrific emotional anxiety over the fear of loss as well as traumatic incidents in his childhood over which he was powerless. Over time sport became the trigger for what was hardwired from early childhood.

In addition to his endless desire for perfection to meet diving expectations, he also was reliving the beatings of early childhood. Smacking ones back on the water is very common when learning new somersault dives. The smacking sound and cutting sting into his bare skin brought back memories of abuse inflicted upon him by his mom's boyfriend. All the fear and helplessness bubbled out.

Despite Jason's difficulties learning more difficult dives, he persevered. And there was no limit to my stubbornness to support his diving. He even dove at one of Greg Louganis' old digs in Mission Viejo, California. For those of you unfamiliar with diving, Greg Louganis is a legend in the sport. That specific trip occurred during a school break. The facility, which had a national reputation, was operating a short week dive camp. Jason was a beautiful diver with superb form and rip entries that earned him the nick name "Moses," as the water seemed to part around his body as he slid into the water. However, he had difficulty moving beyond the basic dive list. He would earn high scores and win most every local competition. But as he progressed to the State level he lost to lesser divers that were performing more difficult dives. The more difficult the dive, the higher the degree of difficulty (DD) number which is multiplied by the diver's score. So a 1.5 difficulty for an 8 score produced a 12; while a 2.5 DD for a 5 score produced 12.5. Getting 8 required near perfection, a 5 was average. Jason always maintained an excellent sports attitude, congratulating winners, smiling and enjoying the camaraderie of his fellow divers. But deep down, I know he hurt. No doubt, his inner barrier all related to his personal fear of failure, which from his view always resulted in loss. So many foster children fear rejection from failure. In his mind the two were synonymous.

One fall day we were off to Mission Viejo. He was cautiously excited. I was hopeful this was the single answer. I never have given up on the simple solution. The coach assigned to him was a former Russian National Champion who spoke broken English. Jason liked him and soon learned his lingo and hand signs. He started brilliantly, and then it was up to the three meter board to work those back and reverse one-and-a-half somersaults. Ouch! However, this pool had a special benefit, a bubbler system. The idea is to create powerful jets of air from the pool bottom that broke the surface and softened the blow if the diver entered poorly, or in Jason's case, flat on his back. Jason was truly gifted in this manner. I'm not sure if it was self destructive or he simply was built off balance, but when he smacked, it was flat on the back. You could hear the smack clearly across an Olympic size pool. Even as a high school sophomore, we witnessed him in tears, barely able to breathe. The bubbler was an ingenious solution. He was resistant at first, but soon worked through his trepidation. He found success at last and it was well worth the investment.

Later that winter he was diving with Barb's U.S. Dive Team at a country club in North Phoenix. The only pool time available was in the evening. As the sun set, the cool desert air picked up. Diving in 50 degree weather, even with a heated pool, demonstrated the great dedication of these children. I was always impressed with their stamina. Late on one such evening under flood lights over a dark reflective surface, Jason missed his call out on a back one-and-a-half somersault and smacked flat on his back. He quickly pulled himself to the side, his eyes teary and barely able to breathe. I complimented him for a good try and urged him back on the board.

"Be tough guy," I said, "it's all part of the sport."

He rejected my every word and quickly swam away from me and the board to the other end of the pool.

"You don't understand how it feels," He cried.

I was embarrassed by his almost infant like behavior and angry that he would not get back up and try again. We had spent so much energy to get this far. He had such a great future. College coaches were telling me he could go far, very far. He had the perfect build, performed with grace, and ripped the water like a true champion. He just needed to advance in the sport. He attended dive camp in the summer, participated on three different US Dive teams struggling to find the right coach with the magic technique. All the coaches started with the same, basics. Weeks were spent on board work and working the spring of the board. He always learned something new from each coach that he would add to his routine. But when it was time to learn the advanced dives, the result was always the same, personal failure. On occasion his body would tense, he'd just suck it up and go for it, inevitably slapping on the surface time and again. This repeated behavior only further reinforced his self-doubt. He was not good enough. He was a failure. At some deeper level was he fighting off the mom's boyfriend who beat him so relentlessly? Was he undermining himself with a fear of failure that would bring my disappointment?

Sometimes fathers can push too hard, either because they are reliving their own dreams through their children, or want so much for them that they miss the whole meaning of athletics for youth. During this period I was one of those Dads. Jason so wanted to please me. At times, he must have felt utter failure and disappointment. Together, we evolved this father/coach and son relationship and he taught me how to let go of my dream and support his personal vision.

On a side note about this country club where Barb's team practiced, Jason commented that it seemed very familiar. After a short time, he remembered. This was the club where Ryan and Marge were members and their daughter swam for a club team. Prior to a practice one evening, he wanted to drive down memory lane. He found their house, but did not want to knock at the door. I now know why. He also took me to the hill where Ryan would take him in his car during rages. He was visibly shaken and I felt most uncomfortable. We left never to return.

Jason peaked his junior year even though he suffered a slight disability. During an early season practice, before competitions began, Jason's dive coach was late, so the swim coach took the reins to teach him a reverse one-and-a-half somersault. Normally you might think this inappropriate for a swim coach to attempt. But in our case, the coach had been a college diver, so he knew the methods well. During one of Jason's attempts he leaned back on his hurdle and after completing the somersault, came crashing down on the board. The result of which was a broken wrist. It could have been much worse. I've seen children face plant the board, clip it with their mouth, or snap their necks backward. The coach sent him to the office for the guards to check it out, and all agreed it was just a bad sprain, no big deal. He continued diving, though protecting that wrist. The next day, the swelling was enormous and I took him to the hospital for the two hour wait for an X-ray. Yup, it was broken just as the dive coach predicted upon her return just after the incident. That was the last board advice provided by the swim coach that season.

A broken wrist was manageable. The orthopedic surgeon cast the hand and provided an athletic excuse for the term. That was not going to fly with Jason so early in the season. Two doctors later, we found a group who specialized in athletic injuries. We returned home with a new water resistant cast and a prescription for X-rays each month.

The first meet was classic. Word was out that Jason was injured and out for the season. He hung around the board donned in his shorts and shirt while the other divers warmed up. The dive order was called out and to their amazement; Jason Hunter was on the list, in fact, first up. You could see their mouths drop as he ripped a near perfect straight forward for eights. He was undefeated that year in his region. The coach commented to me later that she was convinced his success was due to his completely relaxed attitude. He had an excuse for poor performance, the cast. So he just went all out with the anxiety of damaging his self-image firmly out of his head. Diving, after all, is a mind sport. So how did such a mentally damaged person like Jason ever get into it? Jason was gifted that way. And he beat the odds.

By his senior year, I gained such an appreciation for his talent and the enjoyment it brought him; I finally let go of my competitive attitude. To this day to watch him perform a forward straight dive, where he literally hangs six feet above and parallel to the board before dropping into a perfect rip, is one of my most enjoyable moments. Despite the occasional frustrations we both suffered during the height of his high school diving career, we both treasure the time we spent together.

Nothing compares to sharing a common interest. It provides the foundation for continued interaction and dialogue between father and son. This opportunity, at times under great stress, allowed the continued development of a meaningful relationship based on trust. While many teens disown their parents during high school, Jason pulled me closer. Diving was a key activity that forged the path for my paternal relationship to transition from caring for a little boy to honoring a young man. This experience also taught me to have the confidence to back off and have faith.

Coming of Age

Dealing with sexual issues with your own birth children is difficult and for many parents an awkward topic. Most of us provide a book with the words, 'If you have any questions, feel free to ask.' We then quietly disappear, hopeful they'll be advised by an older sibling, school or otherwise through osmosis. In truth, by the time we offer them the book, they already know, or at lease believe they know, more than us. They certainly understand everything in the book and more than most parents would feel comfortable discussing. They also do not see their own parents as sexual.

Our church ran a Christian sexual education program for middle school children that I attended with my son Nick. Parents and children attended separate sessions to learn and discuss issues. At the end of the day, the two groups were brought together. The ground rule was simple, you could ask any question you wanted, but no one was committed to respond. The purpose was to open dialogue. One of my scouts, whose family I knew very well, blurted out while staring directly at his parents during this meeting:

"I just can't believe you guys really do it!" while he moved one figure through two fingers in a loop made by his other hand.

Yes, his parents turned red, and the whole group had a good laugh. It did break the ice, but also made a powerful statement about our children's perception of their parents in American society. Our social consciousness is still very much impacted by our puritan heritage.

Soon after starting his freshman year, Jason fell in love. It was his first real experience with emotional caring for another which was now tied to erotic feelings. His testosterone was in full force. The girl was his age, but had engaged in sex since middle school. The only pubescent sexual relationship Jason enjoyed up until that time was his right hand.

Now would be a good time to educate the reader on a memorable training module provided at my initial foster care education class. We were told that all boys at twelve and over are to be provided condoms. I remember this specific lesson because of the controversy that it stirred by the innocent prospective foster parents. All were stunned.

"How could we do such a thing;" we asked. "Isn't that the same as giving them permission to engage in sex? What about abstinence?"

We were reassured that the agency's position was to teach abstinence. But they could not risk their health and unwanted teenage pregnancies, both of which continued on the rise. And so, all my boys had condoms at their disposal from an early age. For the most part, they all responded in a similar way. They played with them; experimented trying them on, but mostly used them like balloons or to impress their friends. I recently saw a notice from my agency regarding a sex education class they were teaching for their youth. In the description of topics of interest was included a note about a condom demonstration. I guess they figured that would draw them in.

His first high school girl friend was sexually aggressive and apparently got him under the covers soon after they met. He was honest with me from the beginning, looking for my reaction, more resulting from his continued incessant fear of rejection, than to boast. He had been demonstrating great self control from physical reactions to triggers since TNF, but still maintained that instinctive fear that followed his underlying issue: self-doubt. His fear now was making a mistake that could lead to rejection and loss. We talked about health issues, relationships built on common interests, and all that adult talk to steer him away from just sex. But I was talking to a hormone crazed fourteen year old who was also forever seeking maternal love and acceptance; only now, his penis was in the middle of his childlike emotional need. I called Bret.

"What now?" I asked.

Bret was calm. He knew the children had access to condoms as it had become somewhat of a family joke, not that the underlying issue was anything to laugh about. I don't remember if Bret spoke with Jason on the topic, but he took the issue seriously. He too believed Jason was searching for maternal love as much as normal sexual experimentation. I was not prepared for my little boy to start so early. Nick did not engage in sex until late in high school. I was more vigilant of Jason's activities after that, but he seemed as engaged in athletics and school as much as ever.

After about a month, the girl's parents invited me over for the proverbial coffee talk. I was prepared for a rash of insults and threats. The kids were in the backyard, no doubt making out. The father was quiet, the mom outspoken. He broke the ice with trivial small talk. Then she hit home.

"Our daughter says she is having a relationship with your son. Did you know?"

I acted the innocent, surprised, and last to know parent, who suspected without confirmation. The mom continued, telling me about a former affair her daughter engaged in and how hurt she was when the guy broke up. I was confused to what end this conversation was headed. Finally she told me her daughter was on the pill and she expected that I had instructed Jason in protection. She also bluntly asked if I had him blood tested recently. It was time to talk with Bret again, good old Bret.

Jason and I left after a short time. I asked Jason if he knew that his girl friend was on the pill. He confirmed his knowledge. He was head-over-heels in love. Nothing was going to intercede. My attempts were only met with anger and his disengagement from me. I did not want to push him away and damage our open dialogue that took so many years to solidify. I worked at keeping him occupied more and more, hopeful of the old proverb, busy hands keep children out of trouble. After a couple of months the romance cooled down. They spent more time arguing than in romantic pursuits and rarely did anything together outside of sex.

I was in the office paying bills one evening when Jason burst into the living room and threw himself on the sofa, blanket over his head crying. She gave him the "Dear John letter." It was predestined as with all first infatuations, but still emotionally overwhelming for young teens. In Jason's case, the pain was a thousand times more so, as this rejection drove all those years of loss to the surface. Jason was never able to understand this painful feeling that tore at the fabric of his soul. Perhaps he suffered tremendous loss trauma before he learned language, therefore never had the mental capacity to put words to the feelings. But they were none the less real, always dragging his emotional state to very early childhood. As I stood frozen, not knowing what to do, the girl walked in the front door. The expression on her face was one of astonishment. She had been through this event before and was far beyond Jason in the ability to move ahead. She also had no idea or understanding of his past, she was simply too young and immature. She turned and walked out. I never saw her again.

I tried to comfort Jason, but at an adult level, talking about the cycle of relationships at any age. How we need to enjoy the moment, but never get so attached we cannot let go. That was easy for me to say, but honestly, I never learned that lesson well myself, especially when it concerned a foster child placement in my home. Once I offered them my heart and hearth, I could never let go. Certainly, that was the case with Jason.

I quickly learned that Jason would continue to struggle with teenage relationships. He so wanted to have an emotional connection with others but his sexual awakening only complicated his arousing need with his sexual drive. To my amazement, he was also deeply loyal during any affair, never compromising a relationship. For Jason to initiate a break-up would be rare indeed.

After his first romantic entanglement he steered clear of intimate relationships. While working at McDonalds he was invited to a fellow employee's eighteenth birthday. He was not involved with this girl yet, but was just looking for a good time. The party was at a community center at her neighborhood. Everyone from his work was there. They started playing drinking games and things got a little fuzzy after that. Next thing he knew he was making out on top of the pool table with the girl from McDonald's to the cheering crowd. He thinks it was planned, because she brought a condom. Good thing, he was not clear headed enough that night.

I learned about this activity via the internet one day when I was checking his dive statistics. We had a number of long talks about public activity, and the danger of friends putting pictures on the internet. I also emphasized my restriction in dating girls over eighteen. During the remainder of his freshman year he dated frequently, but none developed into a lasting connection. Perhaps he was still reeling from his first affair earlier in the year. His dive coach's biggest complaint during that year was all the flirting around the boards at practice. She swears he dated every girl on the team.

In his sophomore year, Jason dated the swim team manager. The relationship became intimate toward the end of the dive season. They stayed together until Valentine's Day the following year, when she broke it off for another guy. Again, he was deeply hurt. She handed him a note between classes and he immediately broke down crying. The teacher excused him from class that day. He did not date anyone until the next school year. He focused totally on diving which was his escape from the pain of real life. When on the board nothing mattered but the moment. Jason once told me that as he took his steps, the world stopped, everyone's eyes were on him, he was the center of the universe. He loved that feeling.

The next affair began his junior year, but ended after four months when they realized they were more friends than romantic partners. He jumped to a few other girls he knew from diving, but felt uncomfortable due to his feelings of friendship over sexual attraction.

Then Beth entered his life. He met her through an old girl friend who worked with the drama club. Beth, a flutist, hung around these people and that's where they met. Their first date was in my corvette, which impressed her greatly as it was her favorite car. Beth was his first passionate love. She was a year his junior, bright, fun and outgoing. They hit it off quickly. They became romantically involved after just a month.

The relationship moved along well and Beth's parents followed very strict rules. Beth was required to be home by ten any night she was at our home. That worked well for me. Unfortunately, they both enjoyed the spa and on one occasion lost track of time. Her mom appeared at the door around midnight. I was in bed when rattled by the banging on the door. I was the first person to feel her wrath. The relationship was put on hold by parental order.

After the separation, they were only allowed to hang out at school. Jason attended a number of parties the latter part of his junior year. Some were a bit wild. At one such party, Jason describes the action:

"We did lots of truth and dare without the truth part. It then became a topless pool party."

After the gallivanting in the pool, my boy started fooling around with two bi-sexual girls back in the house. They later moved back outside. At only seventeen, at least from my perspective, this was all too much, too soon.

Soon after that party, Beth called. Jason was still deeply in love. The relationship was rekindled. He apologized to her mom for the prior indiscretion and promised to be more attentive to the rules. Jason felt very comfortable with Beth's family and enjoyed their company as much as his girlfriend. After six months or so, the relationship was again on the rocks, though this time not due to parental interference, but rather Beth's fear of commitment. Again, Jason was devastated.

Tragedy & Victory

After three years of only minor incursions, the worst being his ditching class on those days when I traveled out of town, Jason looked forward to an awesome senior year. In diving he was highly ranked at the State level with a good shot to medal. It was also the year that our swim coach of many years chose to change schools. The old coach was a friend of the family and knew Jason well since fourth grade. He understood Jason's emotional issues and was very capable of keeping him in check. A new coach was selected for Jason's last season on the team. As we learned over the years, Jason did not deal well with change, especially with new people who pushed him to change his routine without any prior communication and preparation. The replacement coach was also a new teacher at the school. She had no history of the school or swim team culture, and specific to Jason, had not been shown his IEP. She was a controlling personality who wanted to dominate the team from the start. She had no interest in following in the shadow of her predecessor, even though he was one of the most respected coaches in the state. There was conflict from the start between her and the kids. Many quit early in the season. Jason was anxious with the change and worked to maintain his distance, but was not prepared to surrender all control of his diving to her. After all, he had been doing this for three years and was considered one of the best in the State. He was also the dive team captain.

Early that season during practice the coach came over to advise him that her team wore Jammers, not Speedos. For those of you not familiar with swim fashion, Jammers are swim suits that fit tight like a Speedo, but look like shorts. Many high school teams have gravitated to this type of swim wear to attract more kids to the sport, many of whom shy away from wearing the small Speedo suit that is very revealing for a timid teenage male. He was shocked by her request to give up his Speedo. He was told by the Olympic coaches that in diving competition, the judges preferred Speedos so they could better observe the diver's form. He was also cocked for a battle due to the ongoing conflict between the coach and the team that had been brewing from the first day.

He blew up. She continued arguing, getting closer and closer, putting her face in his face with the traditional pointed finger almost to his nose. He turned away from her and hit a concrete wall. He could take no more and began to use vile language and arm waving. This was his first serious rage in public since prior to entering High School. The teacher was truly scared. She ordered him off deck, and later, had him removed from the team.

This was a personal, as well as family tragedy. I had invested huge sums of money and time in his diving. I was devastated. My reaction certainly didn't help his situation at the time. I'm sure he was feeling rejection and loss enough without the further dejection from my disappointment. But in the flurry of accusations, administrative actions and reactions, I was caught up in the fight and not attentive to his personal emotional needs at the moment. Unfortunately, this coach took the matter too far. In addition to removing him from the team, she contacted his employer (Jason was a lifeguard at the same pool) the city manager, to further damage his reputation and have him fired. We were fortunate that the manager was not over-reactive, and in truth, after a few weeks of the coaches constant battering, was questioning the teacher's motives.

It was a difficult beginning for what should have been his best high school dive season. Fortunately, cooler heads prevailed between the school administration and the city pool manager. Arrangements were agreed upon so Jason was not on deck while the swim team was in the area. This was a hard lesson for Jason to swallow, and though he outwardly blamed the coach and school, he understood his responsibility. The penalty may have seemed unfair and almost vengeful, but the message was clear. Raging in public was unforgiveable and resulted in unpredictable consequences. We did learn later that year the teacher's contract was not renewed by the administration. No pity from our household.

Though the loss of his final year diving was painful, Jason had moved on to focus his attention on a far greater passion, and one that did not involve stressful competition. He followed his childhood dream to care for exotic animals. He applied for a volunteer position at the Wildlife World Zoo that summer; a private zoo that required volunteers to be eighteen years old as they worked side-by-side with the keepers. This was exactly the break Jason privately dreamed of for so many years.

He had no fear or anxiety about facing a crocodile, alligator, anaconda, or Burmese python, just to mention a few of the reptiles he enjoyed. He was fortunate to work under a true enthusiast, an older Dutch born gentleman. The two hit it off from the start and the keeper enjoyed mentoring Jason in animal husbandry, but more, he shared his love and respect for wildlife. Well, except for monkeys. This relationship provided a key opportunity for Jason to build his self-esteem without me on the sideline. We all try to help our children get every opportunity to succeed. With foster children who come with so little, it is easy to over-parent. That is, to over- protect and feel responsible for always holding them up. Sometimes, especially once they enter adolescence, you need to let them fall and learn how to get up on their own. This was a hard lesson for me to learn and implement with Jason. I'd seen so much suffering and hurt, seen the helpless *puppy dog* expression of desperation and empty eyes begging for help. For me to not help was outright abandonment. At times, I was as much a challenge to the case worker as Jason. In addition to my continued drive to always be a crutch for Jason, I was impulsive and never missed on opportunity to email the case worker with my latest concern. He once told me he had advised another social worker asking about an exasperated email I had sent: 'Ask Bill if he is venting or wants you to bring it up chain?'

This new adventure at the Wildlife Zoo was Jason's own discovery. I felt completely out of my element at a zoo. It was an opportunity for Jason to educate me and share his passion. This new experience strengthened our adult relationship even more. In this venture, like scuba diving, I saw him as an equal, not a deprived child. He was becoming a young man, a good man!

Throughout the remainder of his senior year, he spent much of his free time at the zoo. Early on, I also volunteered. I wanted the experience. I guess I still have my child spirit. I worked on Saturdays with a variety of species including the big cats, monkeys and lemurs, wolves, and wild dogs. It was an inimitable experience for someone who spent his entire career in an office job. I enjoyed the people and gained a unique perspective on the relationship that keepers develop with the animals. The animals are not all as wild as the zoo management would have you believe. Still, they were unpredictable at times.

On many occasions Jason and I would volunteer the same day, he in the reptile building which I learned to envy during those hot Arizona summers, and I outdoors riding a converted golf cart all over the zoo. A day in the life of a keeper revolves around preparing food, feeding, cleaning and interacting. The latter is important during each visit to observe the animals for any noticeable changes from which the keeper can deduce health problems.

Jason and I would always meet for lunch with his mentor outside the reptile building. We were occasionally joined by one of the zoo managers, Lance, who coordinated all the volunteers. It was entertaining to listen to the debates from the old Dutchman's ultra conservationist viewpoint, and Lance, the great white hunter. But they enjoyed each other's company immensely, and Jason and I learned quite a bit about their very diverse histories. Lance is the one who, when a tiger had escaped its enclosure once, was on top of his truck with a rifle. The old keeper, on the other hand, was a purist at heart who dedicated his life to animal husbandry and breeding. He once managed a large pack of cheetahs on a private estate in Europe. He found them to be very tame and safe compared to any monkey. Did I mention he didn't like monkeys?

One major downside of zoo keeping is that it is a 365 day a year job, much like parenting. The animals' appetites do not take holidays or vacations. Each Thanksgiving, Jason and I would bring a feast to our friends at the zoo. I laid down a white linen table cloth over a worn and beaten wooden picnic table, bring out the fine silver and china, and of course, the Chardonnay. These guys loved wine. We all hoped the animals were fed before lunch those days.

Of course, after a while, animal loving Jason wanted a monkey of his own. His mentor strongly discouraged it. Eventually, against better judgment, I succumbed to Jason's arguments, not to mention my own childish irrational emotions, and we purchased a Ring Tailed Lemur. It was his first baby girl. And yes, primate young are as unpredictable as Homo sapiens. We named her Precious, partly because she was so expensive. She roomed in the house while still very young. We enjoyed letting her out of the cage to run around with our dog, sometimes riding her back while teasing her relentlessly. Other times they would play hide and seek. The lemur always won the game. The dog just wanted attention, winning was not important. Precious also liked to jump around the kitchen cabinets. As she grew older, her aggressive instincts kicked in and she was more difficult to catch and return to the cage. We soon moved her outside into a large aviary by the pool. Jason would spend long hours sitting in the aviary with her. It became his safe haven as much as hers, his new mental sanctuary.

In the end, our old friend was right. She was a vicious little thing and took a chuck of flesh from each and every one of us, including my poor little nephew visiting from Sweden one Christmas. But once she joined the family, we were not about to give her away. Jason worked with her regularly inside her enclosure, but the rest of us soon learned she was most dominating in her cage. One of the boys dressed in full motorcycle gear including his helmet to enter her cage. But once taken out on a leash, she was tame as a kitten.

The Lemur was one of many pets that joined us during that period. At one point we provided shelter to African spur tortoises roaming the backyard, an assortment of lizards like a bearded dragon, and several species of iguana (the big variety), and snakes. Jason loves snakes. I found one in my bed on occasion until Jason learned to put large rocks on top of the screen. I have learned to tolerate the snakes. They are quiet and require only an occasional mouse or two. The worst, from my prospective, were his sugar gliders. They stank. These are little marsupials that resemble a flying squirrel. Jason was very proud of his personal collection, his little zoo. It was around this time that he was more and more intrigued by Steve Irwin. He felt a special kinship. Sadly Mr. Irwin died before Jason had the opportunity to personally meet him in Australia, but he did get a very special card from his wife that he keeps close.

His passion was strong, but his education was weak. I knew that his dream would be a difficult hurdle. So many foster children have poor educations due to the constant placement changes. Recent studies show 75% of children in foster care are working below grade level, and 83% will be held back a year. The more often they change schools the further they fall behind.[4] They are so focused on survival; they have little interest in school. In addition to the poor academic progress, they never form long-term friendships. Whereas most children look forward to school to be with their friends, foster children typically start each school year, if not more than once a year, feeling left out and alone. This is just another source of loss and rejection. Jason was part of that statistic. Due to his outrageous behavior in the classroom, he was in constant motion. He lost the prospect for a good academic education as well as that all important opportunity for social development. The teachers and administration were simply too pre-occupied with keeping his behavior under control.

Though Jason struggled with school, he always finished with good grades. I should have been more attentive to this issue, but we were always in reactionary mode. I was just pleased to see him demonstrate success on paper. He was so proud that year as he approached the completion of a major milestone, a high school diploma. He knew college was a requirement to achieve his goal to work in a zoo, but had little understanding of the academic demands. We agreed that junior college was the safest bet and so pursued that transition during his last semester. To my utter disgust, he was unable to pass the basic entry requirements even though he had better than a 3.0 GPA from his high school. In other words, despite what the grades showed, he had not learned rudimentary English, writing or math skills. He was required to register for these classes without credit the first semester. He was disappointed, but moved forward like a champ.

Though he did quiet down during high school, he was not totally dead of mischievous thoughts. Jason continued his desert escapades with his friends, though he broadened out from the canal to the greater open desert west of our community. When I was out of town on business once, Jason took my new GMC Jimmy out in a monsoon. For those readers not from the Southwest, let me define this event. Monsoons occur in late summer during very high temperatures, high winds, and high moisture, all resulting in deadly storm weather and heavy downpours.

During a break in the weather, they all took off to do some fun four-wheeling through the puddles. He hit a steep slope, and the car slid down the embankment into a flooded wash. The vehicle sank so deep they were forced to evacuate through the windows. They dug it out and then searched for material around the desert to get traction. Once out, they drove it through more water trying to clean the bottom, only to cause the car to break down. His friend's dad gave them a tow. I returned home the next day to a dead vehicle. The dealer came and jumped the battery and took it to the shop. They reported to me later that my new car had about ten thousand dollars in damage on the undercarriage. These are the times that test a parent's love!

As the school year came to a close I was struggling to find the perfect graduation gift. I wanted to surprise him with a reward that was eternal. Jason appreciated opportunities more than just stuff that either wears or collects dust. I was after something grand. Talking to the guys at the zoo one day, they recommended a trip that would beef up his resume for future animal husbandry work and be a growing experience... Africa. The manager suggested a hunting safari, Jason's mentor, now a good friend, was more subtle and recommended touring places like Krueger National Park, which at over 7,000 square miles, is the largest animal preserve in South Africa.

'What a novel idea,' I thought. I was consumed with the notion and over the next few weeks researched every trip available. I spoke with an old contact in South Africa from business I'd done in that country several years back. He suggested a class for certification as a South African park guide. It was decided, though I had no idea where I would get all the money. After talking it up with Bret, we came upon a plan that would engage sponsorship from both the Foundation and the non-profit organization *Friends of Foster Children.* I provided the airline ticket to Johannesburg. The course was only offered in April when school was still in session. The graduation gift idea was in trouble, but the idea was too good to pass up. So it evolved into his senior year Christmas gift. To make the timetable, Jason needed to make arrangements to get his work completed before departure as well as taking some assignments with him on the trek.

This adventure was an important independent growing experience for him as it was one of the few times since the Westphal Basketball Camp fiasco in 1996 he was away from me. The only other times were Scout Camp, but he was with his friends like Junior or his Boy Scout leaders. I was very anxious, but excited for him. How do you wrap a trip to Africa package for the Christmas tree? This was his first experience where the smallest box was the biggest gift. I simply placed an itinerary inside a small wooden box decorated with stickers of wild African animals. At first glance it appeared to be a box for spare change. He was completely taken by surprise. Even after reading the itinerary with great care, he kept questioning what it really was. He simply could not believe he was really going to Africa.

Soon after he left, I was called in an emergency to a hospital in Albuquerque. My former wife had a blood clot move from her leg to her brain. She was diagnosed with Cancer just a few months before. The prognosis was very poor. The disease was discovered too late and had already spread into her lymph glands. While sitting with her lying semi-conscious, I received a phone call from a hospital in South Africa about a lion attack. I gave them my insurance information. They assured me it was not a major injury and he'd be back on the trail in no time.

My former wife passed away a few days later. Dealing with the family crisis kept my mind so occupied I had little time to worry about Jason. This was the second greatest loss of my life and brought me spiraling down. She was Nick's mom so he too was in deep emotional pain. We leaned on each other the next couple of weeks. Meanwhile, I hadn't heard anything more or received calls from hospitals so I assumed all was well. Knowing Jason, I should have been wiser.

Three weeks later he called from an airport in Europe to let me know he was on his way back home on schedule. Seeing him exit the airport gate area was a proud moment for both of us. He looked terrible, underweight and limping. But he had survived to be a stronger and better young man. After a big bear hug, I asked to see his chest scars from his lion encounter. He confronted his fear of separation from his home, faced challenges and unexpected conditions with no support from those on whom he had depended for so many years. He learned to quickly make new acquaintances, solved problems and dealt with his internal emotional reactions to those hardships, and experienced the pride of success... alone! It was another one of my proudest moments. With Jason, I lived the meaning of *Agony and Ecstasy.*

Graduation was a heroic accomplishment. Many people close to his case would have bet on his incarceration by eighteen due to his long history of violent rages and anti-social behavior. Though the Africa trip did not work for a graduation gift, we decided on another animal adventure: *Trainer for a day at Sea World.* He spent the day interacting with killer whales, seals, sea otters and a variety of other sea animals. I even enjoyed a show in which he participated. His greatest joy was working in the pool with porpoises. He quickly learned that riding these magnificent mammals was not as easy as it looks in the show.

I followed him around at a distance most of the day. These are the rewarding times in our lives when we observe our children so very happy and engaged; oblivious to the world outside the moment. Our relationship continued to transition. He was quickly becoming a close friend and companion with whom I was now sharing some of my most wonderful experiences.

During this period of his life we traveled together as high adventure buddies. Our only purpose at the local book store was to explore the travel section and fantasize about far off places. I was the conservative member of the group, the old guy. Jason, young and vibrant was ready to go anywhere to do anything. He was the push. We went scuba diving in the Cayman Islands, among other adult adventures. While in the Caymans, he also visited some of the local animal preserves, chasing down giant blue iguanas. I have another one of those precious photographs of him with lizard in hand, his clothes the worse for wear. His Huck Finn spirit was still alive and well.

We also spent time in Maui diving day and night. One particular dive to a sunken World War II tank caught Jason by surprise. I always stayed behind him when diving. He was faster, more acrobatic and quite frankly, more perilous. When he saw a dangerous creature, he immediately approached, while I had the very opposite reaction. He glided into the open tank top. I stopped, and then proceeded to follow when he suddenly burst out with a giant green sea turtle in pursuit. Once clear, he turned to converse. That was my Jason. This was also the trip where he made the brilliant decision to put his finger in the mouth of a blowfish that was bloating. He learned firsthand that they have a razor sharp beak.

Perhaps are greatest outdoor adventure was Costa Rica. That was one of those travel books we kept in our library to glance at the pictures and just dream. Jason, of course, had no desire to dream forever. After all, Costa Rica has monkeys and several species were of great interest to Jason: white-faced capuchin, the spider, the squirrel, and the howler. Once more, he was familiar with them all having interacted with those species at the Wildlife Zoo where he worked. The howlers are loud, so earning the name. At the zoo they were housed near the reptile building, and he spent many a day working on his rendition of their unique call. Though we enjoyed many adventures on that trip like white water rafting in one of the world's best rivers, visiting live volcanoes and flying down zip lines in dense tropical forests; interaction with the monkeys in their natural habitat was his chief objective.

After some local investigating we discovered a jungle area where our chances to observe these fascinating creatures were high. We checked in with the ranger who warned us about getting out before dark or risk being lost permanently. He didn't look like he had any interest in looking for lost tourists who were crazy enough to just go out into the jungle. After that quick motivational speech I was ready to head back to the hotel. Jason, on the other hand, was even more intrigued. We were off.

It wasn't long before he looked the part of a young Indiana Jones. If you haven't watched much National Geographic, let me tell you it is dark under multiple canopy trees. It is also thick with lush undergrowth. As was a growing tradition, I followed at a safe distance from Jason. I figured if snakes were about, he'd see it or feel it first. After a couple of hours dripping sweat and sliding on heavy moss covered everything, we heard the faint sounds of primates.

Jason was beside himself, but maintained total control leading us toward a large family actively playing high in the canopy.

I dropped my pack. And with camera in hand, I twisted my neck back to catch a glimpse. At first I could only see a few blurs. But as I focused at one spot, I could see a spider monkey perched with all fours spread apart, dangling from its tail. Near its head was Jason! I pulled back and looked again as I called his name. Yup, that was Jason up with the monkeys, and there he remained most of the afternoon. We saw spiders and howlers that day. And Jason's playful antics and perfect howler pitch caught the attention of these tree dwellers. I spoiled him rotten, and enjoyed every moment doing so.

***

Jason's Journal (17 years old)

A lot of people have been nipped by a stray dog, or scratched by a cat, or even bitten by a snake while camping but few have been mauled by a lion and lived to tell the story. I'm such a person. I participated in a Ranger Training Course in South Africa, a country of diverse environments and cultures not so dissimilar from Arizona, one with remarkable cultural diversity and natural beauty. Traveling in South Africa is one of the most memorable experiences of my life.

Getting into dangerous situations is my specialty, and started on the first day. After arriving in South Africa I met a Danish couple who were taking the same ranger course. Seeing that we had three days before the course started we decided to go on a trip through an animal preserve. Because of my experience working in zoos, the owners allowed me in with the lion and tiger cubs. The tigers were orphaned and shipped to the reserve from outside Africa. They were about 9 months. The lions were about 18 months old. I was surprised how soft they were and also how they enjoyed playing with people. In fact, one was so playful; he tackled me to the ground and sunk his teeth into my shoulder and gave me a big scratch across my chest. The cuts were a souvenir I will not soon forget.

The trip began with a backpack trek up a mountain that peaked at 6000 feet. The map indicated rock climbing gear was suggested, though we never used any. Halfway up I was on a 1,000 foot rock face, where I needed to take a break, so I stood straight up, I forgot I had a backpack on, and I fell straight down the cliff face. I rolled down 500 feet until my backpack was caught on a jagged rock. My knee was hurt badly from the fall, but I had to complete the hike because there was no help for miles from where we were at. The worst part was I had to hike back up where I had fallen with a busted knee.

Soon after the hike we traveled to Dolphin's Coast where we spent the night at a pleasant hotel on the beach. I explored a path that night to see the night life. I saw geckos and toads, and while approaching one of the toads I nearly stepped on a Puff Adder, which is one of the most dangerous snakes in the world. I was lucky that it hissed or else I would have stepped on it.

When I found my way back, I told the group what had happened and they predicted my life expectancy to be 29 years of age due to all of the dangerous and crazy things that I do. These were all memorable near death experiences that added to the adventure of my trip. The remaining part of which was in the African savannah, where I visited some of the Zulu and Swazi villages. My best experience was at the Swazi village where I met Pinky, a baby Vervet Monkey, orphaned as a result of local poaching. While at the Swazi village Pinky stayed on my shoulder during the day, and slept beside me at night.

***

During the African experience, Jason took a gun course where he gained an appreciation for the World War II Mouser. For his eighteenth birthday that summer, he purchased a restored 8mm Russian Mouser. This was not his first experience with a rifle. Prior to high school he had a BB gun which he purchased for target shooting. Like any normal boy, the target got old and the flying birds attracted his attention. Unfortunately for me, he missed one flying past my bedroom bay window. Replacing double pane vacuum sealed windows are not trivial.

With his new more powerful weapon, Jason increased his desert adventures. At the time he had a new friend whose father was a police officer. Not typical of Jason. The two boys often enjoyed a Saturday shoot in the open desert. I never accompanied him, though he asked numerous times. This was one bonding experience I let pass.

On one of those excursions the two boys found a new area down an old dirt road. They proceeded past an open gate down the road, set-up their targets and had a grand time. When departing, the gate was locked across the road. Jason proceeded to blow the lock with his rifle from a safe distance of ten feet. Remember, his weapon of choice was an 8mm sniper rifle used for long range shooting. He took aim and fired his weapon. The bullet struck the lock, shattering it. So far so good, just what he intended. But he immediately felt excruciating pain and his friend saw blood pooling on the ground. Jason must have been sleeping in rifle class when they addressed the topic of shooting targets at a safe distance. The bullet and shrapnel ricocheted back at Jason, cutting deep into his knee. The shrapnel hit both his legs; one large piece nicked an artery. With blood pouring out everywhere, he pulled out the biggest piece of shrapnel which resulted in even greater blood loss. He plugged it with his thumb and then used his belt as a tourniquet.

They drove to his friend's house, pulled out the bullet, which was so hot it burned his fingers, and cleaned the wounds. His friend's mom maintained her calm, avoiding any calls to the police and just considered their antics completely stupid. She offered peroxide and burritos. They returned to our house with Jason's clothes blood soaked. I was kicked back in the family room watching television. Jason called out from the hallway for me not to freak out, and then came toward me. I did freak out, but after he told me the story, I couldn't help but laugh. I checked the wounds and all looked well. I watched the next few days for infection, and brought him to my family doctor (certified in emergency medicine). I explained the situation, but after so many years as our family physician, he was not surprised. He was well aware that Jason was a walking accident. After close examination, the doctor reported that Jason and his friend performed expert surgery.

This was just one of a number of desert escapades Jason and his friends risked that summer. The most dangerous was night time rappelling off the grand stand at a local dog track that had been abandoned for years. They did it over a dozen times. On one occasion with his brothers in tow, they were caught. As Jason was about to take his turn, butt over the edge, spot lights lit up everywhere and a voice over a fog horn ordered:

"Freeze, don't fucking move, we'll tase your ass."

His brothers who were at ground level were arrested and placed in the police cars. Then Jason heard:

"You have ten minutes to get down or we will release the dogs."

He packed up and surrendered. After some questioning and a search of their stuff, they were released with a warning.

While Jason was enjoying his last moments as a mischievous kid, never missing an opportunity for adventure, I was being pressured by the family developer to renew my foster care license in the event of the need for a new placement. Little did I realize just how close I stood to that life changing event!

Life with a Nun

In the fall of 2004, Bret approached me about helping a foster mom with a fourteen year old boy named Drake. He was having behavior issues with the foster mom that resulted in never ending punishment. He was also showing signs of general depression. Bret was concerned. I wasn't acquainted with the mom or the youth, but Jason knew him. His older brother had moved in the same home as Jason's brothers several years earlier, and so he had some familiarity with the family.
    Drake had been part of the same agency as Jason for many years now, but I saw him only in passing, usually at the Foundation parties where he was always cheerful and appeared restless. He was removed from his grandfather's care at ten years old along with the older brother and sister. He was with the agency for several years while living there, so his history was well known. What Drake remembers about the move from his Grandfather relates to an incident at school in fourth Grade.
    He was accused of vandalizing the school bathroom. As the teachers were writing it up they threatened to call his Grandfather. He told the teacher he was scared to go home because he would get belted. They took him to the nurse who checked his body and immediately called the police who did the same. Drake never went back home.

He had been with his Grandfather since he was three years old. His only memory of leaving his parents was a hospital visit and a cast on his leg. He could not remember the features of his mother's face, and remembered his father only from his dirty jokes.

Drake's parents separated when he was very young, and like Jason, the mom brought home a boyfriend that shattered their lives. Drake was the youngest of three children. His older brother was six years his senior and sister four years. The family was very poor, but not so much that the parents could not afford to maintain their drug habit. Meanwhile, the children sold toys in front of their apartment to get money for food which they bought at a local gas station. The boyfriend was very abusive to the children and their mom. He would accuse them of stealing or telling lies followed by beatings until they admitted the wrong. He would use whatever was handy at the moment in a violent rage, an extension cord, belt, or stick; anything with which to lash out against their tender skin. During one of these incidents Drake was pulled down off a dresser in flight with such force to break his leg. At the hospital, the manner of the break combined with other bruises on his body resulted in an immediate CPS removal.

Drake was sent to a shelter, but soon placed in a foster home. His brother and sister were taken from their schools that same day and never allowed back home as well. Like Drake, his sister found a placement fairly soon, while his ten year old brother was lost in a shelter for six months. The grandfather first found Drake's older brother and was granted custody. Later, he brought the other children to his home too. The first couple of years went well, but as behavior issues surfaced and the grandfather's patience wore. Life became unbearable.

Drake suffered a very restricted lifestyle under his grandfather, where daily activities, that most children take for granted, required permission. Cabinets and the refrigerator were off limits. He was never allowed to use or answer the phone. Going outside was strictly forbidden. He had a bike, but was only allowed to ride short periods at a time in front of the house. They never were allowed to go out after school to play like other children. Television was strictly forbidden unless grandpa turned it on. They were not permitted to touch the controller. The internet did not exist. When Drake was dropped off from the bus after school he would walk home as slow as possible just to avoid being isolated in the house. They were restricted from seeing their mom. The older boy heard that she was blackmailed with providing sex to the grandfather for visits. When she refused, the children were just told that it was too hard for their mom to see them.

This mental disability exhibited by the grandfather to maintain total control affected Drake's behavior and the very core of his emotional being for years. Even the simplest chores were done in a very controlling manner. For example, one of Drake's jobs was to pick up the leaves from the yard every Sunday, literally. He was not permitted the use of a rake. He once described one such Sunday when he was out picking up one leaf at a time, when he found himself under a hail of roof shingles. He was alone. Panic overcame his common sense and he ran off. He learned later that his brother and sister were well hidden on the roof from where they threw shingles down at him. The strap was his reward later that day.

Many of the children's stories centered on their grandfather's obsession with women, so it was evident he was highly sexual. He had many girlfriends and his escapades would scare them. One of those antics caused Drake's most frightening memory that haunts him far more than the routine belting. He heard a girl screaming from his grandfather's room late one night while he was trying to sleep. He remembers the sounds being so violent he was scared for his own life. He was very young with no concept of sex.

When their grandfather went shopping he would often leave them in the car alone. Drake remembers the children sharing such stories, trying to make sense of a dark and mysterious world of which they had no knowledge, and at the same time mock the man they so feared.

Their father visited occasionally, but his drug and alcohol problem interfered with any paternal relationship. His older brother recounts times his dad would talk to him like he was one of his close adult friends. Yet the boy was not even a teenager. The dad would offer him beer and share his sexual exploits and dirty jokes. The older children lost all respect for their dad early in life. And worse, continued to live with their grandfather in fear and humiliation.

Drake and his siblings' only opportunity for peer interaction was at school and after-school programs. But when they were too old for after-school activities, they simply sat at home. His older brother once told me about an incident when he was caught watching television and was kicked out and forced to sit in the backyard thereafter until his grandfather came home from work. They were denied the whole social aspect of growing up.

Drake seemed to be the focus of this Grandfather's wrath, related mostly to school issues. The man was so self-assured in his abusive manner, that he would even redress Drake at school, taking him from class to yank his head back pulling at his hair to reprimand the boy. The belt was a standard affair. Along with the physical abuse was the ongoing emotional cruelty he suffered. Drake's most hurtful memory of his grandfather's reprisals was the hard stares from the man followed with the question:

"What were you thinking?"

Drake learned to stop thinking years before. It provided no benefit, just personal torment. Sadly, this harshly constrictive upbringing occurred under the watchful eye of Arizona's foster care system.

Years later his older sister admitted to being sexually abused in this household, and they all lived a life of physical & emotional persecution. Drake never spoke out until the incident in fourth grade. He explained years later that he simply believed this existence was normal.

His story is not unique. The very organization that removes children from abusive homes, in many cases, puts them right back in danger, not just from physical abuse, but emotional trauma as well. If they don't get hurt within a placement, they struggle their whole lives from constant moves resulting in feelings of rejection and loss. Worse, many times they are lied to about the move so that they will not make a fuss for the social worker. The adult is looking for a quick, short-term solution without any concern for the long-term trauma. The foster child's ability to form trusting relationships is innately denied. As these children mature, this paranoia of trust is rarely understood by those outside the system. This can result in years of frustration as they struggle to acquire what others seem to find with such ease: a caring relationship.

When I first met Drake I was asked to provide some advice to his current foster mom. At the time I was no longer interested in continuing in foster care. Though the agency was pressuring me to renew my license, I was very resistant. Jason was now over eighteen and I was burned out. I was in need of respite from the on-going demands of the system.

Now fourteen and a high school freshman, the little boy I remembered from foster family gatherings was greatly changed. He seemed far more nervous, high strung and absent-minded than he had appeared to me years back. It was difficult to make eye contact, as his gaze was in constant motion out of sync with his fidgeting body. He also suffered from an acute breakout and had the habit of picking at the zits until his face bled. His foster mom reported to me that he had no friends and just hung around the house with little outside interests. During the few weekends he came to visit us, Jason was very engaged and enjoyed having a little brother to mentor. They played basketball, enjoyed the pool and most especially diving. Drake was a natural athlete and took to the sport well. Jason was more than proud to be his friend and coach. Both boys seemed to fall comfortably into their roles.

His foster mom was a grammar school teacher. She was a former catholic nun who left her vows, but continued her dedication to society through teaching. I knew even less about her than Drake. She demonstrated a great interest and caring, but seemed to be obsessed with his lack of emotional responsiveness to her. It was clear early on that she demanded his love; an emotion he kept locked deep away and cut out from his external façade. As he grew into puberty he asserted himself, to which she countered with more control to maintain power over him.

A single woman with no prior experience raising children, she found herself helpless to his ever growing apathy. She was desperate for a solution. Her approach had been very pragmatic, not unlike her classroom discipline methods.

Do as you are told, meet my expectations and all will be good. If not, punishment will be doled out. The key problem was that the retribution never ended. Over time, he reduced his expectations for success, and life in general, affecting his self worth and personal drive. He just stopped caring. The more she restricted him and took things away, the less effective the punishment. Drake had evolved into a very passive resistant teenager who rarely showed emotion. This persona only aggravated his foster mom more as she continued to turn up the crank, and in so doing, he tuned up his resentment of her and his placement. They escalated each other.

Near the end of the year his social worker asked if I would take him, pointing out that Drake had shown a desire to be with Jason and me. He had descended into survival mode. I'm not sure Bret even knew to what level he had degraded due to his very passive personality. He could smile and be congenial, but deep down he was void of all emotion for himself, and therefore, for anyone in his circle.

***

Drake's Journal (14 years old)

My foster mom and I lived half a mile from the school in a new home we moved into the prior summer. I was upset that she wouldn't drop me off at school in the morning on her way to work. She made me walk. She would always yell at me about my school work. That's when all the problems started, school stuff. It just built up and up. Homework was a big focus. I played video games too much, so she put a time limit on me. Playing games helped me keep my mind off all my problems. It kept the pain away. I was always grounded, sometimes months at a time. I was always in trouble. Whenever she racked up more and more days, I just told her I didn't care. We were just screwing with each other.

I called my social worker one day and said I don't want to live here anymore. He came to the house that night and met with my foster mom and me to tell us that they had no placement for me and asked my advice. I said I liked the way the Hunter family worked when I visited. That was a place to go. But I really didn't care where, I was ready to go to a shelter, anywhere, but stay in that house another day. I wanted to blow up. My foster mom responded negatively and accused me of setting it up. She was very childlike.

After my social worker left, I went to my room to pack. I didn't know when or where they would take me. I just wanted out. We had a big argument when I was looking for my drawings and I accused her of taking them, but I found them later. I was being stupid too.

A few days later they told me I was moving to live with Bill. When I was ready to move my foster mom told me that I couldn't take anything she bought me over the past years, like my punching bag, PS2 and games, TV, stereo, and my dog Adrian. I was so intent on moving; I just didn't care. I never got that stuff.

***

Prior to his move, I attended an IEP meeting at his high school. It was the end of his first semester. The room was fully loaded with teachers and administrative staff. The message was very clear; he was simply not responsive in class, preferring to sleep much of the time. Like at home, he had learned to escape all demands made upon him. He lost all motivation to achieve beyond the minimum to survive. Once the teachers completed their reports, we advised them he was going to be moved to another school district and we needed to update his IEP accordingly. They expressed no sorrow to see him leave, and politely agreed, providing him work for some extra credit to raise those grades that were borderline failures.

When Drake's foster mom was told he was leaving her, she was infuriated. "That's what he wants," Drake remembers her telling Bret late one evening, "you can't give in to what he wants." Miraculously, my paperwork was done and my license renewed.

He was moved to us the week before Christmas, and to my bewilderment, he came with just some clothes and a broken bike, nothing more. I found that curious for a kid who just spent four years in a single placement. That year, we planned a Christmas vacation in Orlando at Universal Studios, followed by a few days at my mom's house in Tampa. The Foundation rose to the occasion and covered the costs for Drake to join us.

An amusement park environment is probably not the best place to initiate a new father-son relationship, establish household rules or help a new placement get settled in. Drake wasn't complaining. Jason was perplexed. I'm not sure he was too enthused to have a new brother thrust upon him so quickly. Jason did not respond well to change...any change. We had an inside joke at home that if Jason were burned by an iron, just change the color and he'd be sure to get burned again. He was never quick to apply lessons from one learning experience to another situation if it had even the slightest variation to the theme of the original learning incident. Any deviation to his environment or expectations would result in a negative reaction at some point down the road. Too many changes occurring too closely would build to an uncontrollable fury.

That first week set the stage. Drake was fourteen going on ten. He was hyperactive. He was classic ADHD and he was not on any medication. He never walked. Running does not best describe his form of locomotion either. It was more a combination of running, skipping, jumping, hurdling and wall climbing. He likely covered twice the distance we did, using four times the energy. Jason and I watched the entertainment with reservation, asking the question: "What had we gotten ourselves into?" Though Jason used the singular word 'Dad' not the plural 'we'.

We also learned during that week in Florida that Drake had not learned the best manners, table or otherwise, the detail of which is not necessary to divulge. Let's leave it with his personal hygiene habits were not up to standard military specification. Jason, on the other hand, was immaculate about his person and mannerisms, one of the aspects of his personality I noted while he was still transitioning from Cleo Wallace. This difference in personal habits became the center of many conflicts between the two brothers early in the relationship along with Drake's hyperactivity which was becoming a regular irritation to Jason. I was less annoyed by his antics except when he was doing somersaults in the family room while we were watching television. Even I had my limits.

The holiday cheer soon ended, and it was time to develop a family routine. Drake occupied Nick's old room where Jason and I assembled a loft bed. I thought he'd find it cool. He was content with his new digs, but was not neat. Finding the carpet soon became a family joke. He littered the floor and other areas of the house with his clothes. Where he changed, removed shoes or socks, is where they were left. When using any item, it was left undisturbed where he had last used it. Light switches and remotes had only on buttons for Drake. I also learned that he needed the television or radio on when he slept. Perhaps the background noise provided him comfort. It was a need that continues to this day. The two boys enjoyed some activities together such as springboard diving, shooting, and going to swap meets, but were otherwise distant.

Jason was a senior focused on Junior College, a slack schedule and enjoying senioritis. Drake was a freshman needing to buckle down and develop practical study habits and most important, self control and motivation. I soon learned Drake's standard operating procedure. He started strong for the first month, thereafter quietly sliding under the radar until the end of the school year when an IEP was called to address his failing grades.

After a dismal first semester of high school, I was hopeful a new environment would perk him up. His second semester started lonely as he had no friends at the new school. He moved so many times, it really didn't bother him. Drake was never driven to have lots of friends. One is sufficient.

His first acquaintance was Vera who became a long time friend. She too had a traumatic experience, though much later in life than Drake. After her parents divorced she would switch between parents weekly. She became depressed and used drugs. During this period, Vera told a friend about being molested by her father early in life, information that soon spread in the community. The dad was unable to deal with this and committed suicide. The incident affected her deeply, which impacted Drake as well. He hid his emotions, but it did not mean he had none.

With just a handful of friends, Drake kept to himself on campus. Even for lunch he rarely used the cafeteria, but preferred to be by himself outside or with Vera in the ROTC room. He learned early in life how to stay under the wire. He was mellow and apathetic in nature. His school performance was bleak, but he gave the impression he was trying. The truth, however, was quite the opposite. He was not trying at all. In this new school he soon fell back into his old habit of laying his head on the desk and blocking everyone out. His was unmotivated to work. His laissez-faire attitude grew to the extreme. Neither at home nor school could he be motivated to do any work, but did the minimum to keep adults off his back.

His style of adjusting to a new situation was to first determine the lowest level of expectations, and then work to press to lower the curve more by his lack of performance. Drake once told me that he found it difficult to do anything for which he had not already understood the complete solution. Even the simplest task could not be attempted unless he felt comfortable with the outcome.

Trauma is Forever

While Drake was discovering his new freedom, Jason was at the height of his youth. Things were going his way. Still diving but without competitive pressure, fun work volunteering at the zoo, making money as a city lifeguard, and a stable home all contributed to his new found self-esteem. He just came off a very successful high school experience and kept many of his friends. He was able to maintain a sense of stability while most young people his age were struggling with massive change moving on to college or the work place. From his perception, Drake was the only negative. With little in common, they grew apart quickly after the first few months. Though they enjoyed diving together, Drake moved on quickly to more complex dives that always evaded Jason. And his constant criticism of Drake's dive form contributed to a downward spiral in their relationship.

Jason strove for permanence at every level. He still had internal fears of loss of me and strove for a stable environment in general. I could never understand this enduring panic considering the years of turmoil we shared, as well as so many extreme adventures where we stood side-by-side. But for him, they were very real and so deeply seated that he wasn't aware of the connection between his childhood terror and his behaviors and more now, life impacting decisions.

Jason continued to suffer a major case of anxiety, fed by a history of utter helplessness. As a little boy, he never questioned his anti-social behaviors. He was justified. It was the "me against the world" mentality that tormented him.

As a young man, for the first time he had developed formal thinking, the ability to combine and integrate multiple ideas. He was also moving into abstract thinking. Simply said, he saw the world in very different terms. His role and manner of interaction was moving away from seeing himself as the center of the universe, and instead a part of a greater whole. This was a concept with which he would struggle for many more years, but he was thinking, not just reacting. Responses to triggers were less frequent. Building steam to explode was more controlled, except when it related to the foundation of his life: me.

It would take me as many years to truly comprehend this aspect of our relationship, one which Bret was all too aware. How do you break the cured cripple from a wheel chair on which he was so comfortably dependent? For both Jason and me it was to be the last great struggle for closure of a successful father and son relationship and his transition to independent living. We were both resistant, he blatantly so, me more surreptitiously. After all, I was the one pushing him out the door, while at the same time, never wanting to let him go.

Jason did move on to community college, and when not in class, he was working at the Wildlife Zoo. His energy was wholly focused on achieving his dream to care for exotic animals. During this time he expanded his animal collection. He was a regular at reptile shows in Phoenix and Tucson. Attending one of these shows usually resulted in a new resident at the house. Our place was full. We even dedicated one room to a mature male rhinoceros iguana. That was one hostile reptile. My home office also housed multiple enclosures, as did the family room and kitchen. Of course, his bedroom had always been a zoo. Though they were all caged, we had our escape stories. Drake took a large water monitor out for some sun one spring day and made the mistake of turning his head for just a moment. It was gone. Drake distributed flyers, which only heightened our neighbor's fears. A few days later my good friend and neighbor called about his dog having cornered a huge reptile in his backyard. It was the monitor.

During this same period Jason re-connected with Beth. The third time is a charm. They dated regularly, but didn't seem to enjoy common interests outside the bedroom and hanging out with friends. Early in his second college year, he begged me to allow Beth to move in. This is a common request of most boys who stay at home after eighteen years old. It is a question I have been blessed with from each and every son.

"Please Dad, she has nowhere else to go," is the common plea.

I flatly refused. However, the Foundation and I did help them get an apartment a few miles away. This was to be a major lesson for Jason to maintain emotional stability while suffering the stresses associated with independent living that was amplified by relationship issues.

Though Jason had developed a close relationship with Beth's family, he did not know her as well as he thought. While moving to an apartment, she asked him to allow her girl friend to join them for just a few days to help her overcome a recent breakup. As it turned out, the boyfriend issue was recurring every week, or at least so she claimed. This girl stayed with Jason and Beth for several months. This was not Jason's plan and he bitterly complained to me, while justifying his girl friend's kindness. He was clearly torn. Change and insecurity were the environmental constants that fueled Jason's helplessness which always resulted in a rage.

Meanwhile, Beth was at the apartment less and less, showing up only enough to plead poverty when she needed money. Jason suspected she had another boy friend, but he had no evidence other than emotional paranoia. At one point Jason approached her family about their constant financial problems only to learn that Beth was getting an allowance from her father. Once she was exposed, his respect for her collapsed. He still struggled with the fear of her loss, but was building the inner fortitude toward self respect.

One night, I dropped him off at the apartment only to get a call within the hour. He needed to be picked up. Beth had locked him out. He pounded and screamed for her to open the door. It was late in the evening and his neighbors were not understanding of the situation. In fact, one called the police. When I arrived they were already on the scene. Even with their intervention, the door did not open. I fell into my old protective habit, explaining to the police that he was distraught and emotionally handicapped. I promised to take him home with me to prevent any further disturbance. The police cars slowly left the parking area and Jason reluctantly came back to my car. He was still filled with rage over being locked out of his own apartment, though I suspect it was more about those old feelings of abandonment. All he really needed was Beth's reassurance that all was well. The next morning she behaved as if nothing was out of the ordinary and claimed she was in a deep sleep. Was she alone?

After four months and many depressing conversations with me, Jason took the initiative to break off whatever relationship still existed and asked her to move out. This was a major milestone for him. With so much anxiety over personal failure and loss, he overcame the fear and recognized he was being used.

He was alone the last two months of his lease during which time he confided in me his terror of loneliness. He kept himself busy cleaning his now established bachelor pad, no doubt a behavior he picked up from me. Keeping busy is a common method to deal with unresolved stress. Unfortunately, adding to his sense of personal disappointment, the tribulation of the past few months also resulted in failing grades at school. He was forced to abandon the semester.

He moved back home when the lease expired lost in the wilderness of a failed transition. But he was still excited about his work at the zoo. No amount of personal trauma would interfere with that one passion. While healing from this romantic drama, he met Ellen.

Meeting online is a growing trend with young people, and Jason and Ellen are members of that new-fangled club. While suffering the latest loss, he released his hurt on MySpace. Ellen was recovering from a recent breakup as well. Jason found Ellen's MySpace page and asked her to be his friend. Internet talk evolved into phone conversations. What makes this story so unique is that they had already met when they were young children in foster care. Ellen was a Foundation kid. Neither realized this common history until Ellen spoke to her foster mom about the interlude. Everyone at the Foundation knew Jason, for the wrong reasons of course, but nonetheless, Ellen's mom immediately recognized the name and description him as "that problem kid from the Foundation."

Ellen was slight ADHD, but in a comical way. Resembling Jason, she was blond with blue eyes and had light freckles above her checks. Seeing them side-by-side, they could pass for siblings, almost twins. They were beautiful people. Jason was a kind and handsome prince charming, and Ellen was very outgoing and stunningly built. In the relationship, Ellen quickly established herself as the alpha dog.

Unlike any of his previous relationships, Ellen understood his pain, though their specific foster cases and emotional problems were very different. They both entered the system very young, but Ellen had only few placement changes. The relationship grew to be very co-dependent, which in most liaisons is not the healthiest. In their unique case, however, it was core of their immediate success. The danger would be their ability to work together outside the control and support of the welfare system. Despite their strong and positive appearance, they were both very immature with an on-going sense of social entitlement.

When Ellen would get into depressed moods, snapping at Jason, he would launch to his rejection and loss cycle. Ellen would cry and wait it out. She never escalated him. They reconciled without blame. Ellen's main issue was self abuse. She felt so empty and lonely that she would cut herself. Jason typically responded with anger and disappointment, but never walked away. They were a pair who understood each other well having shared the common culture of foster care.

Leaving the Cocoon

When Drake came into our home he was extremely shy and withdrawn. Unlike his prior placement that had smothered his natural adolescent development, our home was more relaxed and open to dialogue. This lifestyle was opposite to the repressive environment of his grandfather and the strict 'classroom' atmosphere with his old foster parent. And so began his adolescent escapades. He was a newly released animal, not knowing what to do with all that freedom. Though he remained remote at home, he began to develop a fixation for girls at school. His relationships tended to be very fast moving. First dates were physical. The affairs also tended to be short lived. I later learned that he had already scene porn in his prior placement and engaged in sexual touching. His first experience was at a local outdoor racquetball court with a friend at around thirteen years old.

   Drake's first girlfriend after his placement with me was a senior who taught him to engage in erotic kissing and exploited him to engage in oral sex. She triggered his hormones into a rage. The relationship lasted only a month or so. His main item, however, was a girl named Vera. Neither of them had any friends when school began so hung together most of that year. He made a move on her the first week which transformed into a flirting relationship. And though he pursued her with a passion and had some foreplay moments; their relationship remained a good friendship, never evolving into real physical intimacy.

At first I interpreted his romantic pursuits as normal teenage behavior. But over time, I saw something very frightening. With each succeeding girlfriend, his actions grew more and more possessive, almost to the point of obsession. When he wanted to talk, he would call, and call, and call. If the girl didn't answer, he would ride his bike to her house to watch the door to confirm his suspicions that she was home and just not answering the phone. On several occasions Jason and I observed him biking back and forth several times within a single hour. During this period he was even more distant than in the past, and worse, short tempered. It was so difficult for me to gauge his emotional well being at times. He could work through a dozen sexual relationships, changing partners with little to no remorse. Then, without warning, the threat to a particular intimacy would result in constant obsessive behavior and if broken, emotional devastation. All his behaviors were centered on himself.

The summer of his freshman year provided respite for all of us. As usual with all my kids with school out, family stress was much reduced. However, his poor academic performance during the school year resulted in mandatory summer school. We had enough of playing the IEP game. He was required to bring up two grades. As always, he was quietly cooperative. Things started well enough and his teacher reported he was ahead of the other students. The summer program was computer based lessons which Drake found easy to complete. The school, however, required him to attend a set number of days, so getting too far ahead had no real value other than leaving him bored in the classroom.

One morning I was called to the school for an emergency. Drake had lit a firecracker on campus. With continued violence in schools and the growing no tolerance policies, IEP or no IEP he was off the campus for the summer. I was surprised they didn't throw him out of school. What we learned later should have been a warning about his character and future behavior pattern. Another kid brought the fire cracker and matches. He was asked to do the honors, to which he was more than pleased to comply. Drake was a follower, always ready to accommodate a peer group for acceptance. He was impulsive and did not consider consequences until after he acted.

That summer we enjoyed our traditional trip to Catalina Island with Jason and his girl friend Beth, and Nick and his wife Amber. Drake was alone. Though comfortable with girls he knew, he was not the type to chase them for a one night stand. His brothers kept teasing and pressing him to hook up, but he never did. Their banter angered Drake, and he responded by distancing himself from the group. I suspect he was more disappointed in his own lack of confidence than the gaming from the other kids. Unfortunately, that was not his most enjoyable Catalina trip with us. He felt left out since Jason and Nick both had their girlfriends. He didn't find the company of his old man much solitude. I don't blame him. What I enjoy about the island is the ambiance. I turn off my mind with a drink in one hand and a book in the other; passing the day under a palm tree staring out at the ocean. Not much fun for a teenager.

After Catalina Drake spent several days with his Uncle and Aunt at Lake Mary in Northern Arizona. During that trip he met a new girl Dana while his cousins were off riding their quads. He broke the ice with her while watching Harry Potter in the resort lobby. Dana was a cute brunette high school cheerleader. He described her as small, athletic and beautiful. He was immediately attracted. He soon learned she lived in the neighborhood of his former foster mom, not far from our home. This liaison developed into one of those obsessive relationships over the next six months.

During that summer Drake continued working with Jason to learn basic springboard dives in preparation for his sophomore year. This would be his first season on a dive team. He had a short spurt on the freshman football team in his prior placement, but it didn't last long. He found learning the play book too difficult, especially after an afternoon of conditioning work. His lack of focus was likely a result of his ADHD. Throughout the summer, I kept a close eye on Drake as it concerned girl friends, or at least I kept alert when females entered the house.

Drake entered his sophomore year with optimism. We also started him on *Concerta®* to get control of the ADHD. The medication kept his head off the desk as well as helping him to conquer his general social inhibitions. Though he had pursued a few girls with the ultimate goal of sexual intercourse, he was yet to interact with the greater peer population for the sake of friendship and school camaraderie. His self confidence was developing along with his good looks. He knew he was attractive in both physical features and personality. People were drawn to him. He was at that stage when boys stare at themselves in the mirror while tensing their chest and arm muscles. They all do it. He was no different.

One time a social worker shared with me that despite the many personality variations and emotional disabilities of children in foster care, experience demonstrated that children who survive the system best share three virtues: good looks, outgoing personality and intelligence; all genetic. Not surprising, though these personality traits are influenced for better or worse by outside forces to include the foster care experience itself. My first foster son Jason had all these traits, but at the time I met him at Cleo Wallace, none were obvious. All were veiled by drugs, depression, and a failure to thrive. Drake was blessed with good looks, but did not show an aptitude for intelligence or an extrovert personality when he joined our family. Over time, however, like with Jason, these natural characteristics, which were locked away from years of abuse, slowly emerged. He was growing into a brilliant star.

Jason, with the help of his associations with the diving community, prepared Drake to make a dramatic entrance into the high school dive scene. He was also starting academic classes with a clean slate. His misconduct during the summer was set aside in lieu of his promise of good behavior. This school worked with the youth to succeed.

His diving went so well that season that, like Jason before him, Drake was accepted on the US Dive team at ASU. He did well working with the advanced coaching staff, but was still suffering from a strong sense of poor self esteem, a block for success in any sport. He found it difficult to accept criticism in a positive way. Rather than motivate him, it achieved quite the contrary effect and knocked him down. But he so wanted to perform well that he battled this internal demon. Despite his best efforts though, his fear of personal failure, impulsivity, and lure toward distractions, led to calamity.

During a routine practice that I had not stayed to watch, I was called by the coach to come to the Tempe hospital. They said he was alright but hit the board. When I arrived he was in the ER, strapped to a back board, blood all about, under observation. Following in the footsteps of his brother Jason, he landed on the board executing a reverse one-in-a-half. This was a dangerous dive for my boys, though they have it down now. In Drake's accident, he hurled himself backward coming off the board, and so landed directly on it, head first. After several hours, he was discharged with a dozen stitches. Dealing with so many emotional issues in foster care, the medical emergencies, though distressing at the moment, caused the least stress for me.

During this period his infatuation with Dana, the girl he met that summer at Lake Mary in Northern Arizona, was also swelling. She was his first intimate sexual partner. This was another puppy love which was complicated by his compulsive obsessive behavior. He was constantly paranoid of any activity that might indicate an interest in another guy.

His obsession lasted until Christmas when they broke up. I always wondered how many relationships were damaged by his controlling behavior which certainly must have made the girls feel uncomfortable. This breakup was one of many issues that contributed to a depressing 2006 holiday for Drake. The falling out started when Dana talked about a girlfriend that was in the midst of a relationship. The girl was upset that marriage wasn't in her boyfriend's plan. Drake made the mistake of agreeing that marriage was not necessarily an outcome of a relationship (he should have read one of those books about understanding girls). Dana was appalled and stopped talking to him. He kept trying to contact her with no success. Just before Christmas her old boyfriend answered telling Drake to stop calling Dana's cell phone. It was over. He was devastated. But for Drake, such feelings were always very short in duration, unlike Jason, who could carry a loss for months.

Returning to school in January, he was depressed over his recent loss. Not so much for Dana, but being left alone. He started hanging out with new friends he had met his freshman year whom he had not associated with while dating Dana. He was rebellious about school because of pressures from the adults in his life, me included. All he wanted from school was friends, while everyone else demanded better academic performance. So he blocked it all out and went back to his old habit of sleeping in class. He also started smoking at that time with his old friends. During that period Drake's smoking was his sole motivation to get up and go to school. The smoking was a means to friendship. He would meet his friends across from the school campus, where surprisingly they never had an incident with the administration. It made him feel grown up and provided an opportunity for peer interaction which was so important to him. The signs seem so obvious now in hindsight. He always left lights and the television on at night, had friends with him whenever going out and even invited friends to spend most nights in his room. He feared loneliness.

He also started using pot at that time with his cousin. He experimented once before with a friend, but all it did was make him hungry. He thought it was counteracting with his *Concerta®*. Good thing at the time. But now the drug was helping with a deeper pain, one he didn't understand and was unable to resolve. Worse, his passive personality left us all in the dark to the problem.

After his momentous injury diving just before Christmas, he healed quickly and rejoined the team. But like school, he had lost interest. Once he shut his mind to an activity, it is over. His case worker made transportation arrangements, so I was not with him at practice. By March the coach called to ask about Drake's poor attendance. Again, parents are always the last to know. Drake was not going into the pool area, but rather, wandered around downtown Tempe. He would go get a drink at a pizza place, find a bench and just sleep. By the time I discovered this problem, he was off the team. Now I was devastated, though we soon had bigger issues to resolve.

Boot Camp

Drake continued to follow his distinct academic cycle. Each year started well, followed by a downturn. We thought diving would help him as it did Jason. We even had Jason's old coach and good friend Barb work with him. Though he participated on the high school swim team as a diver and was very talented, like Jason, he suffered from serious self-esteem issues which interfered in his progress and ability to compete. But he thrived on the peer interaction and attention. During the dive season he maintained his grades, plainly proving he had the ability to do so when motivated. As dive season came to a close in November his grades fell.

The winter/spring semester was always a disaster requiring a quick fix two weeks before school closing to salvage some credits. We reviewed and changed his EIP each year, trying to find ways to raise his head off the desk. He listened, never argued, sounded agreeable, but never achieved success. No doubt his years of being beaten down by his grandfather over school problems caused an internal distaste for the classroom environment. He certainly demonstrated by his behavior that an inert wall imprisoned his capacity for academic learning at multiple levels from childhood trauma.

After the fiasco of the prior summer we decided to send Drake to YMCA camp. He had a long history at that camp from a young age, so he was comfortable there. Jason and Drake were also clashing more and more at home so Drake was actually looking forward to be out of the house. He enjoyed two weeks, after which he was invited to stay for the remainder of the summer as a counselor in training (CIT). He took the opportunity to stay away from home and enjoy his new friends. He benefited from the activities and people he met. It was an opportunity to mature outside the structure of our home and community. He did well and was invited to return as a counselor the following summer. I was once again exhilarated, though I learned some years later that with the goodness of this CIT experience also came some negative influences. To compensate for the lack of pot available at camp, he learned to self-medicate his anxiety with such cold over-the-counter medications as cough syrup and inhaling burning herbal leaves called salvia.

Later that summer while Drake was still at camp I decided it was time to change homes. I had lived in the same place for ten years since returning from Reston, Virginia and needed a change of scenery. I had also spent those years planting a tropical forest around the house which required daily maintenance for which the kids had no interest. I was getting tired of it all. I decided to find something smaller that required less time and energy to maintain.

Don't ask why, because there simply is no explanation. I purchased a home back in our old lake community that was twice the house, twice the land and twice the price. You've got to love realtors. All kidding aside, I wanted the home and Drake was immensely impressed with his new digs. This was truly a dream home. Only one minor problem, I moved right after school started. It was his junior year and he was hyped up for school and diving. Drake was now one of the State's top divers and looked forward to a successful State Championship

After just a couple of weeks of practice, however, because I had changed homes, he was forced to move to a new school just as the competitive season was about to start. I had planned to keep him in his old school for the year, but the principal advised us to move him or he would not be allowed to dive the following year; an issue with the High School Athletic Association rules. I transferred him that week. At the new school we were told that he had to wait several weeks before he could compete; and to make things worse, the school had fall break in the middle of that period and those days didn't count. He could not complete until the end of the season, just in time to qualify for State. So throughout that whole season of his junior year he practiced without the short-term reward of weekly dive meets, he was always forced to stay behind when the team was competing. The camaraderie and team spirit that occurs during meets, Drake was now denied.

He was not a happy kid and his school work reflected his mood. I was enraged when I learned from a director at the Athletic Association that the advice from the first school was wrong. He did not need to move during the semester. Though we were misled, it was too late to move him back. He'd suffered enough change. So we sat and waited it out. In the end, he did qualify for State, but his performance was dismal relative to his ability. He was clearly disappointed in himself and took it to heart. I love diving, I enjoy watching my sons perform no matter how they rank; but that was one season I was relieved to see end.

By the middle of his junior year, we all became very frustrated with his lack of academic progress, and worse, he was hanging out with the wrong crowd. He was less interested in finishing assignments and more desirous of following the narcotics road of weed to deaden his inner pain. Though he had experimented in the past, he now found it regularly soothed all his anxiety. We called an emergency IEP to beg the school for a more drastic solution than the past approach. Most IEP meetings simply resulted in nothing more than changing objectives and allowing more latitude for him to complete assignments, which he rarely did anyway. The assistant principal innocently offered up the theory that Drake was not challenged enough and suggested moving him into a special program at the Junior College that would provide him the chance for more advanced work while getting both high school and college credits. Wow, what an opportunity. Tom and I were excited. Drake was eager for a change. I embraced the plan and went over to the college to complete all the paperwork.

He started with amazing interest. This was a new Drake! He talked about his classes and seemed generally fortified. While he was enjoying his new academic environment, I was under pressure at work to close on a major international opportunity that was expected to open new future markets for the company, so was traveling quite a bit. After a few months I noticed Drake had lost his school fervor and looked very tired. I stopped by the registrar to inquire about his grades, but was denied. After a terse rebuff and request to see the supervisor immediately as he was underage, I was handed a printout. He had been dropped from his classes. I charged over to his counselor at the college who was responsible for all the high school kids in this special program. She was dumbfounded, but promised to contact the professors and call me the next day. It was confirmed and no one had a clue, accept the professors who simply wrote him off, literally.

A college campus represents greater freedom and less structure which was clearly the opposite of what Drake needed to be successful. How could the school administrators and IEP specialists have missed such a basic issue? IEP's may work wonders for the physically handicapped where issues are more clearly defined, but for emotionally disabled students who confound the best psychologists, not so much. I have had limited success with IEPs for my foster children other than the federal protection it provides to prevent the administration from throwing them out of school.

That same week I noticed his eyes were blood shot and he acted very moody. Jason and his girl friend, who were often at the house, reported to me one night that he smelled of pot. When I inquired, he angrily denied it; attacking me on the 'trust' issue.

Marijuana was to be a challenge for our family. Here I am a foster parent with no prior history of use or interest in narcotics. I bring a child into my home with a hereditary history of drug abuse. In Jason's case, he turned against being a user, learning from the horror of his past. Drake took the opposite tack. He embraced it, and as I would learn later, so did his whole family. When he would visit his sister in college, she would show him her stash. While visiting his older brother in town, they would smoke together. Weekend trips to his uncle were opportunities to smoke with his cousins. Some of his friends actually were allowed to use the stuff at home with their parents. Where was I living all these years? He was engulfed by the influence of pot. I was stupefied by his endless attraction to it. Foster children bring more than just emotional baggage; they can bring illicit behavior and threaten the tranquility of your home, if not its very security.

Several meetings with Tom and a drug test confirmed our fears. With the truth out, Drake also admitted to having a sexual relationship with a twenty-five year old student from the college. He was still only sixteen for god's sake! I was overwhelmed with anger and grief. This behavior pattern had just gone on too long. I marched down to the school and confronted his guidance counselor with the facts. They acted surprised, especially that their program manager at the college never advised them of this impending problem. It turned out that the counselor met with all the program students once a week, meetings that Drake rarely attended. From my perspective his lack of attendance should have been a red flag to the school administration.

How he got involved with an older woman was most astonishing. It started the very first week school began. He first met her in one of his classes. She was seated next to him, though he never engaged a conversation until about the third class session. After some small talk, Drake asked her for a ride to school the next day. He was hitting on her and looking for an opportunity to get her away from school. That morning she picked him up at the house, they stopped for breakfast at IHOP. That is when he first discovered she was a smoker, which encouraged Drake into this habit more than his prior experimentation.

After this incident, they were friendlier toward one another which did not go unnoticed by other classmates. She drove him home after school that day and Drake invited her into the house to watch television. Our dog Nala was very excited by a new person in the house and jumped around her. At one point the dog sniffed at her crotch to which she responded: "We know what she wants."

He got the hint and made a move on her by getting physically closer and kissing her. She then asked his age and was shocked to learn he was only sixteen. She stopped kissing him, but did not create any physical distance. She shared her concern about getting into trouble having a relationship with someone so young, but Drake convinced her it was safe and she would not get into trouble. Drake then asked her to his room. Though sex was not discussed, they both understood the meaning of the conversation.

Drake put on some music and they both undressed. They had no shame or fear. They joked about how no one in class would ever guess about the extent of their relationship, especially after only two days of a casual friendship. She soon left before I returned home from work. This relationship continued the entire time Drake attended Junior College.

By the spring of 2007 I had a high school student who lost all credit for the semester, on drugs and engaging in inappropriate if not outright precarious sex. The Foundation and I agreed he needed a wake-up call. No one wanted to traumatize him more than what he had already suffered throughout his childhood, but his current behavior was spiraling out of control, putting his future, not to mention his life, at risk. It agreed he required treatment away from home.

Once decided, the hard question was where to place him. Beds are not conveniently waiting empty for everyone's unplanned crisis. I'd been through this before with Jason when he was moved to residential treatment years back. When the decision was finalized and the facility arranged, reality hit. Many of the emotional fears I suffered when Jason was moved, rose to the surface. It all worked out in the end for Jason, which I kept repeating again and again. So Drake would be alright as well. This was in his best interest.

For a parent, foster or otherwise, the most difficult emotion to manage is guilt. You just can't help to blame yourself; no matter how much you rationalize the kid made the incorrect choice, wandered off the righteous path, and must now pay the consequences. No matter how harsh your reaction seems at the time; no matter how much you the parent hurt, you must charge forward. This was not the first, nor would it be the last time I would suffer this trauma.

After a couple of weeks of research, Tom discovered a facility on the other side of town. Tom was unavailable the day Drake was scheduled to move, so we went to the intake with his old social worker Bret. I had no expectations other than my experiences with Cleo Wallace and The New Foundation with Jason. When the location was described, it sounded very familiar. I later learned the facility, known as Canyon State Academy, was housed on the property formerly known as the Arizona Boys Ranch. How small is our world. When I first arrived in Arizona in 1983, I worked at the Boys Ranch as a relief house parent for several months while job hunting. When we arrived in the parking lot, I experienced déjà vu.

The facility had two programs, shelter for short-term placements and a high school program for long-term residents. Drake was assigned to the shelter program. As we sat in a small conference room off the lobby completing paperwork with an intake counselor, I was overcome with a sense of regret. My heart went cold. He was not coming home with me that afternoon. They asked lots of questions to which Drake answered in his evasive fashion. He maintained his cool, though I noted he was very anxious, twitching and taping his feet and hands about, mechanically picking at his face, head down. He was slouched in a chair, a woolen cap pulled tight over his head to keep his long, wild hair in check. He was advised of his rights, then asked to sign some papers and we were done. It was quick and clinically dry.

What next, I thought? I was preparing myself to help him settle in. But the separation was abrupt. As we left the room, a stocky man, dressed like a typical coach with stretch pants and a polo shirt, met Drake and led him away down a hallway. I waved goodbye as he partially turned back, looking over his shoulder toward me. At that instant, I sensed his panic as if he were holding on to me, his eyes filled with terror. For Drake, it was a significant moment in his life. Leaving the building I saw small groups of youth walking in step, stopping every so often to do calisthenics. This was a boot camp operation.

I was quiet on the drive home. Bret, who coincidently was with me the night we took Jason to both Banner Hospital and TNF, understood my difficulty with loss and gently assured me. But, he also suggested that I assess my own feelings. If I really didn't want to continue with the kid, now was the time to make that decision; I didn't have to take him back. I immediately went on the defensive. I spoke about my commitment to him. I would never turn my back on him; that was flat immoral.

I never told him that I loved him. That word just never seemed appropriate with Drake. He always appeared so mature and aloft. But I cared deeply. I could think of nothing else that first week he was gone. My thoughts flew around my head like a tennis ball. Did I want him back home? My feelings were so very confused. He was all so distant. Could I remember a warm embrace? But he was already fourteen when he joined our family, I didn't expect he needed lots of physical affection. He never addressed me as Dad in conversation. People who spoke with him about his feelings towards me always reported back how positive he described our relationship. I remained perplexed. I spent many sleepless nights working the puzzle for which I had no solution. There were still so many unknowns. He spoke so little about his activities, and less about his past. He was an enigma.

Not to be defeated, I contacted Tom and asked to visit with him as soon as possible. To my surprise, an appointment was scheduled within a few days. As it turned out, because he was in the shelter program, the social worker had extraordinary power to set-up meetings at any time. I learned later that visits for the mainstream children were limited to twice a month at which time all the children would be brought to the cafeteria to meet with their families. It resembled the waiting area of a train or bus station. Dozens of conversations melded together into hollow noise. There was no attempt at privacy.

My first meeting with Drake felt very uncomfortable. I was still hurting from the self imposed guilt of allowing this to happen and worse, from questioning my own feelings and motivation in regard to fathering Drake. I was even questioning my honesty in the relationship. Was the social worker right? Should I walk away now?

***

Drake's Journal (16 years old)

When I first was told to go away I was compliant with everything. I wasn't really scared till I got there. During the trip in the car I was imagining what it would be like, a boot camp or residential place. When I got there it looked like a military school cause of all the land, grass and cottages. When I started asking questions at the intake about what I could bring, they told me I couldn't take anything with me but shampoo. I couldn't take my bag of clothes that I packed. I was anxious, but otherwise detached.

After my dad left, I assumed I would see him the next day. The staff took me to a room and gave me P.E. clothes and washing basics and asked me to change out in that room. I was then escorted to my new home, a group cottage. As soon as I walked in the adult in charge warned me that they don't deal with crap here and after the first offense, I would be punished.

If I did anything physical, I would be managed to the ground by a de-escalation team, meaning they would tackle me to the ground until I calmed down. I told him I didn't have that problem.

At that point I was in a daze and despondent. I felt depressed I went to dinner with my group. I tried to keep to myself. I didn't want to talk to anyone. After the meal we all went back to the cottage. We always sat quiet for long periods of time in the group room. No one was allowed to talk or move hands or feet. We had to keep our hands on our lap in a diamond shape, heads forward. We were allowed later to have some free time to draw or write letters. Bedtime was 8:00. I was still trying to be the tough guy that first day.

I lived a very strict routine at Canyon State Academy. The second day we had group, each of us were asked to talk about what we were thankful for. I was last. I broke down and asked to leave with a staff person who calmed me down. I thought I was there for good, that I would never see my dad again.

***

I was led to a tiny room, just big enough for a small table and two metal folding chairs. The walls were bare; the place felt cold and bleak. I waited, impatient, nervous and insecure about the event unfolding. Drake arrived in the academy P.E. clothes, burgundy colored shorts and a white T-shirt. His hair was still long and unruly which looked all the worse with his head bowed low. He sat down. As our eyes met I again sensed his panic. His legs were shaking. He was as uncertain as me. As we spoke he broke a smile. He reassured me he was alright, but wanted to know how long he had to stay. He seemed to think that it was my decision, but I assured him it was not. All was in the hands of the Foundation and the case worker at the academy, whose decision would be based on his progress and attitude over the coming weeks.

After resolving his immediate concern that he was not staying forever, he drove the conversation to his work on becoming a better person. He shared a letter he had just started that addressed his issues and plans for improvement. He was going to send it to me. The manner in which he spoke appeared genuinely repentant. I felt the dim glow of burning amber. Did Canyon State breech the wall or at least open a hairline crack? It was a short meeting, but we did accomplish an important milestone. We assured each other that the relationship was worth salvaging. He was scared. I was anxious. I was grateful for that opportunity to immediately re-engage with Drake. Had I been separated from him too long in the beginning of his 'incarceration,' I'm not sure how his placement with me would have concluded.

So often the foster care system leans on the side of conservatism, following the standard policy of separation from prior relationships while the foster children get settled into new situations. Risk management will always take precedence over humanity. It is very painful for all parties and I really question the long-term effects on the youth in terms of their ability to form healthy trusting relationships the rest of their lives. In solving a short-term need, the system creates life-long trauma and antisocial behavior patterns. I needed the encouragement to work it as much as he did. Seeing him face-to-face was the strongest motivation I could have received. No amount of therapeutic dialogue could have achieved that same objective so quickly, efficiently, and with as much power. I was committed in both heart and mind. We were both given the gift of hope.

During the weeks that Drake was working to understand his behavior, develop self management skills, and discover a sense of purpose; I was preparing for his return. Summer was upon us and I didn't want Drake sitting at home. If I learned nothing else, it was the value of busy hands. He had recently completed all his certifications for life guarding, and in fact had a job offer from the YMCA just weeks before being committed to Canyon State. That opportunity was lost. Tom and I had been pressing him during the school year to take a counselor position at the YMCA camp in Prescott where he had a very successful summer the prior year as a CIT. He was very resistant, not wanting to leave home. While away at Canyon State, however, he had a change of heart. Being away at camp for the summer was looking very attractive compared to his current situation! From my perspective, it would provide a growth and leadership opportunity; a continuation of his current work. Tom contacted the YMCA camp coordinator in Phoenix who remembered Drake and wanted him to return anyway, more so when they learned he was a certified lifeguard. So things fell together easily.

Meanwhile I continued to visit on a regular basis. When I arrived he always greeted me with a long bear hug. This was new! What happened to that very reserved, 'don't touch' persona? This was the son that would always move to a safe distance if I sat next to him on the sofa watching television. Wide boundaries were a key ingredient of his personality. It was unmistakable. Something was changing.

The Canyon State staff routinely reported back to me regarding his behavior. They were impressed at how he stood out as a model to other troubled youth. He was promoted quickly to leader earning many privileges. We learned that he did well under structure. He proudly advised me of his new position during one of our meetings which always started with that big bear hug.

Our conversations always centered on how things needed to be different, more structured with less defiant behavior. I especially wanted him to recognize that his passive resistance was as painful to me as a screaming tantrum. We needed communications, even if it escalated. His quiet character that had shielded his oppositional behavior would no longer work for either of us. Also, an all important issue he needed to confront was his lack of empathy for others.

One appointment coincided with the standard school visitation period, so we met in the cafeteria amongst, what seemed at the time, a hundred other people. I waited at a large table, partly occupied by another family deep in conversation about personal matters. I was lost in my own thoughts, impatient for Drake to be escorted for our visit. My senses peaked immediately upon seeing him. His hair was cut! Understand that all the children in the school program had military style near bald cuts, but the children in shelter had a choice. After all, they were not part of a long-term residential program. Some in fact, were just being housed waiting for a foster home. Drake loved his long hair. He was animate about this being his property to control. Was he trying in his own remote manner to tell me he was giving up control to me? That he was ready to come home to be the kid, not the parent?

Drake was behind the maturation curve in his understanding and acceptance of social norms, rules and regulations. All his actions were impulsive reactions to an internal need for instant gratification with no concern for others. This resulted in a serious behavior fault that could easily lead to sociopathic behavior as an adult. No amount of therapy could solve the problem without the mental ability to connect the dots. He needed to want the help, engage in the help, and have the cognitive ability to comprehend his place within a greater community. He needed to discover for himself that these issues existed and were a danger to his well being; then work hard to find the tools within himself to address it. His stay at Canyon State was not an instant solution, but it absolutely opened the door for his introspection into his behavior and how it affected his life.

As planned, Drake was discharged from Canyon State with high expectations for a rehabilitated life. He had learned his lesson. He was motivated to succeed and was already talking about finishing school and going to college so he could have a meaningful career. I took him to camp that summer with a renewed spirit for both of us.

While he was working as a counselor under the cool pines, I was working to get him accepted in a private school for the following academic year. I was totally disenchanted with the public high school by this point. We could not afford another failed year. I applied to several schools in Phoenix, but one after the other denied his entry over different issues. In desperation, I spoke with the principal at St. Mary's which had a reputation for supporting a diverse population, not just the elite. The principal was intrigued with his case and agreed to meet with Drake to determine a plan of action.

I drove up to Prescott to bring Drake to this all important interview. He went in alone and after nearly an hour, reappeared with a calm smile. He was accepted on probation. It was also decided he would enroll as a junior, repeating that year so he would have two years at St. Mary's to build a strong academic foundation. As we left the school, I asked him how he succeeded in the interview. He simply replied:

"I'm smooth like that."

The next major hurdle was to petition the Athletic Association for a waiver to dive for the new school. The rule is that student athletes must wait out one year after transferring schools unless they can demonstrate a hardship. This rule was instituted to discourage drafting high school level athletes. Going from public to private school is an uphill battle. Drake presented a good case and was granted the petition on the grounds he was changing schools to improve his ability to succeed after multiple failures in the prior school. Though people have had varying opinions about these athletic unions and their management policies, I found the people I dealt with very understanding and well meaning. Though they never promised any hope for our case when I discussed the problem, I was regularly reminded that their purpose is to support the youth in education; not to develop world class athletes. They were not in business to cause emotional trauma or deny a student a future. For Drake, the road was paved. It was left for him to start the engine and drive within the lines we defined.

First Love

With no children at home that summer, it was easy to arrange routine visits with Drake at camp in Prescott. After so much turmoil, I wasn't leaving anything to chance. I was going to be more attentive to his behavior and mood swings. I was committed to be proactive; attentive to any sign of trouble. This was to be a difficult objective due to his veiled personality. The YMCA offered him a unique opportunity at leadership, an important first step after Canyon State. Throughout the summer I kept in touch with the camp director for regular reports of his performance, and was reassured that he was an outstanding counselor. I soon dropped my guard. I could finally relax and enjoy his company without that typical anxiety of 'when is the next shoe going to drop.'

While Drake was away at camp, Jason was busy lifeguarding at the local city pool and was working hard on independent living skills with his new girlfriend Ellen. Though their apartment was only 20 minutes away, it was a start. Aside from the usual challenges of apartment living, their greatest issue was keeping nearly a dozen reptiles, two cats, a dog and his circus of sugar gliders. The place stunk, though not as badly as his first apartment with Beth where he raised baby ducks he found by the zoo. That was outright disgusting to the non-initiated, though to a dedicated animal lover like Jason, it was acceptable.

As a side note, those ducks are now happily waddling about in our community lake. He is a proud father.

With Jason again on his own, weekends were painfully quiet. I enjoyed the lack of daily drama, but missed the busy household. Occasionally, I would visit Drake to reassure myself all was well. The drive north to camp is pleasant and a desert person doesn't need much encouragement to find an excuse to leave the hot valley for a weekend in the cool pines of Prescott. During the first month he was always very pleased to see me, and like any of the campers he managed, looked forward for an opportunity to get out of camp and go to town for a good meal. We talked and enjoyed the time together. After we said our goodbyes, I would hang around at the main lodge to watch him manage the little campers. I was so proud. As a parent, I always saw him as a child without a rudder; and now he was directing chaos into order. Impressive!

By July change was in the breeze. I would arrive at camp only to be told that Drake was in town with friends. This happened several times which was most disappointing after driving two hours to see him. On one occasion I chased him down in town, but we had little time together as the group had made plans to see a movie that afternoon. Well, at least he was socializing with his peers. He seemed happy, blissfully so.

The next trip to camp I called ahead to coordinate better and get a commitment. When I arrived he was waiting for me at the dining hall with some friends.

"Bill, is it OK if my friends come along?" He was fully energized, his whole body colorfully animated.

The group dispersed to get last minute items while I sat under the overhang of the cabin style porch. It reminded me of my days at Scout camp not so long ago. Watching a bunch of children having a water pistol fight, my attention was caught to one in particular. He was very outgoing, rambunctious and talking up a storm. Outwardly, he seemed to be a normal young teen. Drake scolded the boy over something now forgotten as he came up to the dining hall.

During lunch in town Drake introduced me to his friends, one in particular named Lynn. As the children talked at lunch, I was amazed at their stories. Only one could say they led a normal boring life, the rest came from broken homes, foster care or some other childhood tragedy. Lynn spoke, not of herself, but of her little twelve year old brother she loved, but at the same time feared. Her eyes spoke of his misery and her sense of hopelessness.

She spoke about her family's struggle with him. About his adoption into their family through an emergency placement and how his behavior had caused her parents so much pain. Her voice trembled with deep concern for her mom, who she described as always in panic mode. Her brother was a child who suffered profound sexual abuse and many placement changes in the system. He joined their family four years earlier at nine years old. Afterwards the mother started foster care training, but not the dad. When they were advised that both parents were required to be licensed to maintain the placement, the husband had other obligations and could not commit to complete the training at that time. Their only option to keep the boy, so they were told, was to commit to an adoption.

A few weeks before the adoption court date, the parents were given his records, a large stack of papers which they did not immediately read in detail. His horrific abusive past was never discussed or any specific therapeutic plan offered. These dark secrets were tossed into a filing cabinet, not to be seriously reviewed until well after the adoption.

Things went seriously wrong when he started puberty; and though the family had a therapist working with them at the home for some time, the focus was on the symptoms and cultural adjustment issues; keeping the core problem hidden well below the surface. The therapist later told this family that she could not address his deeper sexual issues because he would not talk to her about them. They were a good family-oriented traditional Mormon household. They embraced him as such and raised him in their faith. Due to his behavior and in part to their culture, he was kept close to home with little social peer interaction outside church members. The more he acted out and rebelled; the more he was restrained and contained. The few times I spoke with Lynn that summer, the topic about her brother always surfaced. She always conveyed the worry about his future with her family and about her parents. Her love and loyalty seemed torn.

Her interaction with Drake was spirited, but guarded. This relationship was to play a turning point in our lives. It was several more weeks before I realized a love affair was blooming. She was very shy with a heart of gold. She spoke softly, rarely speaking a critical word about anyone. Her voice was calming and her gaze embraced you. As the summer came to a close, I learned that Drake had fallen in love with Lynn. So began my mission down a rocky path.

Through Lynn, I was to become entangled with her younger brother named Michael. The one I casually observed that summer playing around the Dining Hall at camp. This child took me deep into the horror of the lowest bowels of social behaviors. I experienced firsthand the impacts of inhumanity to the human body and mind, and how such degradation splits the soul, ever struggling between good and demon. It taught me the difficulties for these hurt children to navigate upward toward normalcy.

Camp ended. Their relationship did not. Almost every weekend I found myself driving Drake to Lynn's home in Casa Grande. Her parents were warm at the very first introduction. I also met a younger sister about Michael's age who appeared very shy and distant. I learned later that she used her closet as a sanctuary, a safe haven from her adopted brother.

In the meantime, school at St. Mary's seemed to be going very well. Drake was on the dive team, though the only member, forced to find his own dive coaching separate from the swim team practices. But at least he was with them during competitions. And to their credit, the students did put out an effort to welcome him into their group. At one event I remember a small cheer group with poster boards rallying behind the boards. But he was distant, rarely sitting with the team. He preferred to hang out with other divers behind the boards. Occasionally Lynn would show up. As you might expect, those meets were not his best. He was focused on the wrong passion. Perhaps the high blood pressure in his lower body put him slightly off balance when performing the dives.

Though his grades were good, I rarely saw him do homework on weekends; those were reserved for the only person in his life, Lynn. After a few visits down to Casa Grande, the family crisis there became apparent. During the long drive home I listened intently to Drake talk about his love for Lynn and fun activities with the family. I was so happy for him. He found more than just a girl friend, but a family that cared for him and he appreciated there interest at a personal level. But at the same time he would always end our conversations with a sad comment about Michael.

He would cry out:

"Poor Michael, the kid just seems to be alienated from everyone else, always getting yelled at, punished in his room or left doing chores alone. They will share food from each others' plates, but never his. He can't win. His mom always picks at every little thing. We can't even have dinner without this going on the whole time."

He also shared with me how he heard Michael cry out at night: strange and eerie sounds. Something was very wrong, but Drake was afraid to speak out in fear of damaging his relationship with the family, and his ability to continue seeing his love. After a few of these weekends, he asked me to speak with the parents and share my experience about Jason. Her parents more than agreed. They were desperate for resolution. Their title 19 adoption was failing. The problem was that such an adoption operates like foster care without the social worker. The family is wholly dependent on the mental health care system for appropriate care.

That day I was invited to dinner to discuss Michael; a relationship began that went well beyond a neighborly acquaintance. I soon became an intimate friend. After the usual warm welcome you expect from a Mormon family, I was seated by a kitchen island while the whole family was busy preparing the meal. It all looked chaotic to the casual observer, but to a chef, all was orderly. They maintained a normal conversation with me as their hands were busily pealing, chopping and mixing food. Michael was at the sink, struggling to keep up with all the pots, pans, and utensils flying at him to clean. I soon understood what Drake had been describing.

Just walking into the house one could feel the tension; most expressly between mother and son. Battle lines were drawn. Both wanted total control of the other. The mother openly admitted she was burned out. She couldn't even hug him anymore. For this, he was required to ask permission. The father was distant as well. He found hugs from Michael to be very uncomfortable from early on. His issues revolved around his own past and a need to protect his wife and daughters from what he perceived was an ever growing threat as the boy continued to grow into a teenager.

It was during this first meeting that the family disclosed his profound sexual trauma which occurred between three and six years old. The details would sicken the most experienced social worker. To compound the problem, his birth mother was an alcoholic and drug user during the pregnancy, and also suffered from her own psychiatric conditions. Despite this extreme history and evaluations done back as early as six years old; little had been done for Michael outside of standard therapy sessions. When the family adopted Michael, they and the community were vulnerable to a behavior pattern that was evolving from this past trauma of which he and his parents had the least understanding.

As I became engulfed by their family crisis, I was hoping for a case worker intervention. From my perspective they were the family's salvation. During one of my visits to the Foundation, venting about Michael's issues with the family, the clinical supervisor had suggested doing an intake, another worker at this meeting advised her he was out of their district so it wasn't possible. But I latched onto her every word.

I learned, though too late, of my lack of genuine understanding of his true therapeutic needs and harsh structural requirements to support his lack of self control. As appalling as his birth parents' crimes and harsh treatment, the foster care system fared no better in the lack of mental health therapy provided to him. His chance for a normal life may forever be crippled due to this deficiency early in his development.

As he settled and worked to manipulate his environment, a survival technique learned through years in the system, he and the family grew at odds. He could rage with such violence that he would punch the tile floor until his knuckles bled. He tried to strangle his mom and once even put a knife to her throat. She spoke of her fear of physical harm which drove her to dedicate time to karate classes. At this point, she could still throw him to the floor; and at times, she did just that. She described one particular incident where she had him on his stomach, arms crossed in front of his head. He freaked. I explained to her that was likely the position in which he was raped as a little boy.

At this time I also shared with them my own childhood incident, discussed in an earlier chapter, to help them better understand how certain positions and sounds can trigger the horror of his past which includes total helplessness at the hands of a stronger, more powerful person. I wanted them to understand the use of physical force would only reinforce the message to him that control is based on strength, a lesson he would likely use when he grew up into a young man. Behind his cute exterior was a powerful demon in hibernation.

After dinner the family cleared off the table with Michael back at the kitchen sink. Everyone sat down to play games and Michael invited me to chess. His father quietly warned me that his son was very competitive and does not respond well to losing. Our game lasted into the night, but ended in a stalemate. He was actually a decent player. Drake and I took our leave and received the traditional Mormon hug goodbye. What I received from Michael was far more. He held me very tight as if he were my own son saying goodbye before a long trip. He tilted his head back and looked deep into my eyes. It was one of those experiences you carry with you for many years. His eyes were wide and vacant. He was pleading for help!

After a few of these visits, I realized that other than school, Michael was under total confinement. He could only play or ride his bike in front of the house. He was required to ask permission even to use the refrigerator. Going to the basketball court in their housing community required a partner the family trusted that would take him and bring him directly back home. His punishment for violating any rules ranged from a spanking with a spoon to long periods in his room. His father's description of the rage and flee behavior was familiar to me after years with Jason. Their response, however, was very different from mine. They nailed his window shut and locked his door. Drake's reaction when he witnessed all this during his weekend visits was more than superficial concern. A deep pain rose to the surface. He was now an observer to the life he once lived with his grandfather. Was he burning inside with rage?

I asked about the availability of respite, to which they quickly advised me that he had worn out his welcome in numerous weekend placements due to his inappropriate behavior. Even in a group home respite, where children are typically under constant supervision, he presented problems. On one such short-term stay he had sexual contact with an older teenage blind girl. It is hard to know the truth in terms of who was the instigator or perhaps more fittingly the predator. In the end, she let him grope her breasts and rocked against his groin area. To this and other stories the parent's relayed, I naively interpreted as normal sexual exploration or saw him as the victim. To the untrained eye, he seemed so childlike with his deep blue eyes and angelic features that reflected innocence and purity.

To help relieve the family stress, I offered to take Michael in my home for weekend respite. Two weeks later on a Friday afternoon, I dropped off Drake with Lynn and returned home with Michael. Both were pleased with the deal. Drake was more comfortable in the home without all the tensions. And freedom rang for a young boy whose mother had held his reigns very tight for years.

That first visit with Michael was one of the most shocking in my twelve years of foster care. Never before did I experience a kid who was so sexually open in terms of discussion topics. I scarcely new this kid other than at the level of an acquaintance, and he was expressing an interest in taking a shower with me, using the approach that it was proper for a dad to take a shower with his son. I was stunned. My quick retort was that I was not his father. It took a great effort to keep him off topic. He even had the boldness to ask about my sex life and how I performed.

When not asking questions about sexual subjects, he was complaining about life at home. These grievances were of great interest. I listened intently so I could report back to his mom and dad. When in the spa one night I noticed a large bruise on his side. When I inquired, he shook his head and shrugged his shoulders. I assumed it was the result of one of those physical altercations with his mom. My attention to this mark of humiliation caused hurt at that moment. I saw it clearly in his expression. I eagerly returned him home Saturday evening.

After that very first weekend, it was clear to me he had significant issues which I shared with the family and Drake's social worker, who at this point had evolved into our family mentor. Jason's mental health case worker once shared with me that he had asked one of the support staff at her agency if she were a virgin. He seemed so innocent, but his questions were not. The subject matter was very mature, though they came off as very ignorant of sex in general. It all added to my confusion of his intent, if he had any at all. Was he driving for sexual gratification? Or had he found the ultimate negative behavior for attention. Regardless, within the social welfare system, sex is a topic that will initiate the total risk management process.

But here is where I failed my family and myself. I walked into a major behavioral crisis that had been evolving for years, trying to help a family with an issue of which I had no experience or knowledge. I understood his humiliation and pain from my own childhood experience, but not the reactions and behavior issues. I broke with my friend immediately after he was raped, so I don't know how he dealt with it all. Their approach was total control and manipulation. My approach was listening, understanding, and observation. At the time, that was easy for me to do. I wasn't the responsible parent. I saw lots of behavior issues with Michael, and unfortunately, I was unprepared in their proper management. I discussed them openly with many professionals, but received no specific guidance in terms of parental management. As critical as I felt about his parents' control method, I soon learned the need, both to protect him and the community in general.

I worked to support the family by participating in IEP's with his school. I had a wealth of experience with my own foster kids dealing with the public school system in the fight for the rights of emotionally disabled students. His initial IEP was dismal at best. With help from a state support agency, we moved forward with a much better defined plan.

I also researched processes and personnel who had authority within the mental health system through my many contacts at the Foundation, in an effort to bring attention to the situation and press for support services. Through this experience I learned how process driven our mental health care system operated, and how, like any major corporation, inside selling was key. Without an advocate inside the system, foster/adoptive parents have little hope to gain the necessary services to bring about positive outcomes. When I contacted the State Adoption Subsidy Board about the dilemma, I was astonished with their response: 'Our job is to contract others, not manage the problems.' The more people I called to find help for this family, the more fingers were pointed in various directions. I soon discovered all the same dead ends the family experienced over a number of years.

During the fall he spent more and more time with me and I could sense the distance growing with his adoptive family. At one point, his parents disclosed to me their concern that Michael may have assumed his parents were transitioning him to live with me. His experience was that each time he had weekend visits with another family; it was followed by a placement change. They assured him this was not the case and that I was simply helping as a friend of the family.

During those weekend visits he spent his time playing around the house. During each visit I would plan a special activity such as a trip to the local zoo, a movie, or hanging out at the local skate park. Like Jason, he loved to poise for the camera wherever we went. During this period he had no interaction within my neighborhood or community other than Sunday church services.

Michael was a chatter box. He was very open about his past and present situation at home. He talked with me about his growing anger at his confinement at home and the physical aggression he felt from his mom. The one topic that always escalated Michael to anger revolved around his desire for contact with his birth family.

"Why wouldn't my mom (adoptive) send the letter I wrote to my mom (birth) if she let me write it?' He would complain to me.

Apparently, birth family relationship issues were never closed prior to the adoption, at least in his mind. Once adopted, the new parents had no interest in developing anything further with Michael's birth family. They wanted his attention and emotional effort focused on the new placement. Michael, on the other hand, did not want to surrender his prior relationships with his birth mom or siblings. Apparently, his adoptive mom allowed him to write a letter for therapeutic purposes, but for Michael it was all very real. He wrote a letter at my home to express his anger over this issue:

I've been very pissed off about you manipulating me about 'you can write the letter to you know who' and then not sending it. When we were at the judge's court we agreed that I had no physical contact, but I never agreed to no contact at all. We agree that I could not write to my mother and family. That promise meant you would send it too, not just write it. Because what's the point in writing without sending it.

In my heart you're not my mom anymore. That's how I feel. Dad said to me if I don't love you then I don't love him. It's pissing me off that I can't love him because I don't love you. I can't believe you would manipulate one that way. Why the hell would you not let me write and send the letter to my mom and family? From now on you're just a friend and I will always sleep outside forever till I'm old enough to find my family and so that's what stands.

This was just one of many issues layered one atop another with which this boy struggled. He wrote a journal of letters to his parents at my house to release his anger. He asked that I not share them at the time. I think he was expressing himself for my benefit more than his own therapeutic needs. He wanted pity in the hope it would lead him into a new placement. He did not understand the true meaning of adoption. He was still wired for foster care.

I was introduced to the birth parent crisis one weekend when I arrived in the midst of this battle between Michael and his mom. I had arrived at their home to pick him up and found myself deep in a cauldron of boiling water. Tempers were still flaring and the initial reaction from his parents was to keep him home as punishment. Drake was distraught. He was now accustomed to Michael not being at the house during his weekend visits.

The prior day Michael discovered that his letter written a long time past was still never mailed. He was enraged and escalated toward violence. He had been waiting, hoping for a response that never arrived. Later that evening he took his blankets to sleep out on the patio, shivering against the freezing November desert night. I convinced them to let me take him as planned so all parties could calm down. Everyone needed respite from this continuing crisis. Little did I realize at that moment but I had just moved the rage from the house into my car. He pounded the seat, door, and dashboard. He was fuming mad. I'd never seen this display of anger with him. I could provide no comfort. After a while he just sat tense, sporadically shaking. When we arrived home, he joined me in front of the television and just stewed. He kept repeating that he would never sleep in his house again. It was a tough weekend.

Finally my agency recommended filing a complaint against the agency managing his health services which was also suggested by the State Adoption Subsidy Board. She was told that the person was on vacation. However, a staffing was scheduled the next week which gave hope to the family that things might change. They were desperate for help.

After another month or so of that goat rope nothing seemed to change for the better, meanwhile Michael continued to decline. All the agency could accomplish were CFT meetings, but no concrete solutions. In December I was invited to join one of his CFT meetings to describe his behavior at my home. I talked about his constant questions about sexual topics, some of which were very personal and inappropriate for a young teenager. I also described some of his aberrant behaviors such as pulling the front of his pants down for no apparent reason, hugging the dogs while straddled over them and thrusting his groin, and how on occasion when hugging me, his groin would gently rock against me. The team members seemed shocked. The parents told me later that the case worker just needed to hear it from someone else outside the family. It seemed that I brought credibility to their cry for help.

The case manager now recommended residential treatment. The psychiatric evaluation promised so often in the past now seemed of little importance. They felt that the current acting out was enough to support this recommendation. Time continued without a placement. Each week the parents would go to the agency with Michael, packed and ready to be taken for residential therapy; they returned with him in tow. He became more despondent and fearful for his future. These episodes increased stress at home and school.

Midway through December he was caught in Math class sticking his finger out his pants zipper. It was enough to get him suspended for the rest of the term. His mom's standard practice when he was suspended was for him to work chores at home during the same hours as he would be in school. She maintained a very structured home and was consistent in her management of his behavior. The stress was consuming the family. His mom was using me as a carrot more and more to maintain his compliance. She shared with me her surprise at how well it worked.

With so much anxiety, she really expected him to rage more. In fact, she started to work at triggering him in hopes that she could call the CPS Crisis Line to send an emergency team to take him to a hospital. One evening she suggested a plot to do just that. She would tell him as he packed that Friday that he could not come with me, with no explanation, even though he had earned the weekend by cooperating with her. She wanted him to rage. I was concerned. Things were disintegrating quickly and I had no desire to be a pawn. I discussed her plan with my social worker who strongly warned against it. His reasoning was twofold. It would further damage Michael, as well as put the family at risk. I relayed the message to his dad. Mom backed off the plan.

I still provided respite during his suspension and into the Christmas season. After one weekend with him, rather than drive him back home in Casa Grande, I met his family at the Mormon Temple in Mesa to see the light show. His dad met us near one of the Temple entrances and led us to his mom who was sitting on a bench with her teenage daughter snuggled close. Michael was unusually clinging that evening. I felt very uncomfortable with this behavior. Walking along the paths, I fell back from the group. Dad was in the lead followed by Mom with her daughter arm-in-arm. Watching Michael was a lesson in psychology. He went to his father, walked close and put his arm around his dad's chest. His dad did not return the affection. He would then go to his mom and 'dance' about her and his sister, trying to wedge between them for the slightest attention, to which his mom would respond with a reprimand to calm down. He then came to me in the rear. I know I hurt him that night, because I also did not respond. It was not appropriate under the circumstances, or at least at the moment I did not feel right. He did this cycle many times that evening until we departed from the parking lot. When I said goodbye, he asked what was wrong. I gave him a strong hug, but I knew he was confused and upset. It was that night at the Temple that I realized just how dependent he was becoming on my affection. It would be months before I realized the depth of his emotional needs and very confused state of mind relative to this type of physical contact.

During the holiday I also took him to see the *Radio City Music Christmas Show*. This was one of those poorly thought out great ideas. The show was wonderful, but Michael couldn't sit quiet. In fact, he does not sit still well at all, rather he fidgets. His constitution is such that some muscle or entire limb must stay in motion at all times. It was also at this time that Michael shared with me his favorite nick name of Oreo. I found that odd until he explained that was because of his choice of black and white clothing.

While I was wrestling with Michael's situation, Drake's love affair with Lynn continued to deepen. His major conflict was the need for physical love. This was not an acceptable practice in the Mormon faith. Like Catholics, the firm rule was no sex before marriage. The family managed the issue by keeping him close at hand, ever vigilant of their daughter's whereabouts. The family really did adopt him and opened up their hearts and family activities to him. I know he was delighted with their caring attitude.

Mormons are deeply religious. If the relationship was going to move beyond friendship, it was necessary for Drake to convert. Lynn, however, had implored Drake not to enter the church on her account alone. She was forever the angel. But Drake was on a path from which he could not be swung. Drake accompanied the family to church every Sunday that he spent the weekend, and even attended church locally when home. I too was attending the local Mormon Church each Sunday with Michael which was expected in my role as respite caretaker. Going to church with Michael was a chore. His ADHD was always in over drive in the pew, his legs waving back and forth profusely. For Michael, attending church was old hand. But for Drake it was a new adventure. He opened his heart to the missionaries, though his motivation was more physically driven than spiritually. I was shocked when he invited me to his baptism: The week of the event. I had no time to mentally prepare. But after so many years with Drake, I should have known better than to expect too much discussion. Why would this act be any less spontaneous and impulsive than any other in his life? Lynn's dad was the attending priest.

Without planning it, Lynn's dad and I had changed roles between families. He was accepting responsibility for my son's soul; and I was accepting responsibility for his adopted son's emotional health. Neither of us could know the difficulty we faced, though I suspect he had a better angle on it than I. Though I would not have, by my catholic tradition, pointed Drake toward the Mormon faith, I was nonetheless proud at his baptism. I also had some experience with the faith and in particular the people in this particular church in our community, where I served as assistant scoutmaster for a year. I was asked to teach a young teacher assigned as Scoutmaster the fine art of Scouting. In return, he taught me about the meaning of family and Mormonism. I did not agree with all his teachings, but left with a very strong trust in their dedication to family values. It was a church of strong faith and caring people. I could not argue his choice. Drake had made an independent decision of faith, a major step toward adulthood. It was a very moving ceremony for me and done in the presence of Lynn and her family, including Michael. Drake's judge also attended. Drake glowed that day with humility and grace.

It's a Boy

During that summer and fall, I was a complete irritation to the Foundation. Drake was turning eighteen and Jason was going to Colorado to attend college to pursue his passion to care for exotic animals. After twelve years, I was not ready to be an empty nester. I survived Jason, and Drake was moving in a positive direction, though with many hurdles still ahead. I was confident I could deal with any foster child thrown at me. The family developer promised to keep an eye out. Meanwhile, I searched data basis on my own for children that I thought would fit the bill, every so often presenting a few cases to the family developer who handled new intakes. She always responded with a kind smile, reminding me that the Foundation was already working a number of new intakes and had parents waiting in line, some who had yet to get their first placement. I was amazed by the irony that CPS complained they had a shortage of homes forcing children to stay in group homes and shelters for long periods of time, while the Foundation had anxious parents with empty beds. The Foundation talked to me about twin African American boys that they were considering placing with me, but after an interview with the children, it was determined that they wanted a black dad.

I remember a sibling pair of African American boys I discovered through an agency web page. The narrative described all the characteristics of fun and active children. The older one enjoyed swimming. I had a half acre and huge pool. Of course, they never tell you the whole truth. With this pair I did get some attention, but unfortunately the Foundation had several issues. Firstly, the children had anger problems (that would have been a cake walk compared to Jason). And secondly, they were black. This was the bigger issue as they called me in to meet with a sizeable group at the Foundation. Strange that this was an issue for the two I picked, but not for the twins they were considering several weeks earlier. I was told that my neighborhood was an issue for such a placement. I lived in a predominantly white community.

"Would they fit in," I was asked.

Did I consider the affect on our family? Did I know that taking a colored child would automatically make my family one of color and did I understand what that meant? I spoke with several mixed marriage families at my workplace for opinions. They presented very realistic issues to consider, but in the end were supportive, believing that more people needed to make such commitments. In the end, the Foundation declined. But within a week or so, they hinted that one of their kids might need to be moved and I was one family under consideration. At the Foundation family Christmas party a few weeks later, I was told to standby. A plan was in the works and they anticipated a quick transition for this youth.

I was excited. Drake was hesitant. He was not ready to share me. After all, he'd been the center of attention over the last few years. I was learning that Drake rarely engaged for my attention. Just knowing I was available provided him comfort.

Jason too was at the house almost daily. He worked at the local community pool, so it was convenient to stop over and relax in our family room most afternoons. This was an irritation to Drake and honestly to me as well. He had an apartment with Ellen. I soon discovered she too was annoyed with the amount of time he spent at the house. He was reclaiming his turf; reassuring himself he did not lose his place with me. He was still suffering fear of rejection and loss that was so profoundly hardwired at a young age. This was the very same emotional trauma that both Drake and Michael battled daily. No one was ready for a new kid in the house. Drake was comfortable alone. Michael took ownership of me on weekends. And Jason was not letting go, to which I was in denial since we had worked this issue for so many years.

Now Jason had Ellen and was leaving for college. He spoke with me sometime later that he was feeling replaced. He admitted jealousy. During discussions about a new placement, he never raised a big fuss and always ended debates with comforting words that he would support my decision. I should have listened better and perhaps inquired deeper into his vast psyche to appreciate his hesitations.

The call came. The Foundation had committed to the change in placement and scheduled an overnight visit. His name was Sam. He was middle school age.

Sam's social worker had just met with him the prior week to confirm his unhappy condition. The family had recently moved from Phoenix to Prescott, a change that did not settle well with Sam. He was also doing very poorly in school. They did not discuss a move; that was left to his foster mom. She called me the next day after telling him he was changing placements. She described a very painful talk. He was taken by surprise. Both were hurting and expressed their emotion with lots of tears. I would soon learn that this was one boy who could cry. He did not hide his emotions.

That very weekend the case worker scheduled Sam's first visit with us. By coincidence, I had already committed to Michael for a respite overnight. I rearranged schedules so the two would not conflict. I took Michael a couple of days early and brought him home just before Sam arrived. I wanted the two to meet, but not the very first visit. Sam had the right to explore the place and have total ownership of me as he was moving in for a permanent placement. Though I cared deeply for Michael's situation at this point, his needs were secondary to the new placement. Drake was excited about having a new brother, but as was normal for him, distant.

It was just before Christmas. The house was decked out in every room with a highly decorated nine foot fresh cut tree that stood brilliantly in the living room. The pine smell of the season permeated the house. Presents were already stacked high and wide. The social worker brought Sam to our home and stayed for a while until he was at ease. He was very cautious at first, maintaining a reserved behavior and manner of speech. He was very polite and seemed unusually calm. I was not accustomed to calm children, mine had all been very athletic and high spirited, and most especially Drake, who was ADHD. Sam was very different. He was composed, and completely in control. He was clearly in observation mode. He was an analyst, the complete opposite of Drake who acted on pure impulse and Jason who seemed always on reactionary mode. I was intrigued how they would relate.

Sam spent that first day hanging out around the house with Drake who found having a little brother a real novelty. I was prepared for Drake to be polite but distant, so pleasantly surprised to see the very opposite. He was engaging with Sam, almost reaching down to the younger boy's level. Perhaps he was making up for his own lost childhood of free and unconstrained play. He was ready to make up for all those years living a constricted lifestyle with his grandfather. Drake was ready to jump back and enjoy the simple carefree childhood that we all take for granted.

The plan was for Sam to stay just one night, but he soon felt comfortable and asked to stay an extra day. He did not stray from the house, but continued a playful relationship with Drake. They played video games, watched television, his favorite show being *Family Guy*, and just hung out together. They seemed inseparable at the time.

The weekend passed quickly. I drove Sam back to his foster home in Prescott to meet his current parents. They were both experienced in the foster care system. His mom was a case manager for disabled children and Dad worked for CPS. During the drive home we didn't talk much though I was formulating questions to draw out his first impressions of us, as well as seeking out information on what caused the disruption from his current home. This child was too perfect. No foster parent in their right mind would give up such an awesome kid. He was very polite and continued to maintain a distant and reserved posture. I was suspicious.

Sam had a fairly uncomplicated past as compared to most children in care. He was removed from his home at an early age due to drug abuse by his parents. His first placement was with a loving grandmother who he adored, and one of the few people he ever trusted. Sadly, she was very frail and unable to care for him too long, after which he was placed with his current foster family. His grandmother died shortly after he was moved. He had suffered loss, but did not act as if he had endured extreme physical or emotional abuse. He appeared very stable, with excellent self-management skills. His greatest hurdle revolved around security and self-esteem.

***

Foster Mom's Journal (The loss of Sam)

As we approached retirement, my husband and I talked about moving out of Phoenix to a cooler climate. In the spring of 2007, we targeted the Prescott area as it was still close enough to Phoenix to see our family. Once our 13 year old foster son, Sam, was assured that he would move with us, he seemed cheerful and talked about living closer to his sister who lived in Prescott. We discussed the move with Sam's case manager, and got approval. Once Sam was out of school, we sold our home in Peoria and moved to a temporary apartment in Paradise Valley while we waited for job transfers looked for a home. In August we still hadn't found a place, so Sam was enrolled in the Paradise Valley School District where he made honor roll for the first time. By November we found a house and moved to Prescott.

Before Sam was placed with us he rarely went outside to play and stayed inside a tiny apartment with his grandmother. When he moved in with us he never wanted to go outside, so did not make any friends. Finally, my husband realized that Sam needed permission to be a child and told him it was ok to go out and ride his bike around the neighborhood. I remember the first time he did so, he came home excited, and said he found out that some of the children from school lived nearby. After that, he still needed to be reminded to "go play", but it seemed to get easier for him. We could never figure out why the Foundation people thought Sam made friends easily. Unfortunately, once we moved to Prescott, Sam regressed.

Initially, Sam seemed excited about the move, and when his case worker visited, he appeared content. The weather was cooler, so we understood that he didn't particularly want to put up his basketball hoop, ride on his bike, or skateboard, but we began looking for activities where he could make new friends.

Then Sam's teachers started calling almost daily to say he was failing and not turning in his school work, and were more interested in socializing than listening to instruction in class. We began having family discussions regarding school which would turn into volatile squabbles, with Sam angry and tearful. He would deny that he didn't turn in work, and didn't have any answers as to why he was failing tests.

We were at our wits end. Finally, one evening, Sam admitted that he hated the school and didn't want to live here. He missed his friends in Phoenix and his school at Paradise Valley. In December, our licensing worker called to schedule a visit and I we told her what was going on. By that time, my husband and I agreed we would have to let Sam move back to the valley if the Foundation could find him a home. Things moved very quickly once the Foundation understood how unhappy we all were. They found another home right away and set up a visit for Sam to meet his new foster father and foster brother.

Typical of many foster children who have to move, Sam was fairly nonchalant and aloof about moving. Sam was to move during the winter recess right after Christmas. After caring for and loving this child for 2 1/2 years, he left big holes in our hearts when he moved away. Looking back, we believe that Sam was suffering from depression after our move.

Sam had two counselors in the past, but didn't seem to benefit from either of them. Maybe a new counselor would have helped, but no one at the Foundation suggested it, and my husband and I were so caught up emotionally that we didn't think of it until Sam was gone. We also found out after the move that Sam's father had a learning disability and terrible anger issues. As fate would have it, our wakeup call came too late. Still, we can't let go. We'll always think of Sam as part of our family.

***

Meeting his foster parents under these circumstances was uncomfortable. This placement move was all arranged through the Foundation and my understanding was the family was giving him up with his best interest at heart. But I still felt like a toad. I was taking their boy whom they cared for the last two years. They were an older couple, near retirement. They had just recently moved to a more secluded and peaceful area of Arizona in preparation for their golden years away from the fast passed and dog hot urban Phoenix climate. They were wonderful people. The mom was gracious, open, and supportive of Sam. When we entered the house, he gave her a warm hug, calling her mom. That cut me deep, but I'm glad I shared it. How these children experience the full emotional meaning of the word "mom" or "dad" is so different than the rest of us. We had a polite conversation during which she spoke highly of Sam and wished the best for him. She really did care; the emotion reflected clearly from her eyes. She was a mom. I left for the long drive home more relaxed about the entire affair, though concerned about how Sam was interpreting events that were unfolding so quickly. Sam was a dream case and the family wanted to be supportive of him even after the move. It was all too perfect.

During those last weeks, it was very difficult on Jason and me. He grew more and more possessive. I was suffocating; and as such, kept pushing him away. My behavior only agitated him more; raising all his old fears of loss to the surface. He wanted more time with me. He dominated the house, like a wolf marking his territory; jealous of any time I spent away from him. He was guarded and interpreted my every act to be a statement of indifference. While he was struggling with his impending move and the feelings of deep emptiness that it raised; I was dealing with the same feelings by creating a physical distance between us before he even departed. We were both protecting our inner anxiety of loss with opposite reactions. An explosion was inevitable. Meanwhile, Drake continued his old survival technique of maintaining distance both mentally and physically. He was spending the majority of his evenings with a bad crowd of friends again during the week and with Lynn on weekends. It was quite a dichotomy between rebellious weeknights and Mormon family oriented weekends.

One day, Jason and I quarreled over my lack of attention to him during a visit to the house. He complained that I always seemed too busy for him. I defended my position. The coffee table went flying, the remote crashed into the wall, and the patio door slammed so hard the hardware fell off. This was a climax of months of anxiety over his fear of losing our relationship. Despite warnings from Bret, I was in denial that he would actually fear losing me after all we had been through over the years. Not only because of my survival of all the traumas from recurring rages, but most especially the good times and activities we shared such as scouting, scuba diving, and world traveling to such adventurous locations as Costa Rica and the Cayman Islands. Jason and I evolved a relationship that was as multifaceted as his emotional baggage. We were a high adventure team, dependent on each other to survive the next conquest. How could he ever think I didn't love him?

Reality nearly hit me in the face as the remote went flying across the room that day. Now 22 years old, twelve years after our first meeting at Cleo Wallace, he still carried a deep fear of loss. His emotional trauma was so hardwired that it utterly consumed him. All this emotional self-bantering was compounded with the news that I was opening my home to a new child, who in Jason's own mind was a replacement. This new foster care placement was occurring at the same period as all the recurring visits by Michael. Jason concluded the timing to be intentional, not coincidental: In with the new, out with the old. Was Drake's anxiety following the same course?

Christmas was a quick affair that year. My extended family celebrated in Florida, so it was just me and the children. I was anxious for Sam to move in. Jason and Ellen were packed and ready for their big move to Colorado to start school. And as always, Drake was in his own little world, mostly focused on his love, Lynn. Though I presented a merry dad celebrating my favorite holiday, I was emotionally withdrawn and deeply hurting. Jason was really leaving.

Sam came for one more visit just after Christmas with the plan to move in a few days later. The visit went fine and he appeared more relaxed around the family. After he left, I completely remodeled the guest room from an old English dark mahogany style decor, to a bright light pecan wood teen paradise. We even had lamp boxes on the walls. It was great fun for me, and despite his conflicted feelings about Sam, Jason helped with assembly of some of the small pieces. I also pulled together a television with a control box to hook up multiple entertainment and gaming systems. The room was wired and ready to welcome our newest family member.

That weekend, Sam's foster parents brought him to our home with all his belongings. Like Jason, this was another foster kid who was not moved with a plastic bag. He had a truck load of stuff that filled his bedroom. He was fully equipped and to add to his golden stash, I purchased him a PS3 gaming system for Christmas, a gift that was waiting for him in his new room. Sam's reserved character was starting to break and I could see a bright and cheerful spirit shining through.

After the first few nights it was apparent that Sam did have security issues. Like Drake at bedtime, he preferred a light on or left the television going. But unlike any prior placement, he would roam the house late at night wrapped in a blanket. I later learned he did better when sleeping with the dog. This also worked in his prior foster home. He had trouble falling asleep, and then staying asleep through the night. Each morning I would find him on the floor in my room wrapped in a blanket. Later, he started showing up all over the house. I immediately advised the social worker who calmly told me to let him adjust. It was a new house and nights were his most difficult time. I called his foster mom to ask about this behavior to which they replied that he had done the same with her, and after a while the parents stayed up later until he fell asleep. At some point they were forced to lock their door to keep him out. They were concerned being a married couple that he might enter at a most inappropriate time. Since we were an all male household for years, I never shut my door at night. I'm also a very light sleeper, so leaving the door open was a deterrent to the children for any roguish activity past bedtime.

None of my children ever roamed at night, at least not without a specific mischievous plan. At various periods of their childhood they would come into the bed in the morning to cuddle, though more often to wake me up to make them breakfast or take them somewhere. But Sam's behavior was completely new. Several times I tripped over him on a late night bathroom run. I followed the advice given and let it go for the moment. Apparently, it gave him comfort.

During the first few weeks he and Drake spent a lot of time together. They played Ninja and enjoyed knocking oranges off the tress in or backyard to either punch them on the fall or cut at them with a knife. Drake took him for rides on his motorcycle, which he really enjoyed. Being around an older youth, Sam was feeling like a big kid, though he would soon mature to a teenage mentality at an alarming rate. On one occasion the boys bought a sling shot and later a blow dart gun. Drake was the instigator and Sam was more than pleased to join in the hunt, at first for oranges, but they soon graduated to rabbits and quail.

One afternoon, heading off on an errand, I saw the two boys briskly walking away from the house, blow gun and sling shot in hand. I stopped to ask where they were going. A casual reply that they were headed to the park to shoot birds was the response given without missing a step. I warned them both it sounded like a bad idea and told them to stick to the backyard. Their plan sounded like trouble with the police. Drake waved me off as an over anxious parent. My suggestion to use the backyard had already been dismissed by the boys as they were bored with that hunting ground. This was one of those parental moments when you must let them learn from natural consequences.

Within thirty minutes my cell phone rang. Yup, it was the sheriff. I drove over to the park as the two boys were being escorted to the police vehicle. I assumed they were going 'downtown.' They were clearly embarrassed and worried. Sam was pale. The officer told me their story about my having just warned them. He found it amusing. I wasn't laughing. The officer, a dad himself, was firm, but felt the boys' tension and after a stiff warning, handed me their deadly weapons and released them with a warning. It was a very quiet (I told you so) drive home. Sam learned a valuable lesson that day. Don't always follow Drake's impulsive ideas. However, it was good to know that Sam was a healthy normal boy! Drake, on the other hand, was still copiously troublesome.

Sam was no saint either. He had his moments. For example, one evening soon after this event while watching Harry Potter with Lynn and me, he came out with a remark that was truly unexpected. In one scene, Harry is turning and tossing in bed from a nightmare.

Sam commented in his subtle and random fashion: "That Harry Potter is a bad seed, look at him jacking off." None of us will ever see HP quite the same way again. Thanks Sam.

I enrolled Sam at the local middle school with a stiff warning to the administration that he was a new foster care placement and should be watched for any unusual behavior, emotional or otherwise. I was introduced to the school counselor who took my concerns with great sincerity and promised to keep in touch. My concerns were over reactive. His teachers quickly reported back that he was adjusting very well, and in fact, was sought after by his peers. He had a very engaging personality, even if he was somewhat bashful. On campus, he was a real hit.

Though it sounded as if he was making new friends at school, he never went out after school, but kept to himself at the house, mostly watching television and playing video games. His friendships at school were still casual. During the first few weeks, reports from school were good, but soon things took a downturn. His grades began to slide south. His teachers still indicated that his relationships at school were doing very well. He was now fully accepted on campus. He just wasn't turning in any work. After talking to his old foster mom, I learned this was not a new issue for him.

One night I decided to be the ever helpful dad. I asked about his assignments and we opened his math work sheet together. He stared at the paper, pencil oscillating between his fingers. The pencil had not made contact with the sheet yet. His eyes were blank. Suddenly the pencil went flying and his language went as far south to crude as his grades. Sam had a potty mouth! That was news to me. This perfect child who was so polite and reserved had a temper, a rather significant one at that. He left the room, carrying his expletives along. I remained at the table with his homework sheet. He returned a few minutes later to the same position; only his pencil was now grasped firmly in a fist that shook at the paper.

"Why can't I do this?" He yelled, followed by a flying pencil and four letter words as he ran from the room again.

His third attempt was a charm. He returned and started writing problems on the sheet. Somehow his brain kicked into gear during the anger episode. Perhaps it was the adrenaline. This was not the last tantrum we would see, but as time passed, they seemed to become fewer, at least around me.

Meanwhile, he and Drake continued their playful antics. During one such episode Drake spun into the kitchen on his roller blades and hit and split a custom kitchen cabinet door. No, the State does not pay for property damage. A call to a carpenter and two months later the door was fixed. On another occasion, Sam was practicing with the sling shot in the backyard. Forever the concerned dad, I warned him to stay away from the house, the back of which consisted of floor to ceiling glass windows and arcadia doors. How could he, being only in middle school, have understood the physics of a stone in flight? He was shooting at a bird. I have no doubt of it. But he kept missing the lucky creature. As any attentive adult could have predicted, a stone hit the patio tile from where it ricocheted into one of the six foot glass doors. I was in the library paying bills. I heard an explosion. Everyone in the family now knows the sound of a double pane glass door breaking. Did I tell you that foster care does not pay for property damage? In one year alone I accumulated losses over $6000. Yes, foster parents stand alone.

Michael continued visiting during the weekends as he had done routinely prior to Sam joining our family. The two boys seemed to hit it off well. Sam accepted Michael as his ninja student and the two spent endless hours in pursuit of pure boy fun. The nocturnal ninja training sessions also took their toll on my property. The roof was a favorite spot with the view of the whole neighborhood. I number of Spanish tiles could not withstand my ninjas' light feet. On another exercise, Sam and Michael were creeping over the wall into the neighbor's backyard dressed in black, including their faces. The top layer of concrete blocks gave way. They just needed more practice at the art of stealth.

Sam's birthday was the first week in January. He wanted a new skateboard from a specialty shop in our area. I took Sam and Michael into the shop for what I thought was a simple selection. No one warned me that you don't buy complete boards, but rather, all the parts which are then assembled in the store for a totally custom build. Three-hundred dollars later Sam was proud and Michael was looking forlorn. How could he possibly keep up with Sam's new top of the line aerodynamic machine designed for the most difficult tricks with his rather bland board? New wheels and bearings were the only answer, Swiss imports of course. Another hundred dollars off the credit card and I was free from that store. I always get cramps passing that place even today. We drove without delay to the local skate park. They flew up and down the bumps, curves, and holes for the rest of the afternoon. It's all in the wheels and bearings. Things appeared to be going very well.

Sam was adjusting quickly and appeared very happy. Drake was re-living a real childhood experience he may have missed earlier in his life. And my visitor Michael, though jealous of Sam taking my attention that had been exclusively his domain the past few months, seemed content to share me with a new playmate.

Then tragedy hit.

You are Loved

Driving south down Interstate 17 from Phoenix to the Casa Grande area, my eyes watered in anticipation of seeing Michael. I was filled with grief for his unexpected circumstance so abruptly tossed upon him, with simultaneous delight for the opportunity to visit him and provide some comfort. He had confided in me just weeks before after one of his respite visits that he was afraid he would never see me again; to which I quickly challenged him. But the fear in his eyes was obvious. He was already feeling insecure about his situation at home. I too was scared. After he made that comment to me driving him home, I broke down crying in front of his parents. They were consoling, feeling their own anguish. I should have been prepared when I was told that his parents decided to sever the adoption. But I was not!

My visit was just two days after he was left at his mental health case management office by his adoptive parents. They were burned-out on his behavior and frustrated with the bureaucracy of the mental health system. I understood their despair. They could see no solution as Michael continued to decline and the family suffered the tension from his behavior outbursts. He was a Title 19 adoption, meaning, the family was promised health care as part of the adoption agreement, to include those all elusive mental health services. Medical services are easily defined and rarely disputed, mental health services, on the other hand, are vague and contentious. What they were never told as part of the adoption was how difficult getting this service is to achieve. This accomplishment requires extensive internal advocating within the mental health care system, and in some cases, a lot of gaming. As the wheels of government bureaucracy turn ever so slowly, the child's mental damage only breeds upon itself, injuring not only the child and family, but every element of the community in which they live.

By Christmas the parents had made the decision to relinquish him back to CPS, though they said nothing to him. I first heard of their intention during a meeting at the Foundation with them over the Holiday season. I had suggested they speak directly with Drake's social worker for advice about the situation. I heard their words, but was in denial it would really happen. He was their son. They just needed support like I had all those years with Jason and Drake. They needed the lifeline of a social worker.

After Christmas the family could bear no more. During a CFT meeting in early January, having notified CPS, they simply left Michael in a cold office. I was still in denial, assuming it was a threat to force the agency to provide mental health services. It was bitter sweet for the parents, but I know from many discussions before and after, that his mom was deeply hurt. At one time early in the relationship, she truly loved him, but his multiple mental disorders, which resulted in daily manipulation for control, dug a void between mother and son that after so many years of conflict could not be bridged.

CPS dumped him in a group home in Coolidge. That night he laid in a strange bed, his senses overwhelmed with unfamiliar smells and sounds, oppressed by a deepening uncertainty about tomorrow. He was officially back in the system, one from which he might never escape.

After two hours driving far from the metropolis of the Phoenix valley, I found the place. It had the look of an abandoned home as it stood behind an old broken metal fence surrounded by endless desert brush. As I pulled onto the gravel drive, I caught sight of him scouting around collecting garbage in the area. He smiled, but was clearly cautious. After introductions with the staff, signing a visitor book, and then a telephone call to the management for approval for the visit, he took me to his room. It was as featureless as the building. The walls were bare with no rugs on the floor. I felt his despair as he organized and reorganized his few possessions placed in a small hard worn dresser by a single bed, one of three in the empty room he occupied. Since he had just a few clothes, I picked up several shirts, shorts, and socks at a local store. He was depressed, with every right to feel so. Getting some new clothes seemed to help pick up his spirit. I also bought him a wallet and put my picture in it for him. It was my way of showing him I would be there for him.

***

Lynn's Journal (Loss of Michael)

Michael. He's my baby brother, what more can I say. I love him; he was and will always be a part of me, my life and my memories.

The first day I met him, he was this sweet little boy, all smiles and energy. All he wanted to do was show me how strong he was, and how fast he could run to a designated point and back. After he moved in, I can't remember where we were, but, he just took my hand, so much a baby and so much a growing boy trying not to show how scared he was of the world and what it could do to him. This cute little nine year old boy trusted me completely. I felt like I was there to watch over him and protect him. I was his second mom, and that is how it has been ever since.

Oh, we've had rough, angry times, where he didn't want to do something or he'd get me frustrated and I'd lose my cool with him. But the next day or even that night he would be there asking for a good night hug:"Goodnight Lynn, I love you" As he stood there in his too short PJ's, he grew up so fast. I loved him, no, I Love Him.

When my parents told me they had decided to annul the adoption after four years of memories and love, I was furious! How could they turn their backs on a hurt little boy? How could they leave him to a world that had ripped him apart? I came up with all these ways to fix things. I even started calculated how much time, money and effort it would cost me to raise him myself, while going to college, I could see it, I really could. But I knew it wouldn't work, deep down I knew my parents were right. I just didn't want to see it. I sat down and thought about why they were giving him up, I mean, really thought about it. I knew they did it purely out of love. They couldn't give him the support, time or help he needed. He had been hurt so badly before, that there wasn't anything they could do alone; they needed help, but couldn't get it. No one gave it, No one!

Walking into that empty bedroom was a shock for a while. I'd walk in and just stop. It was empty; there was no Michael left in that room. There was nothing. I was empty of all life, energy, anger, frustration, happiness, love, hope of a future. There was nothing! And I felt helpless. All I could do was visit him on weekends, but even then things had changed, we weren't a family any more. But no matter how many times he changes homes, we are family.

It hurt so much to lose him. It was like losing a part of me. Now there's a constant ache that never goes away. It fades sometimes; I can distract myself with happiness and laughter. But always it comes back that tightness in my chest and that pain in my throat, the tears and the pain in my soul.

All I can do is watch from the sidelines as he lives his life. If he is hurting or laughing, I can't share it with him anymore. I'm not a part of that world anymore. And it hurts like Hell!

***

We went out to just walk together. He spoke with a trembling voice:
"Why don't my parents call me? Tell them where I am Bill. I'm in a group home, not a hospital. What's going on? Can't I call my mom?"

I was forbidden to say anything, just to visit. I reminded him about our past conversations concerning therapy and his desire to be like other children his age. That was his dream to be free, to be like other kids. He dreamed to be allowed to have friends and enjoy an afternoon playing outside. After walking several laps around the property parameter, we returned to his room.

We sat on his bed, side by side. I was very uncomfortable. His fear was evident. He showed me a card from his adoptive dad he found with the few clothes he had in a small backpack. He wanted my opinion about it.

"Nice letter," he sadly commented.

In the letter his dad apologized for not being a better father and offered hope for Michael's future. It was a farewell letter, but at the moment, Michael was too confused or perhaps in denial to grasp the message.

We played a game of chess and later went back outside to throw a few baskets. With all he was suffering, he spoke with real empathy of another boy in the home who no one liked. He had a unique problem. When he sat on the sofa he would soil himself, so he was confined to a hard stool in the back of the room to watch television. None of the other boys would play with him. Michael felt sad for his situation and offered him his friendship. Did Michael see his own reflection? It was soon time for me to start the long drive home. He offered a distant hug. I left with a promise to return the next day. He walked away slowly, head down, seeming completely dejected.

During that first visit to the group home I committed myself to help him. I returned the next day as promised to keep him motivated and let him know he was not forgotten. This visit was no different than the previous day. We walked the parameter and played chess on the floor in his room. While outside, he showed me where a kid had gotten through the fence and run away the week before. I was surprised with this news since the children were forbidden to have their shoes on in the building. They were always kept locked up. Playing outside, the children were under constant supervision. Michael never explained how the kid escaped. Perhaps he was never told. Michael was certainly fantasizing about the opportunity.

He continued to ask why his parents had not called or visited. He was very worried that they did not know where he was. I struggled to change the topic. Before I left we shared a song off my iPod: *You Are Loved, Don't Give Up* by Josh Groban. I left him disheartened; emotionally drained and alone. He was still visibly confused by his circumstances. He wanted to go home. I would have taken him with me that very day if I had the authority. I did not.

The next few days were tough. I kept in touch with his CPS worker. I conveyed to her my willingness to take him in my home while they worked the details of his case. It was agreed I could maintain contact; however his case worker was working to get him placed in a psychiatric hospital for a short-term evaluation any day. Banner and St. Luke were the two discussed. I planned to continue visits as time permitted.

After a few days during one of these update calls with CPS, the case worker told me they had signed him out of the group home and took him to school with the intent of placing him in a hospital that afternoon. The plan failed. Due to a miscommunication, the hospital had no bed and did not accept him as scheduled. The group home had already given his bed away. The case manager was desperate to find a bed for the night. I wrote to them:

> *I am more than happy to care for him while a bed is located. I have much experience with Michael and can provide some sense of security and stability with all this chaos.*

It was agreed he could stay with us. It was for just a couple of days. My agency agreed to the temporary respite care and I met an agency driver halfway between Casa Grande and Phoenix. As soon as I arrived, Michael jumped out of the car and into my arms. On the ride home he kept asking what was going on and wanted to call his parents and tell them where he was. I told him I would not abandon him, but at this time I was not in control. I could still not tell him about the severance of his adoption. I had to believe he suspected something. After all, he was a hardened foster child. What trepidation he must have suffered during this period? He had no clear understanding of his present condition or his future situation. He could only operate within the narrow confines of the moment.

That fateful day in January when I brought Michael home put me on a path that tormented me personally and disrupted my family. This one action put me squarely between two powerful agencies, the Foundation, who held my foster care license, and Michael's guardian, CPS. This is how I learned about the disjointed, unaligned, and autonomous agendas of a complex system of independent agencies known as Arizona Foster Care. An operation heavily based on independent contracting firms. It is also how I gained the same annoying experience as his adoptive parents regarding the true nature of mental health care in Arizona ... Pitiful.

Our first calamity arose the day he arrived. He was transitioned to me without his medications, a real crisis for children with ADHD. The medications are short lasting. That problem was soon resolved with help from Walgreens. One certainty was that Michael was not in honeymoon mode. He was very comfortable in our home since he and I had already established a strong relationship with which he was secure. His fear related to his place with the rest of the family, especially the new comer Sam.

Michael's desire was to stay with me. From his view, a relationship had already been established that he desperately wanted to strengthen. At that point in time, however, the reality was very different. The placement was very temporary. Though I cared much for his outcome, the immediate agenda was to get him the help that we all tried to accomplish while he was still with his adoptive family. He slept on an air mattress in the family room and kept his clothes in a small pile by the sofa. He was delighted to be out of the group home, so had little objection to being treated in such a transitory manner. I know he felt displaced by Sam who now occupied the room he had used during the many months of weekend visits. He once complained about Sam using a fluffy white comforter that I had purchased just for his use in that room. I bought it while Michael was in respite, so he assumed it was for his exclusive use. I purchased another. What can I say, children and their blankets! But Michael was generally more overwhelmed with the daily fear of being disrupted again to leave time to display too much jealousy.

I worked my employment schedule around our new houseguest who was not in school. Why register a new pupil who was only a short time visitor, not to mention I had no birth certificate or shot records. Day after day, I called at 2:00 PM for the placement news. Each time the answer was the same that no bed was available, and they expected good news the next day. A typical message from CPS was:

> *I will continue to find a hospital bed for Michael. She (case worker) feels pretty certain that St Luke's will take him, just not sure when.*

His anxiety continued to grow, but he was certainly happier in familiar surroundings with people he knew. It was about this time that I noticed how he would bite and ripe his fingernails and cuticles until they bled. This habit correlated directly to his stress level.

After a few days, his case worker allowed him to call his mom. He emphasized how well he was behaving. Clearly he wanted to impress her that he was ready to come home. He still had not been told his parents had filed for a severance that that this break with his family may be permanent. After the first week I advised CPS that Michael

> still knows nothing, and just seems to be living for the moment. He is content in my home, but clearly very insecure. This creates a pressure cooker for him personally as well as the other boys in my home. Please keep in mind that Michael has been under stress about going away since November.

The days flowed into weeks without word about a hospital placement. His fear was acute, especially in the evenings when he would cuddle close to me while watching television. By the second week, he was talking about his parents less and less and occasionally called me Dad. He was testing the waters.

Soon after moving into our home, Michael shared a story with me that was very troubling. He spoke about an incident that occurred over the Christmas break back at home. Since he was very restricted to the house, he rarely went out to play. Over the holiday a fifteen year old family friend offered to take him to the basketball courts. They never went to play basketball. Instead, the two boys went to a nearby park, where they found privacy in a play area and had oral sex. Michael told me he was curious. He wanted to know what it was like. As he told the story his expression screwed up to a grimace. He didn't like doing it. Was he playing for sympathy or wanting me to see him as a victim needing protection? Was he manipulating me or was this an honest confession to test my commitment to him? This form of abuse was very foreign to me and without professional guidance I was paralyzed. I reported the incident to CPS and his adoptive family. CPS seemed disinterested, the family in denial.

Over time he would describe many events from his past, but always, at least from my perspective, he was the victim. Sometimes I was confused between abnormal behavior and normal boy curiosity and sexual growth. Throughout his stay I described his strange behavior and stories to CPS, pleading for therapy. I did the same with people at the Foundation hoping for their intervention. I knew full well I needed help at home. I received empty promises from one and threats from the other. Neither of which was very useful.

Meanwhile, both Sam and Drake were trying to adjust to the dramatic changes caused by Michael's situation. Not only was he very loud, at times obnoxiously so, he was continuously stressed to the wire. He wanted to stay, to be accepted in the family and not be moved. He was very competitive. He worked to dominate my attention, working diligently to prove himself superior to Sam at every turn. Sam, though laid back, became very aggravated with Michael during these competitive episodes. He lectured Michael over and over about how unimportant being first or better really was, but Michael was hardwired. Domination, control and superiority were his only tools to achieve his goal of permanency. Little did he understand that his behavior produced the opposite effect. It was the root of a growing hostility against him.

At times I would referee major verbal outbursts that bordered on physical conflict. Sam always maintained control during these confrontations while Michael stood his ground to taunt Sam into a fight. This conduct only increased tensions and the possibility of disruption. To make things worse, because I was also very insecure about Michael's fate, I tended to take his side, to protect him from added emotional harm. In so doing, I threatened Sam's sense of security and feelings of being wanted and loved. He occasionally made me aware of this issue in his own passive way.

It was during this period I fully grasped the complexity of the state foster care system and its massive bureaucracy. He had a CPS case worker responsible as his guardian. A mental health provider, called Horizon Human Services, which recommended services for his mental health care; and State insurance for general medical needs. In the background always loomed a quiet, but powerful player called Cenpatico, or what I would later refer to as "the bankers." Regardless of what was recommended by staff from these other agencies, Cenpatico had the final approval for mental health care, which for Michael, was his greatest need. They were the underwriters. This was a new experience for me. I had spent the last twelve years shielded from this maze of organizations by my agency, which was my single and only point of contact. The Foundation case managed their foster children. With Michael under the control of CPS, it was very different. I now needed to develop the skills to navigate the State system.

Days turned to weeks and I was told that the hospital plan had failed. He did not qualify as a dangerous person requiring psychiatric hospitalization. Yet, Cenpatico would not approve residential treatment unless recommended from a hospital stay. We were in a catch 22. I spoke with an intake person at Banner hospital one day, who confided that they did not want the responsibility of a child with a sexual history because they did not have their patients under constant secure observation. This was my introduction into the placement tribulations for children like Michael that had a history of not only sexual abuse, but ongoing sexual acting out with other children in their foster care record. This information can be hidden from individual foster or adoptive families, but not from group homes and institutions. They are too savvy.

Meanwhile, Michael started interacting with the community. From the beginning we had a strict rule that he was never allowed out to play, ride his bike, and be out in the neighborhood alone. I required him to have one of us with him. I had reservations due to the extreme degree that his prior home kept him confined. I wanted to take it slow and observe his behavior. However, Michael soon engaged many of Sam's eighth grade friends. Michael was not in school at the time and so had no interaction with his own grade level in the community. I always questioned Sam about Michael's behavior who told he was annoying at times and always seemed to be embroiled in some peer conflict; but nothing more. He showed interest mostly in girls, but then so did Sam. Biking was his greatest pleasure. It makes sense as this one activity represents a child's first taste of freedom. During one of his first rides with Sam, he decided to high-five a tree while riding my mountain bike. Let us just say, the tree got the better of him and the bike. I purchased him a new bike soon afterwards.

This accident reflects the wild spirit of this boy. It was this outgoing, outrageous and mischievous character I came to love and admire so much. He captured my heart during those early days. He enjoyed fishing at the lake or performing stunts at the skate park. During many of these outings I would sit on a bench and listen to my iPod while he and Sam enjoyed the simple joys of childhood. Occasionally other children would stop by for small talk. He seemed content. This was more freedom than he had experienced from his adoptive home. He was and will always remain in my memory, my little Huck Finn.

While the house was in disruption from a lack of stability for Michael; Drake and Lynn continued to be an item. They had a difficult time when Michael first moved in as Lynn felt very uncomfortable coming to our home. It was understandable considering the circumstances of his disruption from her house. This created significant friction between Drake and me. He wanted the kid out so not to disrupt his relationship. I would assure him that Michael was leaving any day, but he always countered with: "He'll never leave."

Drake began striking out with anger and frustration. He also feared reliving the tension he previously experienced when visiting Lynn at her home and all the chaos he witnessed. He was apprehensive about the effects on our family, especially knowing Michael was under constant stress. I remember a number of evenings when Tom would come over to the house and just walk down the street with Drake talking it all out. We were all feeling the stress and sense of helplessness. Drake admitted months later that he was being very selfish. In hindsight, I also believe that Michael's unstable situation brought Drake's own sense of insecurity to the surface. Like Michael at that moment, Drake has felt the fear of disruption most of his life, learning to suppress the pain with a face of indifference.

After a couple of weeks, Lynn was more at ease with the situation and happy that her brother had a home. Drake then relaxed about Michael's situation, perhaps too much so. One night soon after this, Drake and Lynn broke the golden rule and engaged in prenuptial sex. This was catastrophic to their relationship. Drake knew all too well the religious condemnation. But what he did not yet realize was the damage he caused taking her innocence. He was too immature to understand the consequences of setting off a person's sexual drive. Once set off, it cannot be turned off.

For reasons known only to teens, Drake shared his sexual exploits with Sam the very next morning, then me. He felt the full weight of guilt, as much from the knowledge of the religious implications, as practical fear of her father's wrath . . . honestly, more from her father's wrath. I immediately told him it was necessary to meet with her parents. A call had to be made that very day. After speaking with Lynn, there was hesitation, but I insisted. I knew this family and such an act was not to be taken lightly. Worse for me, I had their son in my home. At this point I still considered Michael their child. He was just in temporary crisis. Procrastination was not the better part of valor in this case. Direct confrontation was the only option. We all drove to her father's office for the pre-arranged meeting. No doubt the parents had a notion about the subject.

Drake and Lynn admitted to their transgression with honesty, though the humility in their tone may have been more from fear than true humbleness. Marriage was discussed and methods to manage their behavior were a priority. Lynn was not to stay overnight at our home anymore. And when she did visit, she was to be out no later than ten in the evening. I was to supervise and never leave them alone. Trust was broken. Her dad, who had just recently baptized Drake, was visibly disappointed, but did not lash out at him. This was one meeting where I supported Drake as a distant observer. He and Lynn were young adults and needed to resolve the matter without my intervention.

We all departed friends that evening, but I think it was a turning point for the relationship. Drake was in love, but on his own level, which was very different from Lynn. He was not ready for the responsibility of a long-term partnership and marriage. He was still a teenager searching for his identity, seeking relationships to help him to better understand his value and place in society. Lynn was a traditional Mormon woman already two years behind her peers without a husband. They were on different planes of maturity.

Michael discovered the truth about the sexual liaison in short time and felt anger toward Drake. His Mormon upbringing was ever present in his thinking. Drake had fallen off the pedestal at a time when Michael needed assurance and security. He was also angry at me for not protecting his sister. And lastly, felt alienated from our family as he was the last to know. These were all valid emotions from his perspective. I so wanted to just hold him and tell him it would be alright. I could not. All I could do was repeat the same old verse:

"I am not in control of your situation."

The plan for a hospital placement failed. The next plan was to find a group home where he could stay while an evaluation was arranged. Meanwhile, the Foundation was very discontent that a CPS child was still in my home, a placement they considered to be their private domain for Foundation children only. For them, this was a risk-management issue due to the uncertainties of Michael's past. Though I was very vigilant and advised both Drake and Sam about

Michael's history and what acting out behavior to expect; the Foundation would hear nothing of it. The message was clear and consistent: "Get Michael out of your home."

No child was allowed in a Foundation home without following a strict intake process. I violated that rule for which I would be severely punished down the road. I, who was celebrated as one of their finest foster parents, was quickly descending from grace.

After a few weeks, Michael had moved in. I made arrangements to pick-up the remainder of stuff that was still at his home in Casa Grande. This was another tacit symbol to him that he had a chance to stay. Like me, he was always looking for the smallest sign to help keep the flame of hope alive. Stashed with his things was an envelope filled with letters from his birth mom and sisters. When I arrived home, I gave it to him.

Michael is very emotional and struggles to keep old relationships burning in his heart, even if they are denied him in the physical world. He had no contact with his birth family since his adoption. I sat with him as he read each and every letter, slowly, thoroughly. Some he read several times. He was indolent almost in a daze. I could not consol him. If his internal anger were measured on a scale, Michael wasn't far off the end. He had lost so much in such a short period of time.

On several occasions, while I would be sitting at the computer working, Michael would stand by me and ask how to find his family, especially his two sisters. I am an avid genealogist and pride myself with the ability to find just about anyone, dead or alive. I started doing some family research as he remembered some information as to their legal names and the last place he'd lived in Arizona. While I worked my magic going from website to website, he sat on the edge of my chair and quietly observed my every research method. He is one smart dude. I found some leads, but was concerned moving too quickly without CPS approval. When I called his social worker, she had little interest. I was told CPS had no files with his parental information and it was not a priority at the moment. How cruel to his soul. For Michael, it was the only priority.

He will struggle with birth family issues for many years. It will continue to haunt him, especially when he feels the most vulnerable. Will anyone ever care? He also contacted some old foster siblings while with me. His old relationships are a lifeline that gives him hope. Even foster children have a right to hope, though the system works to drive it from them at every turn.

By the third week in January we experienced a dramatic day that was to impact my family and everyone on the case. I drove Michael to get braces, an anxious experience for any kid. During the trip I told him I had a court hearing to attend. I steered away from why, though he suspected it was about him. I had no expectations. The CPS worker asked me to attend. I was introduced as his current placement. The hearing was very mundane. All I remember was the judge agreeing to Michael remaining in my custody as requested by CPS and agreed by all, including his parents who had just surrendered custody.

When I picked him up later that morning from the Orthodontist, he was in some pain. That was to be expected. While driving home he pressed for information about the court hearing. I could not keep it from him anymore. I told him his adoption had failed and he was with CPS. That is why he was put in a group home earlier. His reaction was cold, his expression empty. The first words from his lips: "Are you keeping me?"

Of course I wanted to just say yes, not to worry, we have a plan. But I knew better and did not want to raise his hopes, or mine. Little did I realize that day how hard and long I would fight to give him that very answer.

As January came to a close, CPS and Horizon were working the group home angle. My plea was for a placement near us so we could maintain contact with the hope of him returning one day. But in the meantime, my focus at home was to begin working toward establishing a new family dynamic, one where Michael was an equal member. We talked as a family. I called Michael son, while he continued calling me dad. I never considered him different than the other youth in my home. They all were permanent placements. It was a model I would learn too late was packed with failure. My message to the case worker was:

> *how about getting him into a day treatment program first, rather than spinning our wheels on group homes.*

It was my way of asking to keep him. I continued to struggle with finding therapeutic help for him that would also provide support to our family. The Foundation, however, demanded the contrary. They wanted Michael out of the house. I, on the other hand, was already asking his social worker and attorney about guardianship. By the end of the month, his attorney agreed to speak with the case worker on this and ascertain CPS' position.

By the end of the month I was given official papers from CPS called *Notice to Provider*. I assumed at that point I was his foster parent, though it was never official through the Foundation. In fact, I was later told Michael was a kinship placement to get around the Foundation. I never requested compensation, though I had by this point purchased him all new clothes and helped him acquire all the things normal for a young teen. Our neighbor gave him a stereo system as well in exchange for chores he was doing for them. The CPS supervisor was most distraught about me not getting foster care payments, and in the end, I was sent fifty dollars per month for food and clothing. This was very short of the thousand dollars a month I received from the foundation for each of their youth.

At the end of January it was clear he was not moving anytime soon, so I asked CPS about enrolling him in our local school. At this point I finally got his birth certificate and shot records. Due to his history of classroom disruptions and several suspensions from sexual acting out, I elected to encourage the school staff to place him on a restricted campus for short-term observation until his IEP was sent from his old school. I was also still uncertain how many more days or weeks he would be with us anyway. The school agreed. Meanwhile, Sam was feeling the stress of our unstable situation, which was showing both at home and in school. I wrote to Sam's teachers:

> *Lots of emotion at home this weekend. I have a CPS case in the home that was dumped by his parents into the system with no plan forward. He is temporary on day to day status. This is creating stress for everyone. It also triggers fears and old memories of Sam's past history. The CPS boy was just sitting at one point looking at pictures and cards from his birth family. Watching this trauma unfold is affecting Sam. However, I cannot just throw the boy out to a shelter. It would be cruel and only leave Sam with a further sense of insecurity for himself.*

I finally received an email from CPS that authorized me to enroll Michael in school, and in the same paragraph advised me they found a bed for him in a group home in Globe, Arizona. Globe was hours away from our town. I was confused and devastated. First I can enroll him in our hometown school, but in the same communication they are moving him far away!

The next day I asked CPS if I could just keep him while they did an evaluation to determine a treatment plan. By this point I had two very upset boys acting off each other's fears. Drake, on the other hand, accepted the situation, but seemed to spend more and more time away from home after school and on weekends. I was now imploring CPS that Michael needed to know he had a place to call home. And honestly, my whole family needed to find some resolution and peace of mind. To help the boys all felt camaraderie in the family; I purchased a family cell phone plan. This single act opened a path for major peer interaction for all the boys. Sam was a texting professional, achieving as many as 6,000 in a single month. Michael tried to compete, but could never get close, plus he really preferred direct contact with people. Both boys found their cell phone to be a lifeline to the community. For me, the phones were my reigns on these boys. I always knew where they were and could contact them at a moment's notice, which I frequently did.

***

My Neighbor's Letter

The day Michael knocked on my front door I was pleasantly surprised to see a boy in the neighborhood for my step-son to hang out with. Michael was very outgoing and friendly and wanted to shake everybody's hand. He just started talking and basically never stopped. My children did not know what to think of him. He wore us out with questions and information about his life. He liked all my children from age 7 to age 15. He especially enjoyed the girls. He wanted to be liked and tried to woo the girls with all his newly acquired material things: cell phone, video games and "cool clothes" and wore lots of cologne. Michael wanted to be helpful and offered to do chores and talked about how he was made to work from sun up to sun down in his former home. He was very likable with his big "brace face" smile and red hair that could win anyone over.

As we got to know Michael we could tell he was prone to exaggerate a little and was very good at manipulating. One morning I received a phone call from Drake that his dad was out of town and Michael was ill throwing up and unable to go to school. I went over and brought him to my home to see what terrible illness he had, and after playing a video game and taking a nap he was suddenly ready to go fishing and wanted to go out for lunch! Several afternoons when my children were at school, Michael walked over and asked if he could "hang out" with my husband and I or ask us to take him to the skate park or fishing. I offered to take him to school and he replied he was too emotionally ill to attend school that day. I tried to convince him to go to school and offered to take him. I refused to take him fishing if he stayed home from school.

As he got to know all the children in the neighborhood, Michael rode his bike to the middle school to meet girls. One day as I was picking up my daughter I ran into him and asked him what he was doing. He replied: "I am about to be jumped" (I guess that means he was about to get the tar beat out of him by a very large group of boys who were following him down the street). I calmly told Michael I would like to take him home. He said "no", and asked me to leave. I very patiently and calmly told Michael it would be a bad decision to stay and "chat" with this group. That it may affect his school options or adoption. As he walked away from me I told him I was going to stay here in my truck across the street until I knew he was safe.

He went back to the crowd for a moment, where some of them were now smoking pot. He soon turned around again and came back to me and said with a big smile on his face, seemingly unaffected. "I think I will take that ride, will you help me with my bike". I jumped out picked up the bike, put it in the back, and drove him home. As we drove, I congratulated him on making a great choice. That moment seemed to clench our friendship. From then on he told me I was his "mom" since his dad was single.

Michael seemed to like to "shock" with some comments and inappropriate questions but we ignored them or told him that was not appropriate language. Michael really bonded with girls. He had no problem telling me about sexual activity he engaged in with a neighborhood girl and seemed unaware that he should not have done this. He spoke freely of sex and girls he liked. Sometimes I wondered if he did this for attention or the "shock" value.

***

After much bureaucracy, Michael was enrolled in school, though it took another week of staff evaluations of his background to get him started in class. I also moved his living arrangements from the family room to my office, to provide him more privacy. At this point, Michael started to believe he had a new family. But his inner sense of security was guarded. In the meantime, I was receiving emails from his case worker that they were moving ahead with a group home interview. With him now desperate to find sanctuary, start school, and continue to develop friendships with other children in the neighborhood, the thought of an interview that paved a different direction scared me. CPS was still reacting to the Foundation not wanting him in the home. He, of course, was grasping for stability, but he really was on standby for a placement elsewhere. His day-to-day instability certainly did not promote any strong motivation for good behavior at home or in school.

Michael remained hyperactive and at times very annoying with his hyper-vigilance and ever controlling attitude, but generally acted fairly normal considering the situation. He was emotionally immature and enjoyed a good tuck-in at night. He lacked social skills at his peer level, but that was expected based on his history of family confinement. He seemed to sleep well, but several nights a week he would cry out like he did at his adoptive home with a freaky moaning sound, or short verbal outbursts:

"Don't take me. Don't hurt me."

Drake ran into him a few times sleep walking, and sometimes crying for me in the dark.

Sam and Michael had evolved a working relationship, which is the best way to describe it. Michael was very outgoing and engaging, while Sam was more reserved and inward. Michael really helped draw Sam out of his shell to become a more active member of the peer community. For this we were very grateful. Sam really enjoyed our home and neighborhood. He developed meaningful relationships and enjoyed hours of hanging out like all adolescents at that age. He tended toward hanging with a small exclusive group, different from Sam who was always seeking an ever expanding resume of friendships.

The boys enjoyed the hot spa that winter. It was a new experience for them both. At times, they would dare each other to jump into the pool which was not heated, so easily between 50 and 60 degrees freezing cold. With a running start, they would leap halfway across the width of the pool before crashing into the water, jerk their frigid bodies out on the other side and hop into the spa. It was all great fun.

On one of those occasions playing this game, after daring each other to be first to jump into the cold pool, one of them asked to skinny dip. I was lounging comfortably in the spa while they were splashing around in the pool. At first I argued against it, but after a few, 'ah, come on' dad requests; I gave in. My naïve thinking was for them to get it out of their system. It was a simple act of acquiescence. After a few minutes shivering in the pool, they came crashing back into the spa, with bathing suits on, and screaming from the prickly pain felt with the sudden assault of hot water on cold skin.

The spa was also a favorite hiding spot for the boys. They would often lay in wait for me with the cover down. While working in the backyard, I would inevitably pass the spa on some chore and they would burst out. They got a jolt watching my heart skip a beat. That is also where Michael first experienced Sam's colossal raging.

They were splashing around one night and Sam got a shot of water directly into his eye. He launched at Michael with a vengeance. His expression contorted from beaming grin to snarled rage. This is what we later referred to as Sam's *Avatar* state. We were all fans of the television series by the same name. Michael tore out of the spa and ran to the house. He was freaked by Sam's quick turn from playful friend to intensely fearsome assailant. Michael's tough guy façade crumbled to one of a frightened little boy.

With family relationships continuing to develop and attachments forming, I contacted Michael's attorney to advocate keeping him. CPS agreed. With this new plan, his case worker began working toward finding services with an agency near our home. Until this point, however, no evaluation was ordered. And though CPS was in agreement with moving forward with a permanency plan, they did not have an approach on how to resolve the issue with the Foundation. Options discussed included guardianship or finding a method to transfer the title 19 adoption from the prior family to me. CPS contacted his lawyer for advice.

By early February the Foundation was contacting CPS directly to press their case for Michael to be removed. We were clearly working at cross purposes. Each child placed in my home had a different social worker. All these social workers were continuing to support their charges as independent parties. No one was supporting the family unit.

As Michael's placement with our family continued, I permitted him more and more independence in the community. I continued to question Sam and other kids' parents for any sign of issues. I heard nothing to warrant keeping

Michael under constant supervision. In fact, the parents reported to me that he was a complete gentleman. He was described as charming, cute and well spoken. Our neighbor told me he was always asking to help out and showed kindness and empathy.

Though the school had accepted his enrollment and assigned him to a confined campus, things were still on hold for a bus. I lost my patience and so I transported the kid myself. He had a great first day. For him, it was symbolic of his chance for permanency. On the same day I received a call from a group home to schedule an interview with Michael for a new placement. I contacted CPS immediately for clarification. I was now completely confused. To add to the conflicting messages of that day, I received an email from the Foundation management requesting a meeting later that week to discuss Michael's placement.

That meeting occurred on Thursday of his first week at school. The message was blunt. Michael must leave the Hunter home. With panic in my heart, I sent an email to CPS advising them of this situation. I also emotionally unloaded my concerns about Michael's ongoing behavior issues and tensions in the home. As anxiety mounted, Michael fought to maintain control and personal possession of me. I contacted residential treatment facilities myself to determine how I could take on that financial burden, but it was simply over my income bracket. The case worker was back on the path to find a group home. Meanwhile, I was hopeful of a placement in the local area so I could support him for a return home and end his constant moving. I was completely taken by his heartrending situation. In just a month, I let myself grow from an advocate, to a loving parent.

I am certain I portrayed myself to CPS and others as indecisive. I never wanted to lose Michael at any time, but felt torn between the wants of the Foundation and constant changes in placement options from Michael's own agencies: CPS and Horizon. My family was trapped in a void without rules or boundaries. Each time we took a step forward, the final goal became less clear. We were living in a fog. Personally, I was burning out which only compounded the already heightened insecurity of all three children. Thank God Jason was in Colorado. He would have flipped out, triggered to rage, escaping to the roof.

***

Drake's Journal (18 years old)

One Saturday morning we all went to the store for Sam to buy a new PS3 game. He and I checked it all out and picked a game together. We both had a gift card for that store and I took the game to the register. As we left the store I threw away the receipt on accident. I wasn't really thinking about it.

When we got home, the game didn't work, it wouldn't load and Sam got totally pissed off at me because I didn't have the receipt. When I said I threw it away, he had a shit fit like it was the end of the world. He kept calling me stupid to make me made and upset. Dad was not so worried and told us to get in the car and he would bring the game back. While driving back, Sam kept yelling at me with vulgar language. It got really annoying and I told him if he kept doing it I'd punch him in the face. I was mad at my dad for not saying anything.

When we got back to the store dad went directly to the garbage and found the receipt. Sam kept nagging at me, and I told him again I'd punch him in the face and got in his face, and then he backed down and started making sense saying that losing the receipt really made him mad.

This was as angry as I'd seen him since I pushed him in the pool with his clothes on. In was January and the water was really cold. I saw him freak out. His face was crazed like he wanted to kill me. I helped him out because he was too shocked to pull himself out. He was threatening me and cursing at me. He then went into the spa and calmed down.

After that he made a revenge list of what he was going to do to me. He never did, it was all take and he never got in a fight with me. He would always calm down. It was like a one sided fight. This stuff happened more when he first moved in. After he settled with us, he didn't lose his cool like that again. But he was sarcastic when he got upset, always very defensive with people.

After awhile he found a way to deal with his boredom and anger. First he would punch oranges off the tree, and soon graduated to attack the oranges with knives. He would throw an orange up in the air and slice at them. I liked doing this too.

We also hunted birds together. Our neighborhood was populated with quails and pigeons. We built a box trap and waited hours for the right moment to spring it. We caught a quail and a few pigeons. A crow once got trapped, but it was too strong and got away.

***

While we were all working hard to appear living normal lives, everything came to a sudden stop when I was called to the scene of a motorcycle accident. It was Drake. The family was temporarily distracted. I rushed to the scene which was near his friend's house. The ambulance and police were already on the scene, with medics checking his vitals and patching his road rash for transport to the hospital. I rode with the ambulance crew, my heart pounding with every moan from his weakened body. Upon arrival he was immediately taken into the crisis center where a regular drip of morphine calmed him. By this time all the children were in the waiting room with a friend from work who had always remained quietly in the background during my many years in foster care, always ready to help. Everyone's thoughts were on Drake. Michael was panic stricken fearful that Drake would die. He was always so dramatic.

Standing over Drake as he lay there shaking from both pain and fear; I was completely drained of all the recent family issues. He constantly repeated how sorry he was for having the accident. I tried to console him, but he would have none of it. He was in confession mode, a result of the morphine I'm sure. He went on to exclaim his love for me and that he never wanted to lose me. He began to cry, big tears rolling down his checks. During my four years with Drake I had only seen him cry once before, when he learned his sister had been molested by his grandfather. Tears and emotions were not a strong element of his fundamental character. He kept his pain hidden deep, protected by a dense wall of granite blocks. He spoke gently about Michael. I could hear his sense of responsibility and genuine care. He had grown to love him in his own way.

The next day, Drake woke up in agonizing pain. Meanwhile, Jason and Ellen drove down from Colorado to help us. Later that day he was discharged to lay helpless in bed. With burning road rash and deep gashes he was unable to perform the simplest task. I awoke the next morning to incessant moaning and was shocked to find him seated naked on the toilet crying, his body shivering. He was unable to move. He felt completely vulnerable. For an athletic eighteen year old, it was dreadful. He was the center of attention for the remainder of the week.

Now might be an appropriate time to note that young ADHD drivers are two to four times more likely to have a car accident than non-ADHD drivers. This motorcycle incident was only the first of many traffic incidents I would suffer with Drake. Within the first year of his acquiring a license, he damaged both my cars.

The police told me at the hospital from this first accident that he was speeding at near sixty miles per hour in a residential area. Imagine if a child had been playing in the street. I cringe from the thought. The following week after he returned from the hospital, his friends brought over a video of the accident. Luck was never on Drake's side. The home directly across where he lost control of the bike had security cameras running. I watched in amazement as cars drove by the cameras at normal speeds around twenty-five miles per hour, then suddenly Drake explodes into the scene, loses control, his body takes flight over the top of the motorcycle like a lifeless dummy, then thud on the pavement. I am a believer in statistics.

Around the same time Michael had an interviewed for a new placement in a nearby group home. The interview went badly for a local placement. The final decision was for a move back to Casa Grande due to his past history. With all the turmoil and differing positions of both my licensing agency and CPS, I sent a *Declaration of my Decision Regarding Michael* to all concerned including his court appointed attorney. It was a formal commitment to a young boy who had been lost in a world of fear and discrimination. It was a rather long, terse document that expressed my utter frustration with the system as much as with Michael himself. The last paragraph read:

> *As the Foundation is fully aware, my son Jason Hunter who came to me through the Foundation, still suffers the traumas of loss from so many moves and methods used to provide those moves with the least resistance. At some point, someone in the system needs the courage to accept the youth with all their baggage and stop pushing them off. That is the gift that the Foundation social workers have given to me. Michael has a home.*

I realized at this point that I was held prisoner between the wishes of the Foundation and my desire to keep Michael. The longer I had him, the more attached I became. And I continued working toward making him a complete member of my family. Throughout his stay, I found myself over-protecting him from the constant attacks from outside the home.

It was also at this time that the school staff told Michael that his IEP from Casa Grande had finally arrived from his old school and did not support him being on a restricted campus. In fact, his IEP called for only thirty minutes of Special Services per day. All his studies were in regular classes, though when he was placed in the temporary shelter in January, a shadow was provided by Horizon. He and I were told a meeting would be convened that week to assign him classes on the main campus.

The meeting was postponed for two weeks, during which time Michael acted out to such a degree that the school re-wrote his IEP to keep him in the restricted campus. I refused to sign the new IEP. This new decision by the school staff became a sore point for Michael throughout the semester. The school psychologist agreed with my position that Michael would respond better back in the environment to which he was in Casa Grande. However, the administration would not agree to move him without the benefit of a shadow. Michael was caught in a trap that I created and neither of us had any power but to follow along. I pleaded with Horizon for such service and was promised one on and off. Eventually, Horizon backed off this position and advised me that I needed to request a new staffing for such action to be considered... another CFT? I was tired of them all. CPS took no action against the school district for violating his initial IEP. In the meantime, the school cancelled future IEPs to change his status.

After the disappointment not being returned to an open school campus, he was told of the plan for a shadow. But like so many other statements made to him, this option was not fulfilled. I told him in early April to forget any hopes of going to the main campus that year. He was so angry he told me in frustration that he was willing to give up his home with us to get out of that school prison.

While we were fraught with school issues, his case worker was still deciding on a placement, while I was researching evaluation and therapy options. This was a continuous irritation for me and the prior family who were promised an evaluation over a year prior to this point. A therapy firm, The Resolution Group, came highly recommended. I pushed for a single case agreement (contract between his mental health care agency and the Resolution Group) for these professionals to begin an evaluation. At this point, despite Michael's rebellious attitude about school, he was thriving at our home and very open to getting therapeutic help. We were told it was only a matter of days to close on a contract to get services in place. Ultimately, he was provided services by another group which closed two and one-half months later.

In mid-February, I was advised that a new CPS social worker was assigned to the case and supported Michael remaining in our home. I was greatly relieved to hear that Michael was going to stay. Little did I realize at the time, but Michael and I were now in the middle of a serious battle between agency interests. From this point forward, the Foundation and CPS were only concerned with their individual youth placement. What was lacking was concern for the family unit. During the next few weeks the new social worker was getting up to speed on this ever growing complex case. And I was still asking about guardianship.

February 22 was Black Friday for my family. A CFT was arranged at the Foundation to discuss Michael's placement in my home. Horizon participated by phone. It was a short meeting. It started by Horizon hesitating about sharing mental health information on Michael due to confidentiality issues, but they were willing to discuss issues at a top level. The Deputy Director waived them off with a simple statement that they would never do an intake on him, with the words:

"We don't take children with those kinds of severe problems."

The meeting ended in with what the CPS social worker termed "emotional blackmail." The words used by the Foundation were:

"Get Michael out or we will remove your Foundation children."

I was given the weekend to decide. The supervisor raised her voice at me, with firm blame that I knew what I was doing when I brought Michael into my home. They had warned me all along that he was a danger. I felt chilled to the bone. What cruelty. Michael posed no threat to Sam who was older and far more mature and able to manage his own body. Neither child had sexually engaged the other at any time, nor did they demonstrate any interest in doing so. They respected each other as brothers. As we left the building that afternoon, Michael's social worker was distraught. She looked me straight in the eyes expressing her sorrow over the decision so abruptly thrust upon me. We both left dejected.

Little did I know that day, but the Foundation, like many agencies, was more concerned with risk management issues than saving a child. Perhaps I am being unfair here. As a business they have the luxury to evaluate the cost of saving many compared to one. Humanity is transparent. However, families do not have the luxury to think along those lines. No matter how many experts the CFT may draft, and how many lawyers are contracted to the case, none can equal the care of a family. Let the state provide medical and mental health care insurance, but leave the parenting to core family values. The State needs to bow out of the business of parenting. I applaud the States that follow this path.

When the Foundation Deputy Director contacted me the following Wednesday for my answer, I told him that I wasn't throwing anyone out. He was blunt. Sam would be moved. Drake was not an issue due to his aging out of the system in just a couple of months. Within days, I was contacted and asked to partner with them in this move to help Sam understand the issues. How do you explain risk management theory to a young teenager? I felt trapped. Servitude was a more appropriate term than partnering, as I was held hostage to do the dirty deed. I was ashamed.

That very Friday, the Deputy Director and Sam's social worker came to my home to discuss the move with Sam. The Deputy Director was his former case worker of several years. That fact should have provided Sam a sense of trust and security. Sam was told he could not live in the same house with Michael, that it was a risk. Sam was surprised by this and asked how. He was given no concrete examples. His anger grew and he shouted:

"What! Do you think he's gonna kill me or something?"

No response from the Foundation. I just sat on the sideline helpless as Sam's rage grew. He was shocked and fought back hard.

"Why do you keep moving me?" He cried "I don't want to go!"

He was resolute that he would not move. The case workers were calm and understanding, but held their ground. His fists were clenched and he cried that it seemed to him they enjoyed moving him, and when they said they don't, he became more agitated and responded with:

"So why do you keep doing it?"

At that point the Deputy Director told me to explain the issue to Michael. I stuttered it out that I was forced to make a decision based on the Foundation's threat. They were not happy with that answer and pressed me to just tell him I made the decision to keep Michael over Sam. Here, we had to agree to disagree. We had different perspectives of the same issue. For them, I chose Michael over Sam. From my view, the stage was set by the Foundation demanding me to cut the family in half, thereby forcing me into a position to decide on who needed the placement most. Who needed the most protection at that time? My response to them was simply I would not force anyone out. In other words, I refused to make the decision. From the Foundation's view, my refusal to remove Michael was a decisive statement to prefer one child over another.

Though a meeting with the new family had been scheduled that very evening, Sam's explosive response forced a postponement to the next day. After the case managers left, Drake and I explained to Sam the decision that was thrust upon me in more detail. We talked about how I took Michael out of a shelter and could not in good conscience send him back. I tried to soften the blow to Sam with the statement that he had another home to stay without losing a heartbeat. He was more understanding and sympathetic to Michael's plight than any of us anticipated. He certainly should more empathy more than the Foundation. He did not want Michael to lose his home, though he was in no way ready to throw in the towel. Drake too was inconsolable. As for me, I was lost in a battle for which I had little real understanding.

That evening Sam called his former foster mom for help. This is another foster parent that has no fear standing up to the system. She is one tough woman. She advised him to call his lawyer and gave him the name and number. He immediately did so. The next day I was called. The lawyer was confused who I was. She was never notified Sam was moved to my home back in December, a requirement in the foster care legal process. I was not surprised. Did the Foundation violate family court process? They forgive themselves, but never anyone else. This lawyer was his Guardian et Litem, responsible for his best interest, not necessarily what he wanted, but she was certainly interested to hear him out.

The next day Sam was in no mood to meet a new family. But he reluctantly agreed. We were all anxious that morning. I asked Drake to come along for emotional support. We met the Deputy Director at the new prospective home and he quietly participated with arms crossed over his chest, face sullen and lowered. When the conversation ended, he had no questions and just left the room to hang outside with Drake. I stayed behind to talk more with the family. I did discuss Sam's nocturnal roaming issue and how they should expect him on the floor in their room. The dad was unabashed and told me his children jump into their bed in the morning and he was comfortable with it. I was surprised with that answer but only because of what I was dealing with at home. I guess I had forgotten the freedoms birth children enjoy that foster children cannot. Sam abruptly returned to the living room, plopped down on the sofa and announced his position to this family to whom he was just introduced: He had no intention of leaving his home.

"I'm sure you're really nice people, but I'm not living here. I'm not leaving my home," he spoke defiantly.

His reaction to the visit was a complete surprise to everyone. This was especially disheartening to the new family who expected Sam to move in that very day. They were not advised of the issues confronting the boy at our home prior to this visit. Typical of placement moves in foster care. Keep everyone in the dark to provide the least resistance. Once outside the home, leaving these poor people shell shocked, Sam cursed at the Deputy Director. The man told me later that it was at that moment he realized Sam was no longer the timid little boy whose case he had managed in the past.

The trip back home was terrifying as Sam raged in the car. He was physically distraught, screaming with anger, fists slamming against the car interior. He kept repeating that he would not be comfortable in that house. He couldn't be himself. He didn't want to move. He was tired of moving. I called the Foundation Deputy Director when we arrived home to advise him of Sam's raging, making it clear that if they intended to move him that night or the next day, they would need to force him out. Due to this firm stance and how he was demonstrating that he was more mature than they previously thought, the Foundation agreed to re-think their position. They did not want to muscle him out of my home.

Things remained quiet for a few weeks while we all hung on hope. Sam was now waiting for the next shoe to drop, along with the new family who were now on standby.

Michael, meanwhile, was also in shock. I had made arrangements for him to be away from the house with my friend from work the Friday Sam was first told about the impending move. I wanted to protect him from this traumatic crisis. Sam apparently sent a text message to a girl friend when he was told about the impending move. She in turn spread the word across town, including a text message to Michael. When he heard the news of Sam's move he cried and raged in my friend's car. He feared that if Sam was removed, he would not be far behind. It was from this point onward that I saw more acting out behavior at home, more rebellious behavior in school, and observed his general sense of depression. This attack on Sam's stability by the Foundation was a pivotal point that eroded the family morale. For the first time since Michael moved into our home, he realized I was not all powerful to protect him. His trust in me to shield him was shattered. This agency had power over dad's house. My promise that I would never abandon him had lost steam. If Sam could be threatened, so could he. By mid-March I was begging for support services. I wrote to Horizon:

He needs intense therapy and needs it now. Sexual trauma is only one of many psychiatric issues. The longer we wait on that one the higher the likelihood he will be a predator. All the other issues relate to his inability to function at school and within the family environment and they need to be addressed as well.

Looking back, the key issue for Michael was his lack of safety in our home. We were constantly under attack and he sensed it. Generally his sense of security should have improved as he settled. But, how could he calm down under such a confused and ever changing environment? How could any of us? To add insult to injury, during one of Michael's medicine reviews that occurred monthly, his psychiatrist told him the loss of his adoption was entirely his fault. His social worker was taken aback, but had no prior warning. Michael was again devastated and enraged when he came home.

Both Sam and Michael continued to react to each other's insecurity over disruption from our family. No doubt, they each blamed the other. By the third week in March Sam was told he would not be moved, as the trauma of a placement change outweighed the risk of keeping him with Michael. Also during this period, Michael's social worker came for a home visit to assure him he could stay with us as well. He was overjoyed. This was everything he had hoped to hear. Great news! I expected him to drop his guard. He did not. He was still cautious. He was more experienced in foster care then me. I wanted to be optimistic and embraced her every word. The air mattress disappeared. I purchased a full size bed for Michael that I had been promising him for some time. His room was complete, good news for me as well.

Since he came to our home, Michael too occasionally came to my room at night. Unlike Sam, who rolled himself in a blanket on the floor, Michael came to my bed. I would move him back, though that ritual could go back and forth several times. If I were very tired, I'd leave him in my bed and go sleep in his room. I found the air mattress very uncomfortable. The new bed provided a better night sleep.

With summer approaching, the pool warmed and Sam, more than Michael, really enjoyed splashing about with Nala. Golden Retrievers find water irresistible. I can never look out to my pool without seeing the perfect *Lassie* image of a boy with his dog. Another special memory of Sam happened when I was talking with Drake's social worker in front of my house. He was truly happy in his placement with our family.

Within days of the good news, I was informed by the Foundation that they still insisted on getting a full evaluation of Michael and would only allow him to stay if they felt he was not a risk. I should have held off on the expense of the new bed. They had now involved CPS in Maricopa County (District I) to support their position against the CPS in Casa Grande (District V). They were committed to disrupt Michael, who at this point was in a placement prepared for guardianship and adoption. The family was back in turmoil. A chess piece had been moved, but we were tentative of the impact. And of course, still no evaluation or therapy approved by Cenpatico.

Around the time when all this drama was in play, we experienced a very moving drive into Sam's past. Sam, Michael and I were in Phoenix for a meeting with the Foundation, and I decided to show them Drake's school, St. Mary's. I wanted Sam to see some options to public high school. After driving past Drake's school, I then drove further north to another private campus, Brophy

High School. Sam immediately recognized the area and asked if he could see his old neighborhood. I was game and let him navigate me deeper into this old worn neighborhood. He was familiar with the streets and directed us to his old home where he lived with his mom and her boyfriend. He was going down memory lane. He seemed excited as he shared little tidbits of his past. He pointed out places where he did some yard work and neighbors with whom he had developed friendships. He talked about his mom's boyfriend who was always high on drugs, at times screaming naked in the front yard that he was Jesus. The excitement gave way to an uncomfortable silence. As we left the area, he started weeping. Michael felt very sad for him, but reassured him that he had felt the same when thinking about his past. Driving down Central Avenue, Sam pointed out a corner convenience store where his parents forced him to panhandle. He remained emotionally distant driving home. Michael's attitude mirrored Sam's sorrow.

At the end of March, yet another staffing was scheduled for Michael. This time, however, the head of mental health services for the local CPS district was in attendance. Finally, an evaluation was ordered through CPS since the mental health provider was still paralyzed. It was also determined that a Guardian et Litem should be assigned to provide Michael better legal support. But in terms of any change to his current situation, nothing was happening. I wrote in despair to Horizon in early April: "Still waiting for action, not issues, problems and hurdles."

Oblivious to this escalating political drama building around them, the two boys continued playing around the neighborhood like normal young teens, though they were settling into different routines. Sam, quiet and reserved, tended to stay home more, while Michael was rarely in the house. He preferred the excitement of peer interaction. Both boys, however, had mischievous moments. On several occasions Sam arranged to meet his friends at our town lake after ten at night. Of course, that would be after his bedtime. I learned much later that he even went to a girlfriend's house that had another girl spending the night. He snuck in and stayed until two in the morning. The free spirit of youth!

Michael heard of these nighttime escapades and tried his hand at the scheme. One night he waved off his usual bedtime tuck-in. I was suspicious. A little later, I checked in his room to find him dressed lying on top of his covers. He curtly told me he wanted to be ready for school the next day. I thought differently. After a short debate, he admitted he had made arrangements with friends to meet at the lake around ten. I foiled his plans and he tattled on Sam. I quickly confronted Sam that very night. He quickly confessed his past discretions, though he was angry at Michael for telling. They were acting like normal brothers.

These two were also often embroiled in young teen love. 'Going out' with a girl was of primary concern with all the boys in the neighborhood. Mind you, this does not mean they date and go out alone to the movies. It is more a concurrence between two parties that they singularly like each other which may include permission for a kiss. These relationships can last as long as a week or two, but typically disintegrate within days . . . for Michael, within hours. I remember one great crisis involving half-a-dozen children that played out at my house with the girls gathering off to one side of the room and the boys on the other. This all centered on one girl who wanted to dump her boyfriend for Sam. Michael, by his very nature, couldn't help but be caught in the middle, trying to be the peace maker and enhance his position with Sam. Be advised that both boys involved with this girl were part of this soap opera at my house. Only middle school children could create such a dramatic situation. It all played out to Sam's advantage that night when Sam was accepted over the other youth amidst great emotional trauma and tears. But the relationship fell apart as soon as the next day and the girl returned to her old boyfriend. Sam was angry and Michael soon lost his reputation as the matchmaker. Both boys learned a valuable lesson: Don't try to understand women, especially young ones.

Michael's evaluation appointment was scheduled for mid April. Finally we achieved a key milestone. It took 104 days from the time he was turned back to CPS by his adoptive parents. If we go back to the original written request by Horizon in August of 2007, it took 8 months for this evaluation.

Things continued to deteriorate for Michael at our home across the board. School issues, behavior issues, inappropriate peer interaction and we needed help. Michael was extremely high strung, nervous, and easily agitated. His moods swung from high to low. My continued frustrations and anxiety with his behaviors and inability to get him any help, combined with broken promises from school staff, fueled these negative behaviors.

On a positive note, he was rapidly maturing. The little frightened child who entered my home in January was acting more like a teenager. Requests for a tuck-in at night declined, though occasionally he would ask. His attitude seemed more as a check-in of me than a real emotional need. He was spending more and more of his time with Sam or other children in the neighborhood. He had also discovered an undeveloped area not far from our home with large dirt burs that the children worked into dirt jumps for their bikes. He enjoyed it as much as skateboarding. More and more I connected with his Huck Finn character.

The peer activity he most enjoyed was church youth group. He attended almost every week at our local church. It started with dinner for everyone, followed by age groups splitting off for religious discussions and group activities. The young teens had a special place to associate in a separate building, formerly the minister's home. It boasted table tennis and informal areas for the young people to just relax and talk. Adults were quietly present in the background. I looked forward to picking him up each week because I knew he would be all smiles. That was one of those special times when I felt content and secure he had a home. Thinking back now brings pangs of sorrow. He was just so happy!

Michael did face some discrimination from the community. Most were suspicious of a child who did not attend the local school. Several times I was told that when Michael started a new friendship, the parents would call the school to ask about him. His teacher told me she never disclosed information, but did tell them if he was assigned to her special education campus that should be a clue. He so desperately wanted to be on the main campus like his prior school with his adoptive parents. His reasons were social, not academic. Michael had drawn the battle line on this issue and fought the entire term at that school. He played the role of rebel.

He was dismissed from school two hours earlier than the main campus; so he would ride his bike there and wait for that school to end to hook up with people walking home, primarily girls. On one occasion, he initiated a conversation with a girl, and another boy quickly intruded warning him to get lost. He became irate and aggressive and stood his ground. The boy soon gained a group of other boy supporters who threatened Michael. He did not back down. The whole group moved away from the school grounds while the action continued. This was observed by my neighbor who had developed a close relationship with Michael and suspected he was in danger. Fortunately, this caring mother followed with her car and Michael safely left the scene with her.

This neighbor is one of those all maternal people who adopts all the neighborhood children. I know she had a special place in her heart for Michael with which she struggled at times. When he was feeling down and needed bolstering, her home was his destination. This was also his safe haven when he decided to play hooky from school. Remember, he dreaded the restricted environment, and some days he just could not get motivated to get on that special education bus. I was always gone for work by six. Sam woke him up around seven for the bus at eight. That was the ritual. It was also common for me to get the seven forty-five phone call from Sam:

"Michael says he's feeling sick and not going to school. You know he's faking it Dad."

In the beginning I did not. I'd leave work to check him out. He was smart and knew how to play my heart strings. But after a short time I would just get him on the phone to tell him to get his butt on that bus. I would then call the school to confirm he arrived. Sometimes he just ignored me, but that was rare and usually due to a prior day's crisis in the classroom. Those were the days I'd tell him to walk over to the neighbor. She was kind, understanding, but firm. She was an experienced mom. But if she couldn't talk him into going, she had him do chores around her house. He always returned from her home with a broad smile and bright eyes. Living with a single dad drove all my boys to seek out a maternal figure in the neighborhood. For Michael it was my neighbor.

I know Sam also spent time at her home. Well, she did have a teenage daughter in his grade, so it was not unusual to see a group of these pretty things conversing on her front lawn. Sam was never shy to drop over and join the conversation, cell phone tossing in his hand, never losing a beat. He could carry on a conversation while simultaneously texting to the rest of the community. This was a very traditional and safe family. The mother maintained a strict household keeping close watch over the children. These children would not be found roaming after dark.

I was not giving up, but felt so helpless at the moment watching Michael spiral with no therapeutic support for him or our family. I felt isolated from the Foundation and out of patience with Horizon and CPS. During this same period in April, the school sent home a report in an unsealed envelope which Michael read on the bus. In this document he read about the teacher's concerns for his class behavior and general mental health. She discussed his complaints about stomach aches, small accidents throughout the day, weekly vomiting and picking at scabs causing them to bleed. The most hurtful statement he read was:

Michael displays behaviors that indicate he is at risk for suicide. Michael presents himself as a very unhappy child.

He came home that evening outraged as he handed me the report. Later that evening he was despondent. I immediately advised his social worker of the incident. It seemed no matter what we tried to do, we could not find peace in our home. To me, Michael seemed very happy with the family, but miserable in school due to how he was treated from the very beginning on a restricted campus managed like a boot camp. He was outgoing and engaging. To be isolated from other children was emotional torment. He was also such a free spirit, that the more they squeezed him to submission, the greater his rebellion. Thomas Paine, author of *Common Sense and the Rights of Man*, would have been proud of his fiery soul.

During this time we also suffered the first major physical explosion in the household since Michael arrived in January. It was in the making for months waiting for an ignition. Our greyhound dog Capri was the catalyst. On several occasions since I adopted her two years past, she would escape from the backyard to race down the street at forty miles per hour. Greyhounds are big and easy to spot, but not so easy to follow at such high speeds. We also lived just yards from the golf course which was the home to many small fuzzy creatures. Once in that territory, she was in pure race mode. All we could do was wait it out; then search her out lying down panting.

One fair night, one of Drake's friends left the back gate open. She took off. Michael, who was in the driveway and quick to the mark, grabbed her collar hard to drag her back through the gate. Drake, reacting to the rough handling of the dog, ordered him to release her. He did not. Drake was surrounded by his friends and in no mood for a defiant kid. Michael, unaware of Drake's attitude, was wholly focused on being the hero that put the dog back in the yard. This was an opportunity to enhance favor with me. Drake yelled, grasped Michael by the throat and tossed him. Michael ran into the house, called the police, grabbed a camping knife, and proceeded to stab the living room walls in fury. The police and emergency services arrived quickly, and immediately turned their focus on the kid with the knife. Not at all what Michael had planned on.

The matter was resolved without the police taking action, though it raised tensions even more. Michael did suffer a small cut on the finger from mishandling the knife that required a Band-Aid from the emergency vehicle. That was a five hundred dollar bandage. While the action was in play, it drew quite a few spectators from the neighboring houses, huddling and speculating on the incident before them. I live in a sleepy town, not much happens.

Later that night Drake apologized to Michael and promised never to lose his temper like that again. Drake scared himself as much as Michael. That was one of those nights when Michael asked if I were giving up on him. We all recommitted ourselves to his membership in our family. We were not going to give up on him. I knew this act of absolution gave him new hope. Drake asked for his forgiveness which was not given until the next day.

I was feeling more and more helpless. And overwhelmed with the daily battle swirling around us, I was not providing as strict a regime required for such a diverse mix of kids. I did not have a strong disciplinary attitude toward Michael, as I was waiting for a therapist to provide guidance. I was not secure with his mental disability and unsure how to implement any consequence without escalating his behavior. He was still sexually acting out such as pulling the front of his boxers down, which was always accompanied by a blank and meaningless stare when confronted with his inappropriate action. I didn't want to make a big deal about it, hoping if I ignored the behavior, he'd get bored of it and stop. I had no understanding of the depth of his illness and could find no one to provide guidance. As much as I complained to all the agencies, including my own, no one offered specific suggestions for me.

Lynn spent most weekends at the house throughout this period. I assumed she would be more guarded due to her loss of innocence earlier. But I learned she was actually more desirous. Drake, on the other hand, was having opposite feelings after the last lecture from her parents. He was not ready for marriage and did not want to escalate the relationship. On several occasions she would complain about being too tired to go home and spend the night on the sofa. Youth being what it is, they gravitated to one another during the night.

Once again, we called a family conclave with Lynn's parents. This time the meeting was at our home. Drake was indignant. He felt that the family was blaming him for this indiscretion, when it was the daughter who was the passive aggressor. He realized, however, it was his initial act that created her new desire. This meeting was more strained than the first. Marriage plans were a key topic, which pushed Drake further away. Perhaps that was her parents' intention.

After the family left, Drake was fuming. I called the mom to explain his position and recommended that her daughter limit her weekend visits. Within weeks, the relationship was on the rocks. Lynn held tight, but Drake was already distancing himself emotionally. After nearly a year of intense emotional connection, the relationship ended. Due to his own emotional baggage and immaturity, Drake sent a text message rather than initiating a personal meeting, assuming that would bring closure. He had no emotional understanding of himself, let alone empathy for others. He was not being cruel. He was just that distant from true human emotion. I was now seeing the real Drake and the core issue that drove his many antisocial behaviors.

Under so much continuous stress, I went to see my doctor for help. My blood pressure was pulsing at 180/120, and that was on medication. Drake was with me that day as I vented over my stressful life with the children. He was my family doctor from the time Nick was a little boy in the mid-1980's and knew me and the brood well. He cared for all the children, even my newest additions.

He had recently examined Michael and was aware of his history. I was impressed how gently he handled the gentile examination as Michael was animate that no one was touching him down there. He was very nervous when the doctor came in the examining room. At the time, Michael had a major yeast rash. That was the key to checking his groin and the rest flowed smoothly.

As I continued venting, the doctor interrupted and told me with complete candor, it's time to get rid of the children. He wasn't joking. Drake jumped into the conversation to tell the doctor we already dismissed that option, and further asked the doctor to just give me a prescription to calm my nerves. He was a good front man. We left with a prescription in hand. Fortunately for me, I was able to stop the new medication in a month in lieu of more natural outlets such as working out at the YMCA with Drake and bike riding. God bless endorphins.

The day arrived for Michael to have his evaluation, immediately followed by a staffing to close on a single case agreement for therapy. On the way to the evaluation, I stopped off to see Michael's adoptive dad. He had offered to let me have copies of prior evaluations done by CPS years past. I grabbed a thick stack of documents and rushed to the appointment. Michael was very nervous during the drive to the therapist. He was constantly rubbing his groin and talking about unrelated topics that had no meaning. We drove around longer than planned, getting lost finding the office which was located in a house in a run-down neighborhood

After a short wait in the lobby, the psychologist introduced himself and led Michael away. He was curt and appeared bland of personality. A short time later, he sat with me to ask some questions about Michael's behavior in my home. I gave him the highlights and handed him a bunch of papers I pulled from the stack of documents provided by his dad. I thought at the time the information would help him.

Michael was physically, emotionally, and sexually charged leaving the psychologist's office after the evaluation. First thing out of his mouth was a complaint about all the questions. He said there were hundreds, so he just filled in answers randomly to get it done fast. That made sense with his ADHD. He then told me he really liked the guy and they talked a lot about sex. Michael likes to talk about sex. He will engage as long as he has an attentive audience. He said the guy had him take his pants down and gave him an erection that he liked. I did not react, but just drove on. One needed to have filters when listening to Michael. It was a fine line between reality and fantasy in his mind. He also never really accepted responsibility for telling stories; rather if caught in a lie, he would come back with the line: "I was joking!" What was unexpected to me during that drive is that he pulled his penis out of his pants right in the car with me driving. This was not his common behavior. And in this instance, he was fully erected. Whatever happened in that office, his testosterone was in full overdrive! He could be scary at times.

What was really happening for Michael that day would require a highly skilled professional to fully grasp. Was he angry at me for pushing for the evaluation and making him fess up to his issues? Was there more to him then I could possibly have known and now it was all out on the table? He was acting very sexual and annoyed at the same time.

We attended the staffing to choose a therapist. We agreed on the Resolution Group, but there was some concern over contract issues with Cenpatico. Driving home that afternoon, his penis again flipped out of his pants. It was clear to me he was under extreme stress that day. Perhaps he knew he'd be moved now and that all his efforts to secure his place with me were lost. From that time on, he was more distant and exasperating at home.

The next week Cenpatico contracted with a different therapeutic firm than I had requested due to contract issues. This other firm required him to participate in group with children on probation for sex crimes, even though he had never been arrested or convicted for such behavior. It caught me off guard and I overreacted to the implications of such treatment. In hindsight, I wish the therapist had taken the time to discuss the approach and Michael's anticipated reactions, so I would have been better prepared. To keep us all on our toes, Michael had a football accident just before the intake which required a hospital visit and splinting. Fortunately, such injuries heal quickly. But, he missed more school.

Immediately following the intake with his therapist, I requested that he attend Group immediately which was indicated as part of his treatment plan. I wanted things to start as soon as possible. After the very first session, Michael began acting out more under this new stress. He felt enraged that he was put in the same category as the other kids in the program. Unfortunately, I was frightened by some of his statements due to a lack of understanding; a fear I disclosed to his social worker. He told me that the therapist confronted him about having sex with little children and dogs. He acted shocked, like he didn't remember. I tried to be consoling, but was freaked myself by his statements. The conversation ended with him telling me that there was stuff I didn't know.

Was he giving up on us, thinking we would reject him knowing the detail of his past? Or worse to me, was there things happening in my community. How many teen girls and young children did he have contact with during those months since January. He had talked about a girl, or was it two, but I never knew if he was making up stories to boast or really was involved in sexual activity. If so, how many children did he try to hustle? With so much turmoil, and being confronted with his past while trying to grasp the reality of his current situation, he struggled for control. He was acting more combative than ever.

I arranged a meeting with his new therapist to understand the rules of his confinement now that it was determined he needed to be managed at all times. It was less than I first expected based on Michael's input to me the prior week. So many issues could have been handled with less stress if the adults had better communicated. My recommendation would be that a therapist should discuss all issues involving a change to a child's care with the parent prior to such a discussion with the child. Otherwise, as with me, when the child overreacts, so too could the parent. Such an approach also can set the stage for the communication of false information, since children will express their reaction more than the objective data provided them.

In addition to now being restricted to constant supervision far worse than what I initiated back in January when he joined our family, I turned off the internet in the house and had our greyhound adopted out. The dog slept with Michael, which was a significant concern of his therapist. Though I never noticed anything unusual, the therapist simply stated that I did not know what was going on at two in the morning. I was appalled by the innuendo, but complied. I did not want to lose Michael over a dog. My fears grew, however, was Michael engaging in bestiality?

She was gone the next week. A pure bred is easy to place; more so than children. The whole family felt her absence. Of the two dogs, she was the most active. The house felt strangely quiet. Fortunately, I held off taking any action with Nala. I raised her from a pup and she had formed a close bond with Sam with whom she slept every night. Jason heard about the loss of Capri and called immediately to ask about Nala. He was happy I still had her, but warned me he would take her in Colorado if need be. He made it clear in his tone that giving away Nala was not an option.

Soon after therapy started, the psychologist's report was submitted to CPS with a recommendation for him to be placed in a therapeutic foster home where he would be under constant supervision. I was advised he was a danger to the community. Around the same time, his therapist was evaluating possible options for him to stay with me such as day care after school and a shadow at school. This Therapist acted as if he did not want Michael to lose his placement. A new staffing was held the first week of May.

Prior to that meeting I had asked CPS not to discuss the move with Michael until a placement could be determined to avoid anymore undue stress in the home. I was advised to discuss this issue with his therapist, which I did, and who agreed with my position due to Michael's impulsive behavior and unstable condition. Unfortunately, we were ignored by CPS. Michael was told of this impending loss anyway, and then allowed to return home with me. He was given no indication of where or when he would be moved. The CFT team made a point to give him comfort with the promise he could see me as often as I had time. They even asked for my concurrence in front of him. This is the partnering manipulation used by CPS to maintain control of the child. It was another lie in his life. He was forbidden contact as soon as he was moved.

Foster children learn early that people in authority are not to be trusted. I believe this sets a pattern of distrust that impacts their ability to be good citizens the rest of their lives. Never trust anyone in authority, and fight society to get what you want and stay in control.

Since CPS returned him to my home, after concluding he was a danger to my community, Horizon did offer to provide a support person in the home to be with Michael from the time he returned from school until I returned from work: a shadow! By midweek the shadow arrived, two in fact. I was home to greet them, only to be shocked that they were told nothing of his background or about the rules he had to follow and expectations of his behavior pattern. Does the ineptitude ever end? I called the agency to get the same old apology. It was all too little, too late.

I found it more and more stressful keeping Michael on a leash after he had enjoyed such freedom over the past few months. I sent an email to CPS with a sarcastic comment about not wanting to be his jailor. On one occasion when Drake and I accompanied him to the local skate park, we were shocked when an older teen rolled by Michael asking how he looked naked.

Drake reacted immediately: "What the hell!" and bolted toward the teen in fury.

The kid got the message and fled the area. Michael just casually brushed off the remark saying the kid was just fooling around. Was he? Or was I the fool being manipulated all this time?

With pressure soaring and everyone's security at an all time low, Drake announced he was dropping out of high school. After all the effort to get him into St. Mary's he was walking away. He was eighteen and throwing his weight around, though in a self-destructive way. I appealed to his common sense, but failed. He was spending much of his time away from the stress at home, hanging out with older youth. He was envious of their transition lifestyle living at home, but out of school. These kids flaunted their freedom, something Drake strove to attain his entire childhood. One planned to go to Texas to make big money at an oil rig and Drake talked about going with him. This was familiar talk. Prior to going to Canyon State, he spoke about going to Alaska to be a fisherman. He simply wanted to escape his current condition, and in many ways, run from himself.

After he left school I made it clear he was not going to just take the summer off. If he were done being a student, it was time to join the work force. Tom made arrangements for him to visit a professional training school for welding for which he had shown an interest for some time. After several failed attempts due to immaturity and indecision, he did visit the school. The amount of work and time commitment far outweighed high school. His enthusiasm faded. Meanwhile, he was offered a job lifeguarding.

I reported Michael's condition regularly to CPS and worried daily about his behavior as well as the impact on the rest of the family. We continued in complete turmoil. Sam was advising Michael to rage and show them he didn't want to go in hopes of getting the same success as he did with the Foundation. For me personally, the knowledge he was now leaving after all the effort to keep him, was emotionally overwhelming. I forwarded some suggestions to CPS and Horizon regarding employing a full time nanny, but I was drawing at straws. The decision was made and it was time to move forward.

Later that week, he had his first major tantrum with me directly. Walls and doors got the brunt of his feet as he poured out his anger. How disappointed he was. From his perspective, I failed him. He was suffering the anxiety of yet another rejection and loss. He took off on his bike saying he was running away. I contacted his therapist immediately, and after Michael returned, we went straight to see him.

It was a difficult drive. Michael just wanted out. The pain of losing his new family he had struggled so hard to maintain was overwhelming him. For the first time since January, he called me Bill. He also argued with me in the car that I was not crying over him leaving. He was justifying his actions. We spoke with the therapist who handled the situation with great calm. He spoke to Michael about the wasted energy beating the door. It would change nothing. He kept asking Michael to raise his head and look at him, to which Michael despondently responded. The boy calmed down and agreed. I broke down in front of Michael. The therapist asked him to leave the room which he did. He was uncomfortable with my reaction. I cried like a baby, blurting out things like:

"I tried everything. I love him so much. I don't want to lose him. I don't know what to do."

After I regained control I said to the therapist the most terrifying words any parent can say aloud:

"They (CPS) won't let me keep him. Will they?" He nodded in affirmation.

He was lost. At that moment I understood the sheer agony of losing a child to illness after a long battle, never knowing from one day to the next any certainty of the outcome, but you keep fighting, begging the doctors for any new drug to give you hope. I witnessed this very same situation with my dad. During his last days at the hospital my mom was searching for any medical procedure to hold on. After days of unconsciousness and the doctors and nurses restating the hopelessness of his case, she let go. I was by his bedside when my mom held him tight, giving him permission to 'leave.' He passed on that evening.

I knew that night this turmoil had to end. The boy I loved as a son was not mine to keep. A boy who adopted me as a father needed to find a replacement. Michael came back into the room about that time and we embraced. It was the most painful hug we exchanged. All the blood and sweat invested was for not. We were both agonizingly aware that this was goodbye. It was the end of a struggle we both worked so hard to win, but failed.

I advised CPS and Horizon the next day that I would bring him to the Horizon office in Casa Grande. I had no faith in a quick solution based on the last 4 months. I felt the need to push, rather than wait for the pull from the system. I let him sleep late that morning. I was committed to the decision to break this ongoing disruption by the system. The time for departure was upon us.

When he awoke, I told him it was time to leave. He threw a small fit of anger, but he knew it was over. Our battle was lost. I reaffirmed I would continue to advocate adopting him, I would not abandon him, but the power was in the hands of CPS. I'm not sure he believed it. Honestly, I was skeptical of something positive occurring anytime soon. Trust is so fleeting, and truth had rarely been our ally. He packed, as I'd seen him do in the past, with great care, meticulous to the end. He was lethargic that morning as we drove down to Casa Grande. He kept his cell phone until the end, texting all his friends about his departure. Children were crying in class; teachers confused, classrooms disrupted. He had left a mark in our little town. He had many friends and established his presence as a member of the Hunter family. Many of these children still call and stop by asking when Michael will come home.

Once again, Michael had a guardian angel and he was placed in a wonderful therapeutic home that very day in our general area. The good news was he found a home quickly, but like so many times in his past, the new foster parents were not told of his sexual past until after they accepted him. This is a recurring pattern in the system.

I was not permitted to take him, standard operating procedure. I was good enough to hold him when they had no placement, but now I was to be thrown away, tossed out with the trash. Drake and I drove home in silence. What could possibly be said that had not already been expressed so many times in the past? He was gone. I can never listen to Josh Groban again without seeing his wide smile and bright blue eyes.

It was Friday, with no time to properly close with the new family on all the rules. Hell, the agencies didn't even have time to pass on the most basic information about him such as the fact that he was just diagnosed a sexual predator. When he arrived at his new home he had the mom call immediately to tell me he was alright and asked for his things. The social worker would have been fuming. Though he assumed that what he was told at the CFT was the truth and he could contact me, he would learn in 48 hours, it was not. My other foster children warned me that we would never see him again, and that the whole story of visits after removal was to get him to move without a fuss. I was naïve, or like Michael, just hanging on to hope. My other foster children knew the truth. They lived this form of manipulation.

I did bring him his things the next day and was grateful for the opportunity to have met these people and help Michael get situated in his new room. He was excited because the room had two beds, so he assumed he was going to have a foster brother with him. I tried to bring him back to reality. He hadn't said anything about his past to his new foster parents and may have convinced himself he would have a new start and escape all the turmoil he suffered with the recent therapy. I was hopeful that he would respond well and follow the direction provided by the therapist.

While sitting on his bed taking a break from moving furniture around, his new foster mom and I talked about my hope for his return one day. I felt her warm, maternal instincts. They glowed from her inviting smile. While we spoke, Michael broke in saying he assumed this new mom would adopt him. Looking down to the floor he asked if he should be Michael R or Michael H. He was very confused, still trying to grab onto just a tiny slice of security. All he wanted was a family which continued to be denied him. Later, while we sat at the kitchen table, he casually asked what I thought of this placement with an African American family. He explained how shocked he was getting out of the car to her welcoming arms. She admitted the same about seeing a very white boy with red hair and blue eyes. I gently assured him he was in good caring hands and that is all that mattered for the moment.

When I returned home, I sent an email out to all involved in his case over the past five months to recommit my desire to adopt Michael despite his mental disability. However, CPS made it clear that they were taking their time (moving at a snail pace in their own terms) to determine the best placement for his condition and recovery. I would continue the fight for his return; even though I knew from experience I was climbing up a dangerous path. The fight seemed timeless and wore me down; burned me out. If ever he returned after eighteen, he would know that someone in his past did not give up on him, a statement he confronted me with many times during his stay with us. He will know that one person kept his promise.

On Monday I spoke with his new foster mom who was trying to get him to school not knowing his schedule or even where the school was located. I offered to help. That is when I was told about no contact with Michael. The promise of the CFT was all a ploy. What CPS ignores is that the children never forget these lies. Such experiences only fortify their distrust and hatred of authority which can play out in deviant behavior later in life.

After Michael was gone, our home quickly settled down, too much so in the other direction. Suddenly, all was dead quiet. Michael was the squeaky wheel that kept things lively. He was high spirited, at times too much so. He was a taker, a behavior pattern that had burned out many of his former foster parents in the past. His absence was felt by all, and like is so often the case with foster children, his departure was bitter sweet. We all loved him and appreciated his companionship, but at the same time found his domineering behavior hurtful as he always labored to stay in control.

Throughout this period I remained in contact with his social worker. Even though it was a transitional placement, it was important for his therapeutic work for him to settle in and not be confused with prior parental relationships. It's always a trade-off with which social workers wrestle: maintaining prior relationships to reduce the trauma of loss or complete separation to support a new start. Sadly, as children get moved from placement to placement, they often lose past connections, some of which are more powerful than case workers at first recognize. The children bury the pain deep down, only for it to resurface in the form of depression or worse, external rage. As a result, they are unable to form meaningful relationships in the future, or just refuse to do so to protect themselves from anymore suffering.

My son Drake is such a case. Growing up in my home he never allowed himself to get hurt. He never knew true love either. This problem only festered. When Drake entered puberty and felt the first surge of lust, he knew only the physical attributes of sex, not the warm spirit of love. My first foster son Jason raged with such ferocity he frightened most everyone around him at home, in school, and in the community. Michael has shown me both sides of that coin. I have seen his rage as well as his utter despondency. His former mom witnessed such raging demonstrations where he would smash his knuckles until they bled. I have seen the sullen eyes and morbid heart as well. I fear how much sorrow he can endure before the inner demon takes control.

Final Moments

Just three weeks after losing Michael, Drake had the episode with the bong. As this act played out, Sam's social worker appeared at the door with her supervisor. This was one of the Foundation people that participated in that ominous CFT where I was told to throw Michael out of my home or Sam would be removed. I knew from experience something was very wrong; this clinical manager never came to my house.

The social worker went off to talk with Sam in his room to have what I assumed at the moment, her monthly check up meeting. Then the supervisor suggested Tom take Drake for a walk as she sat down and immediately began with:

"Seeing me here, you know something is happening. It is not about Drake, not that what he did isn't serious."

This is when your system shuts down, your heart skips a few beats and your mind goes hazy. I was still focused on reprimanding Drake about pot and the bong, and developing an approach with Tom to get him drug free and back on track.

The supervisor disclosed that I was under investigation for neglect of Michael. That the allegations were such that it was rated a level five, but something had changed, moving it up to a level three which required all foster children to be immediately removed from my home. She was blunt and to the point.

When I asked what I had done that was considered neglect, she was unable to share any details other than the allegations came through CPS and not the Foundation. They only knew because they held my license.

The walls moved in as my mind raced through a movie of past incidents that would be neglectful. I was thinking in terms of physical neglect and the type of incidents that cause CPS to be called to take a child from one's home. I was unable to center on any specific issue other than Michael's general behavior problems that I dismissed since he was placed back with me even after the decision was made to move him away. I was left in a state of emotional and mental confusion.

I remembered the phone call from CPS advising me of the evaluation report and the need to move Michael into a therapeutic home. I asked what happened. What did he do? What did I do? Everything was confidential. I asked what I should do different while he was still in my home, in my neighborhood. The answer still shocks me today: "Just keep doing what you've been doing." Even then, I was still not given specific guidance. My stomach just clinched tight.

Sam entered the family room with a bag in hand, nothing more. He was clearly as shocked as me. He had fought so hard to stay. He had the fortitude to call his lawyer in the past and beg for help. He was determined to battle the Foundation and physically confront anyone who dared to force him out. The move by them was brilliant. Sam was caught off guard. What could he do or say. He assumed Drake was being removed also.

As we all stood about, no one really knew what to say. The supervisor continued that she was uncertain how long the investigation would take and Sam needed to be prepared to be away for several weeks, perhaps more. I asked him about his *PS3*. He acted with indifference replying that he had no bag to take it. I rummaged in the garage for a plastic storage container and helped him pack it. We both went through the motions but said nothing, avoiding each other' eyes. Back in the family room we said our goodbyes. I asked if he could take his cell phone so he could stay in touch with his friends. The supervisor agreed. He left the house a dejected child. He was gone. He was very angry, as much at me as anyone else. I had disappointed him greatly. I did not fight; I showed only submission to those he least trusted. As he drove away with his social worker, he was filled with frustration and fear, countered only by a glimmer of hope to return. Tom said goodbye to Drake. The supervisor offered condolences and drove off. Drake and I were alone. Drake left the house to cry. That was my final defining moment in foster care.

Some part of me knew I would not see him for a long time, if ever. But my never defeatist, optimistic character was already moving into attack mode. I needed to quickly move this investigation forward. What could I do? The supervisor had given me the name of the investigator, but I was too overwhelmed during our short conversation to write it down. That evening I felt empty. The house was cold. Several weeks earlier it had been so energetic with both Michael and Sam, two young active teens briskly seeking out their next adventure. Now I sat in an empty shell, staring out into space with the television for companionship. Drake tried to provide comfort later that evening, but was presently besieged with personal grief and self-doubt. He certainly felt some responsibility with both the bong incident and Sam's departure occurring at the same instance. He must also have felt an uncertainly for his own future.

I was depressed and anxious about Sam. He had sent a few text messages, the most significant being: *Am I coming home?*

I often think back to February. Had I made a different decision to have Michael removed and not Sam, how different it would have played out! Our life would have calmed down immediately. Sam would never have been removed. Michael may still have eventually gotten his evaluation, though it may have taken a number of sexual encounters with other children in the group home to provide the catalyst. One can never second guess a decision. I soon forgot the circumstances, emotions, and pressures of the moment. If done over, I would not have left Michael in the shelter, and I would not have tossed him out under outside pressures. During some of the most difficult times with my other foster boys, they would often tell me: 'I am who you see, accept me for that.' Am I so different?

Twelve years of good service with the Foundation was destroyed by a deed that could be interpreted in hindsight to be foolish, even ignorant. I defied a major foster care agency to help a child whose own future was unknown from the very beginning. A therapist found my actions to be questionable at best. How could anyone give up their family's stability, job security, and health for a mentally disabled kid, even one they may have known from a family friendship? It defied reason, and of course, therapists always must define a behavior based on psychological motivation and mental condition. To commit to another human being for love alone, for that person and nothing else, apparently does not easily fit any textbook definition. I must admit, however, I do receive great joy from their happiness and from advocating for their best interest. Sometimes just fighting the fight is motivation enough. Unfortunately, in Michael's case, I was consumed by the battle.

***

Drake's Journal (18 years old)

One day, a friend and I decided to buy a bong together with our first pay check. Things went as planned and we had for a couple of days, and one night he and I got irresponsible with trying to keep a secret and got really stoned and didn't know what was going on. We left the Bong and paraphernalia on the picnic table in the backyard. I was still feeling the effects the next morning and looked for the bong. My friend and I panicked, first thinking the pool guy took it. We were still shaking from smoking that night. I took off.

When I returned to the house my case worker was there with my dad. They were sitting having a serious conversation, and I knew exactly what they were talking about. Well I immediately shut down and lost touch of reality. I got numb cause they pretty much had way more than enough of that shit and I didn't know what they were going to do. They could've thrown me on the street. I thought it was going to kill my dad; he looked as if he was going insane, crying and crying. As I sat down and began breaking the ice that was between the three of us, the Foundation people walked through the door. At the time, I had no idea what was going on. I thought they were there for me, but I realized something else was up as Tom asked to talk to me outside. We talked about the bong, and how seriously bad the situation was and that Sam was moving. Tom insisted that he didn't know why Sam was leaving other than it had nothing to do with me. After that we went back into the house and I had to get out of there before I exploded into tears, so I called my smoke buddy and went to his house. I loved Sam.

They stole my brother.

***

Farewell

Sam was gone. When he learned that Drake was still with me, he was furious. He blamed Drake for some of the issues at home as much as Michael. He was the only innocent one of us. He knew it. The Foundation knew it. But that did not save him this personal loss and humiliation among his friends.

After a number of phone calls, I setup an interview with the CPS investigator the following week. I wanted this to end. It was one of the most depressing periods of my life . . . hopeless, helpless, and empty. I was lingering on the edge of an abyss to confront unknown allegations.

Sam was sent to his old foster home and we exchanged a number of texts that weekend. Sunday afternoon I drove over to bring him some clothes. He was scuttled out of the house so quickly that all he packed was a pile of dirty clothes, including a bed sheet, from his hamper. He was a teenage boy after all! When I arrived, the foster parents were surprised. Apparently, Sam did not communicate his invitation to me very clearly. I gave him his clothes and sat down to chat with his foster dad. Though I felt very uncomfortable under the current circumstances, I was relieved he was with friends. After he left that home in December, I kept the relationship alive with phone calls and visits. Thank God. How much more difficult this would all have been if it was the first time we all spoke since Sam left them back in January, which was done quickly and under somewhat difficult circumstances. In many ways, the current situation was similar to the move to me in that Sam was confused and not fully engaged in the transition. Rather, he was just torn away by a powerful rip tide of decisions made in his absence. What was significantly different this time was that he did not want to move. His soul and mind were defiant.

The investigative meeting was at my home and lasted perhaps an hour. The concern was over the one skinny dipping activity the boys engaged with back in February, allegations of them going in my room, and if I thought Michael was "coming on to me." Even at that time, I did not fully comprehend the meaning of the questions. They did skinny dip. They did come in my room at times, Sam even slept on the floor occasionally when he was lonely. Michael tried to do the same, but I usually carried him back to his bedroom for another tuck-in ceremony. The last issue was better addressed by a professional, not me. I was still naïve to the whole issue of Michael's sexual disturbance. From my perspective, he was a very immature child reacting to his past. Clearly others saw something much darker and deviant.

The investigator remained pleasant and impartial throughout the process. Considering my level of stress and feelings of loss, I was very appreciative of her kindness. After she left, Drake and I just stared at each other in disbelief. That was it? Sam lost his home over those allegations? Behaviors that a social worker could have easily discussed with me, lectured me, given guidance, and if necessary, slap me over the head! Would CPS take children from a normal family under such allegations? There must be more, I thought, but she did tell me in her opening statement that she was disclosing all the allegations under investigation. I was lost. If foster parents have rights, I was missing the point of it all. Sadly, Sam had no rights but to endure more lose.

I was told the following week that the allegations were unsubstantiated. It would take two more months for the report to be written that said the same. However, in the risk management business of foster care, you are guilty until proven innocent.

Throughout this period my health continued to suffer, which by this time was already in decline. I was losing weight and lost another fifteen pounds over the next month. Throughout this time friends told Sam and I to remain optimistic. They had no reason to think otherwise. But no one could know the total complexity of this case and the Foundation's tremendous disappointment in my decisions over the past six months with Michael. I did not partner with them. I defied them at every step regarding his placement. And in the end, they were right. He was a risk, but as it turned out, to me!

Meanwhile, I was in regular contact with Michael's social worker about his situation. She made it clear that they wanted to move very slowly. At one point I was told that adoption paperwork was done on my behalf, though only to be prepared in the event a decision was made for him to return. I did not want to do foster care, but a straight forward adoption. The Foundation was angry that I was still pursuing this issue. They reaffirmed they did not want Michael in my house. It may have been a critical error of judgment to keep pressing so early after Michael's departure as it set off an alarm with the Foundation that the battle was not yet over.

My final meeting with the agency I had worked with for the past twelve years lasted less than fifteen minutes. The management made it clear that I demonstrated very poor decisions regarding Michael, and most distressful, I did not partner with my agency. Sam was not coming home and the Foundation was not going to renew my license after the end of the year since they had no intention of placing new children with me. I was done with foster care. After twelve years, the walls came crashing down.

We shook hands amiably. I was still caring for Drake and we would continue a long and fruitful relationship working for his successful transition to independent living.

As I left the building, I was calmer than I would have predicted. And driving back home that day, I felt a tremendous weight lifted from my shoulders. It was not that I was pleased not to have Sam return home, but rather, not to have an outside force commandeer my family life. The war with my agency and the foster care system ended.

I was free.

Closing Thoughts

I had only a few cases during my twelve years in foster care. All the children entered my home suffering from various abuses in early childhood, as well as trauma sustained in the system. In every case, I was not provided full disclosure of the child's history, either due to confidentiality, lack of information available to the case workers, or simply to bait the hook. This veil of secrecy or ignorance dooms any opportunity for meaningful dialogue between the state and the foster family and can result in disruption unless the parents are committed without reservation, no matter what the issues.

I also learned that the Child and Family Team is a cover for the DES management team, of which the child and foster family are mere spectators. Though at times, the foster parents will be drafted to implement the team decisions as they are the only people the child trusts. Older children, however, who have been deceived in this manner, soon learn not to trust even the intimate relationship with their foster parents. DES has removed the "C" and "F" from CFT. A close friend who is a social worker told me he once recommended putting the "F" back in. He was ridiculed. And as for the children, they can never honestly be an active member. They are too scared, overwhelmed, and easily manipulated.

The children have an advocate appointed by the court, but don't expect to see that lawyer more than once a year at best. My children never had an advocate visit. Ask them their lawyer's name and you will get the proverbial shrug of the shoulders. Some have a guardian et letum who represent the best interest of the child. They are better, but only know the facts as presented by the foster care agency. Rarely do they spend enough time with the foster parents or child to know the true depth and scope of the problem. The children have but one advocate, the parents and case worker. In the case of the social worker, they are forced by circumstance to always balance the needs of the child with the demands of their employer. As for the foster parents, most stay in the background rather than face the wrath of the system. Over time, many suffer the same trauma as the children. A few advocate with great power and find success.

The foster family does suffer the impact of the multiple mental health issues of these children placed in their care. Rarely can they know the depth of the damage and predict the influence on their family's stability, and in some cases sanity. No one can walk away unaffected. As Jason raged for years, I felt his trauma and in time, suffered my own. Nick was the most intelligent; he kept distant to protect himself from this distress. With more children added to the delicate balance in a foster home, the greater the likelihood for disruption and shattered lives as they each struggle for survival.

Jason reacted to his situation with extreme externalized anger. He did not bury the anger, but allowed it to explode in a never ending cycle that was the core of multiple disruptions and physical abuse during his childhood. While the system worked to cure his behavior, they only added to the trauma, and therefore the rage. With each move he amplified his negative self-talk and reaffirmed his fear of rejection and its consequence: lose. This emotional abuse was compounded with new abuse at the hands of caretakers who were not equipped to deal with such a damaged human being. Jason is a model example of a victim of the system; the consequences of which he will carry for life.

Drake confined his emotions so deep; his mental state remained unknown to everyone for years, only rising to the surface in his late teens. Our greatest frustration was education, with which he may struggle his whole life. This problem is likely the result of physical abuse by his grandfather tied to events at school, all under the watchful eye of the foster care system. These problems, however, may only be a symptom of a much more significant mental health issue that will impact his ability to manage relationships and ultimately to transition successfully into the greater social community. We remain unsure.

Michael and our family struggled against incredible odds together. The children supported each other and began the process of building a bridge to a successful relationship. Sadly, our success was always under attack by one party or the other. We were never given the opportunity for total family support under a solid acceptance by the system.

CPS is responsible for the placement of a then assumed sexual deviant in a home and community without prior notification, training, and therapeutic support. This is especially alarming since Michael had just transitioned from a title 19 adoption, meaning his mental health history should have been current with the agency providing services. CPS and Horizon (the mental health service agency) are responsible for not providing an evaluation and therapy soon after he joined our family despite pleas for help. Again, this is worse yet because Horizon was well aware of his recent sexual history with his prior adoptive home. Would Horizon plead innocence and point the finger at the banker Cenpatico who sit quietly in the background holding the stamp of approval?

What of Michael himself? What of his own responsibility? Both CPS and Horizon were notified by me that he had sexual contact with a teenage boy just a few weeks prior to his placement with me. At the time, I assumed he was the victim. Was he? If he had received mental health services earlier could his adoption have been saved or at least not have suffered a temporary severance? And even more important, could his inappropriate sexual behavior been corrected earlier in his life?

The Foundation was my greatest disappointment. And they have said the same of me. I depended on them for the past twelve years and felt abandoned with their disapproval of Michael in my home. They had two other youth placed with me when Michael arrived. I expected them to provide the most family support. With appropriate guidance, I would have made better decisions relating to Michael's behavior and its effects on the rest of the children. But, I received nothing but criticism. I violated the golden rule and accepted a non-Foundation child in my home. I did not throw him out. For this, the Foundation will never forgive me. The Foundation is responsible for maintaining pressure on the family to disrupt, resulting in continuous stress on us all, most especially Sam and Michael who felt the least safe. That stress escalated negative behaviors that affected us all as they struggled for security.

All these agencies are under the direction of DES. Had they cooperated with compassion, communicated for the benefit of the youth, and been more expedient to meet the family needs; Sam and Michael may not have been moved. Our family would not have suffered so much loss. My family could have endured the wave of turmoil and evolved into a stronger family unit.

Sam lost his home, never to return. During his short stay with us he suffered constant anxiety over a placement change he did not want. He lost more than a home, but a school and friends, in short a whole community. Sam was as close to sainthood as any foster child can be, though surely damaged by events in our home during his short stay. He was innocent of the disruptions that played out all around him that eventually overcame his happiness and drive for stability. His situation is evidence of how the system damages their foster children simply from environmental circumstances of a placement without added negligence or abuse.

Drake suffered untold anxiety under the stress of a disrupted family after so many years of stability. He dropped out of high school, hung out with a bad crowd to avoid being in the house, took up pot, escalated his smoking, and fell into a depressed state.

Jason was most fortunate. He left for college before Michael joined us. And though he felt jealous of being so quickly replaced by the two young teens and angry at the loss of my attention during this period, he was not directly impacted by the daily trauma. He simply worried from a distance about his dad's health and welfare.

Epilogue

Jason (adopted) and I share a spirit beyond unconditional love toward one another, but he continues to struggle with abandonment fears. So far, the PTS syndrome has maintained control of his psyche. He attempted college with a curriculum focused on zoo animal care, but always found distractions that blocked him from completing a degree. His dream is to follow in the path of his hero: Steve Irwin. From his enthusiasm for the natural world, I learned the love and appreciation of wildlife. I have spent more time in zoos since having Jason than at any other time in my life. He opened the door to that world in such a deeply meaningful way. I learned scuba diving with him as well. He gave me the courage to take the plunge and watched over me during each and every dive. He also accepted my name early in life and uses it with pride; and in so doing, he honors his father.

Jason will continue to battle his whole life against the emotional traumas of his past. Though he considers himself mentally healthy, I am not so confident he has won the war. He must allow his present experiences to define his perception of the world, rather than those from his early childhood. His love for humanity is genuine and remains the core of his gentle being and hope for the future.

And where is his lemur Precious? She is now a resident of the "Out of Africa" animal reserve located near Verde Valley in Arizona. If you make a high pitch call like a quall, she is the one that replies back. When you find her; think of Jason. He cannot visit without shedding some tears and asking me: "Dad, do you think she feels like I abandoned her?"

I question who he is crying for most. Will he ever truly recover his lost soul?

Drake (adopted) continues to seek the righteous path. Drake wasted most of his high school years struggling with many of the same issues as Jason. But his character was such that he locked away the hurt. After eighteen and a legal adult, he was diagnosed with attachment disorder. Many professionals will argue that it is too late to change the depth of emotional loss. He may be condemned to a life without that spark of life we all call humanity. My soul says different. I am a parent, not a clinician. I feel his love, as deep as he may keep it locked away from me. I am filled with compassion, too much so!

The loss of Michael and Sam was a turning point in his life. For the first time in many years, he allowed himself to feel emotional loss. He cared about them. Both boys may never know the depth of that brotherly love since Drake hid his emotions behind a featureless mask. He experienced a complete family disruption in just a few months, stimulating many of his past traumas. As a child he had stopped caring about himself and with that, everyone around him. He learned to manage his expectations to want and anticipate nothing, so he could never feel the hurt. It was a brilliant childhood survival strategy that back-fired as a teenager. Something changed and put him on a new, more positive path. He has done some new therapeutic work with EMDR and the results have been astonishing. He is now showing the ability to receive and harvest our love.

Michael was forced by the system to endure more disruption and change in a life already filled with multiple rejections. His story would over flow a single volume. He struggles to find security, even if just for a moment, still searching for a foundation from which to grow. He wants nothing more than to be a normal kid, which may never come to be. His soul is tormented by a sexual drive he is too young to understand and possibly control. With a much damaged sense of worth and denied parental affection, he is expected to demonstrate more self management behavior than the average teen boy, while caged in a dysfunctional mind.

Soon after Michael left us, a foster board hearing was held. His former adoptive mom was amazed at how the case worker brushed over the essence of the case. She wrote:

Epilogue

It is funny how they gloss over things, but I don't think that the current case worker believes Michael has many options. She is saying all of the pretty things but her body language as she says them speaks loud and clear. She really does not feel too optimistic about Michael and his case is stressing her out (those are my opinions).

Immediately following his move from my care, he suffered like a prisoner of war in a foreign land. I was helpless to comfort him as he lived behind a system through which I had no entry. While in the therapeutic home after me, they accepted another teenage boy placement who shared his bedroom. Michael was again tormented by perpetration, or at least so he claimed. Meanwhile, his anger grew as he realized he would not see me again, and worse, he was being told I didn't want him. He finally disrupted from the therapeutic home with violence toward the foster mom who filed charges against him.

From this placement he was tossed into a shelter from where he ran away a number of times. He learned new negative behaviors to survive within the lowest bowels of the system. During one of these escapes he called me. I found him lost in Phoenix. He called me from an all-night corner convenience store. When I arrived, he came out from behind a large garbage dumpster with a small dog on a rope that looked as homeless as him. He looked a mess; his hair overgrown with a sullen expression. He transmitted a strong nauseating odor from a distance. Well, he had been living in the streets a couple of days.

I immediately drove him back to the shelter. To my surprise the staff person on duty that night refused him entry. It was eleven in the evening. I was left with only one realistic option: to bring him home for the night. I was too tired to do much else. I would never take him to the police like a common criminal. He was disoriented, but exhilarated to be back in his old home. Of course, he cried the next morning when I called CPS to take him away.

His legal case is overflowing with complexity and uncertainty. I made a promise to Michael back in that shelter so long ago: "I will never abandon you." My last gift to him was finding a caring Lawyer for the Public Interest with the help of the Bazelon Center for Mental Health Law. I saw nothing but a life of ambiguity filled with emptiness and broken promises. For his part, he continued to misbehave and act out against his handlers. This attorney jumped in with both feet to help.

Nearly seven months after he left me, he was moved to residential treatment. But at what cost to Michael in terms of new traumas and negative experiences? Begging his adoptive dad to hold on, and engaging an attorney for the public interest to support his case was my last act of love. I can do no more except pray. I am confident we will see him again later in life.

Sam is gone with more trust shattered. He will never forgive anyone this defeat. He did nothing wrong. He was a pawn in an agency battle over risk management and power. Staying in contact with his old friends provided hope, but once lost, he disengaged quickly. At one point he discarded his cell phone to stop the calls. I am finished with partnering to manipulate emotions. The agencies hold all the cards. I will always keep him close to my heart. My door stays open to him. His grateful smile will warm the hearts of our family forever. I cannot control his destiny, but will remain his loyal supporter. His aunt stood up to take him, but just prior to the move, she backed out. He was then placed with a favorite cousin. I was told by the Foundation he was doing well. He was happy. I learned from his prior foster mom that he was doing very poorly. He was unhappy and unable to meet the demands of his new home. I continued to hear from the wind that a disruption was building. He moved again. Let us all hope this is the final disruption with only a few years left of High School.

Our family suffers inconsolable rage that would drive anyone to dark impulses. But rather then submit to this primal fury we make the choice to channel this anger into something positive: unconditional love and advocating for change.

    We care!

***

Jason's Journal: Last Entry

A lot of people might not believe my story or think that I am making it up, but I don't care. I have the scars to prove it and scars don't lie. Cuts may heal and scars may fade, but our memories of them remain forever. It is how you live and deal with what happened to you that make you the person you are today.

***

Notes

1. U.S. Department of Health and Human Services, Administration for Children & Families, "National Child Abuse and Neglect Data System Glossary," (http://www.acf.hhs.gov/programs/cb/systems/ncands98/glossary.htm).

2. Lawrence CR, Carlson EA, Egeland B., "The impact of foster care on development," University of Minnesota, Developmental Psychopathology, 2006 Winter; 18(1):57-76.

3. Karen Bowers, "Wild at Heart," Denver Westward News, March 09, 1994, part 1 of 2.

4. "National News Roundup-Arizona, "Children's Voice," Jan/Feb, 2006, Vol. 15, No. 1.